THE KAYAKING BOO[K]

Silhouetted against flatwater, a kayaker practices maneuvering through slalom gates. (Ledyard Canoe Club)

THE KAYAKING BOOK

Jay Evans

former U.S. Olympic Coach

THE STEPHEN GREENE PRESS
Brattleboro, Vermont
Lexington, Massachusetts

PUBLISHED MAY 1983
Second printing June 1984

This book is manufactured in the United States of America.
It is published by The Stephen Greene Press,
Fessenden Road, Brattleboro, Vermont 05301.

Library of Congress Cataloging in Publication Data

Evans, Jay, 1925–
    The kayaking book.

    Rev. ed. of: Kayaking. 1975.
    Bibliography: p.
    Includes index.
    1. Canoes and canoeing   2. White-water canoeing.
I. Title.
GV783.E94   1983   797.1'22   83–1470
ISBN 0–8289–0501–0 (pbk.)

Contents

Acknowledgments

This book on kayaking owes a great deal to many who freely offered their assistance, time, and effort during its preparation over the past two years.

I am particularly indebted to L. K. Fink, Jr. who kindly offered suggestions about sea kayaking; to Linda Harrison, five times national whitewater slalom champion for her overview of competition; to Arthur Miller and Mary Metcalf for their helpful suggestions on editing; to Nichols Productions for their assistance in listing available kayak films; to Carol Fisher and Eric Evans for their loan of outstanding photographs; and to Perception, Inc. for help in compiling a list of kayak schools.

Many manufacturers and distributors (too numerous to mention individually) were also most generous in supplying information on equipment as well as photographs.

However, the content of the book is my responsibility, and errors of omission or commission are mine alone.

Introduction

THE LURE OF OPEN WATER

Water is a fascinating thing. Next to the air we breathe it is probably the most significant thing on this planet. Certainly there is more of it around than any other material, for three-fourths of the earth's surface is covered with it, and over 80 percent of the human body consists of it. It is the universal fluid: we drink it plain, or we doctor it up by adding color, flavor and gas to it. We use it to create power and light for growing food, washing our clothes, mining for rare metals, and transporting goods from here to there.

Of all the substances on earth, water has some of the most interesting characteristics. First of all, it is wet and slippery. It slithers around unless penned up, and it works tirelessly to escape its bonds so it can rush downhill until it eventually joins the ocean. If dammed up it will quietly bide its time and then descend as rain somewhere else on earth in its relentless journey to the sea.

Fresh water is quite heavy, weighing about 62 pounds per cubic foot. This means that in addition to having the quality of weight, it can create a lot of force. The kayaker discovers this when he tries to dislodge his boat from a rock in the rapids: water can exert 8 to 10 tons of force against a boat hung up in a fast-moving current.

Water also has personality. It appears alive. It can sparkle; it can look ominous. Its gentle sound can lull you to sleep, its boisterousness can tingle your nerves, or its forbidding roar can fill your heart with apprehension.

Water is incredibly versatile. As a liquid it is most common, but as a solid it can cool you off on a hot day or store itself up for the spring runoff. As a crystal it gives birth to the world of skiing, tobogganing, snowshoeing, and snowmobiling. As a solid it can be skated upon.

Water, as a liquid, is dynamic. It can form the tiniest ripple from a trout nibbling on the surface of a quiet pond, or become a 50-foot tidal wave roaring across the wide expanse of the Pacific Ocean.

One of the greatest moments in the history of mankind must have been when man first discovered that he could move in water either by swimming himself or by riding on a log. Together with the invention of the wheel and the use of fire and metal, man's ability to propel himself in water marked a major breakthrough in the development of civilization. No longer landlocked, man had a whole new horizon extending before him, much as space travel in our own age now lures us on to the distant stars.

And as he mastered water, he learned to play in it. Actually, there are only two ingredients necessary to enjoy boating on water: an ability to swim reasonably well with confidence, and an appreciation of and fondness for water—even if it is cold. If you enjoy the smell and touch of water, are fascinated by moving current in a river, calmed by the placid feeling of a quiet pond, or thrilled at the sight of rapids, then perhaps kayaking is for you.

In general, people of all ages enjoy kayaking. Children just barely big enough to see over the cockpit and strong enough to lift a paddle have been seen kayaking merrily around millponds and gentle streams. The Eskimos began to teach their children the Eskimo roll as soon as the child had reached the age of 12.

Experience has shown that youngsters of 8 and 9 often have a remarkable sense of balance and movement and can handle themselves smartly in the water. Of course the fact that these little folk probably weigh only 60 pounds or less certainly gives them an advantage, for with so little weight in the boat it rests as lightly on the water as a leaf and seems able to turn at a mere suggestion.

During the adolescent years and in the 20's those who enjoy kayaking will often be caught in the competitive urge, will turn more serious about the sport, and will train their bodies to a fine pitch to improve their skill. Still others will be drawn to travel our wilderness waterways. Many schools, colleges, and youth groups are taking up kayaking as an ideal environmental sport.

Perhaps the golden years of kayaking extend from age 30 to 60. By the time persons are about 35 (if they are realistic about themselves), they will no longer try to keep up with the college crowd to win the coveted racing championship, but will gladly settle for the veteran or senior racing class. And many more will be content simply to attend a race, sharing the excitement that prevails in the campground and taking part in the activities.

Older people should not shy away from kayaking either. Steering your own little craft around the coves and inlets of a wilderness pond, in search of fish or wildfowl or even an elusive view of a sunset, can be a rewarding experience. If, gliding along silently, you round a bend and suddenly come upon a deer—or better yet, a moose or an elk—the day will long be remembered.

A well-known set of rapids that has given you many good times in past years will always welcome you again as a long-lost friend. And what can be more satisfying than introducing a young paddler for the first time to one of your favorite whitewater runs?

As therapy, kayaking is unmatched in its ability to wash away the pressures of a too highly charged modern society. A weekend trip, or even a Sunday afternoon paddle, can rejuvenate your spirits for a taxing week ahead.

Thoreau was right: rivers are a constant lure to the adventurous instinct in mankind.

PART I.
BOATS, EQUIPMENT, AND SAFETY

1. Kayaks

From Sealskin and Driftwood to Fiberglass

The Eskimos

Over the centuries, the earliest known inhabitants of the Arctic regions of North America developed a remarkable craft for traveling over icy bays, inlets, and even open ocean. These light and fast moving skin boats were designed primarily for hunting and fishing. Called "kayaks" by the Eskimos, they were masterpieces of primitive engineering. Made of driftwood and the skins and sinews of animals, the ancient Eskimo kayak was a remarkably resilient and durable craft, both light to handle and swift in the water.

There were no official dimensions—it depended upon the materials available—but many were about 18 feet long and less than two feet wide.

Two Eskimos in a skin kayak were photographed near Nunivak Island, Alaska, in the early 1900's. The hole in the bow is a built-in grabloop. Note the unusual single-bladed paddle. Most tribes used double-bladed paddles with the blades in the same plane, unlike modern paddles with blades set at right angles. (U.S. National Museum)

Sharply pointed at each end and streamlined, they were not only easy to paddle but also quite seaworthy even in the wildest water. Sealskin was stretched tightly over a frame made of bone and driftwood carved to fit. Seal sinew lashed the frame together. The deck, particularly in the stern, was often quite flat to accommodate an inflated bladder and line attached to a hunting spear. The bow deck sometimes held a spare hunting tool or paddle.

Eskimos sat in their kayaks, rather than kneeling, in a small cockpit built into the midpoint of the deck. An Eskimo could sit in this cockpit, chaise longue style, and fasten his waterproof parka around the rim of the cockpit to make his craft watertight even when the largest of waves broke over him.

Since rarely could Eskimos find driftwood wide enough to provide efficient paddle blades, many of their paddle blades were less than half as wide as the ones used today. Nevertheless, they used both single- and double-bladed paddles of various lengths.

Aside from the remarkable engineering feat of the kayak design itself, the Eskimos also provided today's kayaker with other inspirational legacies:

1. *Grabloops.* Carrying kayaks overland or fastening them down in a storm could be tricky, so a waterproof hole was made near the tip of the bow (and sometimes at the stern as well) to provide a place to grab the kayak or to tie it to a tent stake, post, or rock. Most modern kayaks are made with a short line looped through the bow and stern which serves the same purpose. We call them grabloops.

2. *The Eskimo Roll.* Since the Eskimos designed their kayaks for speed, this meant that the craft had to be quite narrow. A slender boat is unstable and is in danger of capsizing. A tip into the freezing waters of the Arctic can be lethal. The Eskimos cleverly developed a maneuver employing the paddle to bring a capsized kayak back into an upright position again without getting out of the boat. Since their parkas fitted tightly around the cockpit, by using their paddles effectively they could roll back up without taking in water. This remarkable centuries-old technique has been handed down through the years and is now known as the Eskimo roll. It is considered a basic self-rescue technique for all people wishing to learn the art of kayaking. It will be covered in Chapter 6.

3. *Light Materials Technology.* The Eskimos also set a standard for lightness and flexibility that today's science has been hard pressed to match. Dried sealskins, sinew, and driftwood are very light materials. Many Eskimo kayaks weighed less than 26 pounds. Even with modern technology in plastics and chemistry, only highly specialized racing kayaks weigh less than this.

Kayaking as a Sport

As early as the sixteenth century, English explorers in the northern seas saw Eskimos using kayaks to travel and hunt on water. In 1865, Londoner John MacGregor built the famous "Rob Roy" kayak and toured many of Europe's rivers in it. Later he founded the Royal Canoe Club of Great Britain. (The English refer to kayaks as canoes.) The club held kayak races on flatwater in 1867. Annual competitions were held beginning in 1874, and by 1885, kayak races were held on the continent.

Before World War I, people in southern Germany looked longingly at the fast streams flooding down the mountain slopes of the Alps. The traditional open canoe, although known in Europe, was simply not maneuverable enough for safe navigation in whitewater, and without a deck cover, it tended to fill with water from the splashing waves. The Eskimo kayak, though far more maneuverable and with a covered cockpit, also presented a problem. Its length made it awkward to transport from place to place— especially by train, the way many Europeans traveled in those days.

The ingenious Germans devised a collapsible kayak, one that would fold and could be carried like two large suitcases. One package contained the folded wooden frame, the other a rubberized fabric outer skin. Called a *Faltboot*, it could be quickly assembled on the river bank by inserting the erected wooden frame into the fabric. After a day's boating, the Faltboot was easily disassembled and packed away for the trip home. Thus the collapsible kayak became the first major technological breakthrough since those of the Eskimos, and it ushered in new possibilities of adventure and sport.

Other refinements were also taking place. Those interested in racing kayaks in flatwater soon discovered that while the old Eskimo design was fast, by making a few subtle changes here and there, the kayak could be made to go even faster. To aid in turning such boats, rudders were affixed to the stern and controlled by wires connected to pedals in the cockpit. It is generally believed that Hans Eduard Pawlata in Vienna made popular the so-called Eskimo roll to right a capsized kayak in 1927. Much of his technique, of course, was borrowed from the Eskimos.

Racing down the rapids from a starting point to a finish line became popular as early as the 1920's in Europe. It was called *Wildwasser* or wildwater racing. In 1936 the summer olympic games were held in Germany and flatwater kayak racing became an Olympic event.

In the early 1940's, a national championship wildwater race was held on a six-mile stretch of the remote Rapid River on the border between New Hampshire and Maine. On the Rhone River in Geneva, Switzerland, the first world championships in whitewater slalom were held in 1949.

Over 80 competitors from 7 nations came to test their skills on a 12-gate course located where the Rhone flows through the heart of the city. Ten years later, the first world championships in wildwater were held on the Vesere River in France. In the United States, the first slalom sponsored by the American Canoe Association was held on Delaware's Brandywine River in 1952. In the early 1950's, more races were conducted on some of the fine whitewater streams in Colorado. During these years, touring and exploring rivers and lakes by kayak continued to grow in popularity.

The Advent of Fiber Reinforced Plastic

In the 1950's kayaking took another major technological leap forward. Just as foldboats were an advance over the ancient skin and driftwood boats, fiberglass emerged as an exciting new material that could be adapted to the construction of kayaks. Fiberglass made it possible to construct a kayak without any major interior framing. These boats were light, flexible, durable, and required little upkeep. As a bonus, with this new material damage could be easily and permanently repaired right on the river bank without sophisticated tools. (Fiberglass kayaks have been repaired and refloated within two hours of having been broken completely in two on rapids far away from civilization.)

Fiberglass (or as the English prefer, glass-fiber) created a minor revolution in kayak building. It increased the availability of inexpensive kayaks as well as their ability to take unusual punishment. The new, easy-to-work material encouraged backyard design experimentation. This, in turn, promoted the development of new techniques and the running of rivers formerly considered unrunnable. Kayaks became more responsive to the paddler's touch, and fierce rapids no longer restricted the boater who now knew that he had a very durable craft under him.

The Modern Kayak

Even in its various forms, the modern kayak is still an extremely simple and functional craft. It consists of a deck and a hull and a seating arrangement for one or more paddlers. Kayaks range in length from the short junior models or those used for surfing or kayak polo—between 9 and 11 feet long—to racing kayaks and ocean-going craft that may be 15 feet or more in length. They are all about 2 feet wide and their height amidships is rarely more than 18 inches. Some kayaks weighing only 10 pounds have been built, although most modern kayaks tip the scales at 20 to 30 pounds.

Let's take a look at each of the major parts of a modern kayak.

The Hull

The subtle shape of the hull is the major factor in determining how the kayak performs in water. Long, narrow, sleek hulls are fast, but less maneuverable. Those that are wider and flatter provide better turning capacity but are not as fast in the water. Slalom racing kayaks are flatter, wildwater racing kayaks narrower, and cruising kayaks strike a happy medium between the two extremes.

The Deck

A kayak's covered deck has two basic purposes: to help keep water out of the craft and to define the place for the paddler to sit. Decks are customarily less ruggedly built than hulls because they are less likely to come in contact with the river bottom.

The Cockpit

This is where the paddler sits (in the middle of the boat) and controls the craft. It consists of the seat itself, a coaming (the convex lip around the outside of the cockpit), and part of the bracing system that supports the paddler's hips and back. The seat usually rests not more than an inch or so above the bottom of the hull, and attached to the seat are adjustable hip- and backbraces that provide a comfortable and snug fit. These braces permit the paddler to feel as if he were wearing the kayak, not just sitting in it. Seats in some oceangoing kayaks can be adjusted forward and back. Hipbraces prevent the paddler from sliding around in the seat. The backbrace—usually an adjustable strap across the back of the seat—provides a firm support for the lower spine.

The coaming acts as a ledge under which a spray cover (also called a spray skirt is fitted. The spray cover prevents water from entering the kayak.

Footbraces

Most kayaks have adjustable footbraces attached to the inside wall of the hull forward of the cockpit. With the backbrace, a paddler, by pressing his feet firmly against the footbraces, gains the excellent longitudinal sup-

The complete bracing system of a kayak includes footbraces, kneebraces, and hipbraces.
(Old Town Canoe Company)

port essential to good paddling. Most footbraces are adjustable to accommodate paddlers of varying heights.

Kneebraces

Flatwater racing kayaks do not normally need kneebraces, since lateral motion is not required to propel the boat forward. But oceangoing kayaks, surfing and kayak polo boats (and actually any kayak intended for white water) should have a firm, comfortable set of kneebraces. Situated directly under the coaming and sometimes part of the under deck, kneebraces help provide marvelous stability to a kayak in rough water or to one that needs to be turned quickly.

Grabloops

Most modern kayaks are designed with some means for grabbing or tying them at the bow and stern. Not many boats use the old Eskimo-type hole; instead a line is looped through and attached to the end of the kayak. Such a grabloop offers a handy grip for retrieving a kayak in the water, for lifting a kayak, or for fastening it to the top of a car.

Types of Kayaks

From a distance most kayaks simply look like long plastic tubes with a hole in the middle for a paddler. Yet, closer inspection shows even subtle differences in contours make a big difference, not only in handling characteristics but also in how the boats can be used.

There are many basic types of kayaks today to choose from. In a real sense, kayaking—like many other sports—has become specialized. No longer can a paddler take a comfortable cruise on a river on Saturday and then on Sunday, win a slalom race using the same boat.

The most common form of kayak in use today is yesterday's slalom boat. It is a single seater with reasonably high volume. It is fairly fast, maneuverable, and comfortable. The serious slalom racer, however, must use an extremely low volume and highly maneuverable craft. A wildwater racer needs a super-fast model, maneuverability not being quite so important. This type of boat, of course, tends to be quite tippy; a characteristic not suitable for the weekend tripper.

Today's outdoor adventurer has a wealth of types from which to choose. Specialized recreational kayaks have evolved for riding the ocean's surf, for playing kayak polo, and for long distance paddling at sea. For flatwater racing, single, double, and four-seater kayaks are available. Demand still exists for folding boats and those that are partly or totally inflatable and for others to which a modest sail can be attached.

The Basic Recreational Kayak

Quite often a beginner will be attracted to a stable, single-seater that is easy to handle. Usually it's an older version of a slalom kayak and may even conform basically to the regulations for slalom length and width. It will have enough interior room for comfort and to store a limited amount of duffle. Manufacturers refer to these as "general purpose" or "touring" boats. These are excellent craft and suitable for a modest weekend trip on a river; they can also be used if you wish to try your luck in an informal wildwater race. But don't expect to take first place using this kind of kayak—it is not designed for it. Older, secondhand slalom models can also be perfectly suitable for the beginner, and they sometimes can be purchased quite inexpensively. These recreational touring kayaks are good starter boats for beginners.

The basic recreational kayak.

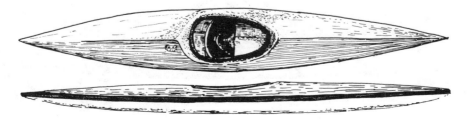

Recreational *short boats* are also popular. These kayaks are about a foot shorter and a little wider than the approved slalom boat, whose dimensions are governed by international racing rules. Originally they were simply reconditioned slalom boats with the ends chopped off and recapped. Now, they are built a little wider at the cockpit to provide greater stability and maintain adequate volume. They are extremely maneuverable in whitewater and remarkably stable. The short boat is an ideal craft for those not interested in slalom racing or long expeditions but who prefer short whitewater trips and playing in the rapids.

Some manufacturers build junior kayaks for young children. The craft is similar to a slalom kayak except it is likely to be as much as two feet shorter and have good volume and stability. For young people weighing less than 110 pounds, these smaller kayaks are easier to manage. Children big enough to hold and control a double-bladed paddle will enjoy such a boat, but they must be very competent swimmers and learn all the basic safety techniques for handling a kayak.

The Slalom Kayak

Next in popularity are kayaks that are a bit more streamlined and maneuverable. To meet international racing regulations, they must be not less than 13 feet 2 inches (4 meters) in length or narrower than 23¾ inches (60 centimeters). A slalom racing kayak is extremely light, some weighing less than 20 pounds. A pronounced upward sweeping curvature of the hull at either end provides great maneuverability. The bottom section of the hull is quite broad and flat. Recent trends dictate that the boat be low volume—that is, with little room to spare between deck and hull, and with sharp sides. (In contrast, touring kayaks have high volume, meaning greater fullness throughout their length with more rounded sides and less of the slalom kayak's pumpkin seed appearance.)

The slalom kayak.

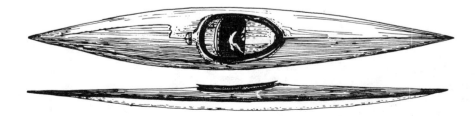

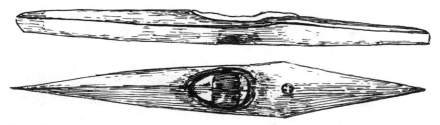

The wildwater kayak.

Slalom kayaks have seats and braces that fit very snugly so the paddler can maintain full control of the boat at all times.

The Wildwater Kayak

According to international rules a kayak designed for racing in wildwater must be no more than 14 feet 8 inches (4.5 meters) long and at least 23¾ inches (60 centimeters) wide. Speed is essential here, maneuverability secondary. The long, narrow V-shaped hull cleaves the water cleanly, but sacrifices some stability and turning ability. The hull does not turn up much at either end, just enough to slice through the waves and slide over submerged rocks. The bow and stern are extremely sharp, and the deck is designed to part the waves. Its widest point is behind the cockpit. This makes the wedge-shaped hull on either side and in front of the paddler a straight line, facilitating a more powerful and efficient forward stroke.

Like a speedboat or a racing car, the rakish wildwater kayak looks fast. When efficiently paddled, it is by far the swiftest boat in the rapids.

Flatwater Racing Kayaks

Flatwater racing has been an Olympic sport since 1936. It is a highly specialized, competitive activity requiring great technique and bursts of power and endurance. The types include a single seat kayak (K-1), a two-seater (K-2), and a four-seater (K-4). All flatwater racing kayaks are remarkably sleek and narrow, requiring precision paddling especially in the two and four paddler boats. Some flatwater racing kayaks are made of fiberglass, others of molded plywood. They have steering rudders. Sometimes they do not have spray covers; kneebraces similar to those in whitewater kayaks are not needed.

In flatwater racing specially designed canoes are used as in whitewater racing. A discussion of these canoes is, however, beyond the scope of this book.

The flatwater racing kayak—K-2. (Dr. Carol Fisher)

The flatwater racing kayak—K-4. (Dr. Carol Fisher)

The Folding Kayak

The fiberglass revolution in kayak construction did not spell the doom of das Faltboot (folding kayak). This unique portable craft that can be stored in two bags still appeals. Its knock-down feature can be a distinct advantage, since it permits the apartment dweller the pleasure of owning a boat without having to find major storage space. Once at the river, its tubular framework is erected, fitted into a rubberized canvas skin, and held rigid with a snap lock fitting.

Folding kayaks come in many models and sizes. Their chief use, however, is for flatwater cruising and camping. They tend to be larger, more spacious, and quite stable. Moderate whitewater streams can be run in folding kayaks. These boats find favor with family groups. Often a sail can be attached complete with a mast, rudder, and leeboards; small outboard motors have also been attached to folding kayaks. The cockpits in folding kayaks are generous in size and often have back rests. Spray covers are not generally used except in rough water.

The Whitewater K-2

Two-person recreational kayaks are manufactured primarily for the non-competitive market; they are not used for racing. One paddler sits directly behind the other. In some K-2's, one large open cockpit suffices for both people. In other K-2's, separate cockpits are provided. Although positioned close to each other toward the center of the boat, the cockpits allow ample leg room between paddlers.

The K-2 designed for whitewater is used primarily for touring and camping. The Scandinavians design two-seater kayaks for extensive travel along the seacoast and fjords.

The whitewater K-2.

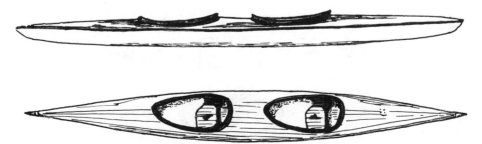

Kayaks for Surfing

Kayaks built for surfing in the ocean may be the sportiest boats of all. They are short (usually around 10 feet long), with a very flat hull and a broad, upturned bow shaped like a duck's bill. The cockpit is located a little behind the midpoint and contains the customary bracing of a slalom kayak. More extreme design eliminates the deck entirely. The paddler sits in a customized shallow seat with two indented places forward for his feet. This deckless kayak has a hull thick enough to provide for sufficient flotation, and the top of the hull is shaped so that it does not ship much water.

Slalom kayaks have been used for surfing, but their pointed noses cause the boats to dive forward into the sand lying just under the breaking surf. Wildwater kayaks are unfit for surfing; they knife through the waves rather than riding over them.

If surfing appeals to you, it is better to stay with the craft that has been so ingeniously designed for it. Advantages of a surf kayak over a surfboard include the fact that you can enjoy surfing from a comfortable chaise longue position rather than balancing precariously on a slippery board. Also, with the aid of the double-bladed paddle, you can turn your craft around, head back out, and get in many more runs in an afternoon. (More about surfing kayaks can be found in Chapter 12.)

Caution: Never go surfing alone, and never surf in the vicinity of swimmers. A collision with a swimmer could be unfortunate.

Bat Boats for Kayak Polo

Kayaks suited for playing polo are hard to find. Most of them are made in England. If you take a slalom boat with its unusually good maneuverability and chop the bow and stern back about a foot or so and patch the holes with rounded tips, you'll have a perfectly adequate "bat boat."

Bat boat.

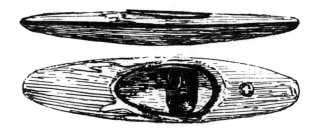

Kayak polo, in which players use their paddles as mallets to hit a water polo ball toward the opponent's goal, is a popular sport in indoor swimming pools during the cold winter months when the rivers and lakes are frozen.

The sharp point of most kayaks precludes their use in pools for kayak polo: they might damage the side of the pool or an opponent's boat. Thus the distinguishing feature of the bat boat is the blunted bow and stern. Like slalom kayaks, bat boats also need a good seat and firm braces to facilitate quick maneuvering.

Oceangoing Kayaks

It may be hard to believe, but in the 1950's a German physician paddled alone in a kayak across the entire Atlantic Ocean. In 1977 kayaks rounded dreaded Cape Horn at the southern tip of South America.

Single-seat kayaks for ocean travel are truly the Rolls Royces of boating design. Regal and stylish, their long, graceful, upward-swept bows and sterns allow them to ride smoothly over the largest ocean swells.

Since maneuverability is of secondary importance, oceangoing kayaks tend to be quite long—some are 16 to 19 feet in length. In addition to the customary braces, many models have waterproof hatches in the bow and stern decks to make it easy to get at stored gear. Common accessories include a compass and light, a sliding seat, a pump, a horn or whistle, a rudder, and deck fixtures to hold your paddle or to store a spare paddle. (Chapter 11 provides further information on these craft.)

Inflatables

A leading manufacturer of airships (dirigibles) in the late 1890's created the first modern inflatable boat in 1936. Inflatable kayaks now come in one- and two-person models. The single-seaters are usually a little longer than a slalom kayak, while the two-seaters can be as long as 17 feet. More

Inflatable kayak.

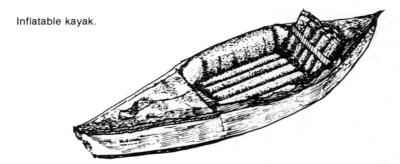

complex inflatable craft use outboard motors, but double- or single-bladed paddles can be used to propel the simpler kayak designs. With their flat hulls, they may be the fastest turning kayaks of all. Inflatable kayaks have open cockpits, hence no bracing to speak of. They are seen at lake shore summer cottages and elsewhere and are especially popular with children.

Kayakamarans and Kayachts

The kayak version of the traditional two-hulled catamaran, the kayaka-maran consists of two large-volume touring class kayaks fastened to-gether side by side complete with a rudder assembly, a 17-foot mast, a 59-square-foot mainsail, and a 31-square-foot jib. It seats two people easily and could carry four in a pinch. The kayacht is simply a single-hull version of the kayakamaran with a lateen sail, seating one person only.

Kayakamarans and kayachts are available commercially, either in kit form or already assembled. They can be transported on car tops and are ideal for lake cruising, coastal marshes, and bays, as well as the ocean itself.

Kayakamaran. (Kayakamaran)

Other Self-propelled Whitewater Craft

I would be remiss to suggest that the kayak is the only proper design suitable for heavy waves, rough water, and rapids. The traditional North American canoe has been refined so that it, too, can be responsive to the demands of whitewater.

Most common is the closed-deck one person canoe. Called a C-1, it can be mistaken for a kayak unless you notice that the paddler is kneeling in the cockpit rather than sitting and is using a single-bladed paddle. Such a craft is more often used for racing than for cruising. According to international rules, the C-1 can be no shorter than 13 feet 2 inches (4 meters)— the same as for the slalom kayak—but it must be at least 27½ inches (70 centimeters) wide.

C-1's are also used in wildwater racing. They must not exceed 14 feet 1 inch (4.3 meters) in length or narrower than 31½ inches (80 centimeters).

Braces are arranged in the cockpit for feet, knees, and thighs. The modern C-1 is a remarkably nimble craft that can spin on a dime and still challenge the slalom kayak for speed. The only medal ever won by an American in whitewater slalom in the Olympics was accomplished in a C-1.

The two-person closed deck canoe (C-2) follows the pattern of the C-1. Both paddlers kneel, use single-bladed paddles, and the C-2 can be designed for either slalom or wildwater racing. The C-2 slalom canoe must be 15 feet (4.58 meters) long and at least 31¼ inches (80 centimeters) wide. Wildwater C-2's cannot exceed 16 feet 4 inches (5 meters) in length, and 31½ inches (80 centimeters) wide.

Advantages in C-2 paddling include unusually effective turning control when the power train (the paddlers) are placed toward each end of the craft. Since there is no equivalent class in whitewater racing kayaks, the C-2 provides the spectator with a marvelous opportunity to view co-

C-1.

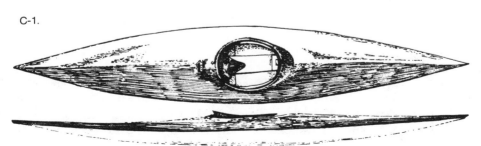

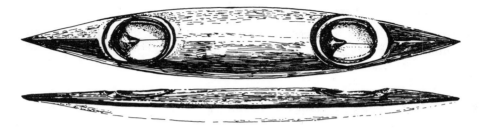

C-2.

ordination and teamwork on a race course. Paddlers working in unison are a beautiful sight to watch.

Boat Materials

Boat designers (and everybody else) want a material that's strong, has high impact resistance, is somewhat flexible, yet durable. It must be light, easy to form and repair, and still be inexpensive. Sound like a tall order? True, but in space age plastics, such materials are available. Applied to the construction of kayaks, the resiliency and versatility of these materials have encouraged design innovations that have brought about many new and exciting paddling techniques.

The chemistry of these new materials is highly complex. But, like electricity, we don't have to understand it perfectly to harness it to our needs. There are only three main components: resin, fiberglass cloth, and a catalytic agent or hardener to bond the cloth and the resin together. When all three components are mixed in proper ratio, a chemical process takes place that cannot be reversed. The new product formed in the desired shape is ready for use.

Types of Cloth

Fiberglass cloth comes in a variety of weights and weaves. Quite common for kayaks are six ounce and ten ounce (per square yard) cloth woven into basket weave designs. Chopped strand mat (without a weave) comes in a variety of weights and thicknesses and is used mostly as stiffening reinforcement, since it lacks the flexibility of woven fiberglass cloth. If you wish to get exotic, you can purchase teakwood print cloth to make your kayak look like a teakwood boat.

Nylon, aramid, polypropylene, S-Glass and Kevlar® fabrics resist tearing, yet are extremely light, flexible, and durable. (Some are used in making bullet-proof vests.) Often, a combination of these fabrics molded together will provide the ideal material for your kayak. Improvements and new designs in fabrics continue to be made.

Types of Resin

The liquid medium in fiberglass kayak construction varies in texture from the color and viscosity (but not the aroma) of molasses, to a very heavy jelly-like substance. When chemically bonded, resins can be either soft and flexible, or hard and brittle according to need. Some chemical firms blend these characteristics to achieve the balance they wish.

Two common kinds of resin used in the construction of kayaks are epoxy and polyester. Epoxy resin is stronger than polyester, but more difficult to handle, more toxic, and much more expensive. Polyester is quite easy to handle and is generally suitable for most kayak construction. Polyester resin is also toxic, but less so than epoxy. Any kind of resin work should be done in a well-ventilated area.

Other plastics are used in making boats, with great success, but they require special techniques and special equipment. For the most part, these plastics are used by commercial manufacturers.

Interior Structural Support

Most kayaks are built to be light, but in so doing there's the danger of building a craft whose deck or hull is so flimsy that it might be dented by heavy waves. There are several ingenious ways to counteract this and still have a lightweight kayak. One is to stuff a three foot section of two-inch wide ethafoam on edge into the bow and stern cavities of a kayak. (Styrofoam can also be used, but it is less desirable because it tends to chip away.) The ethafoam fitted in vertically will help preserve the shape of the kayak in the roughest of water, prevent the hull or deck from denting, and also help provide flotation at the same time.

Other means of stiffening the hull and deck include the bonding of inverted T-shaped pieces of fiberglass mat to the inside of the hull and deck and bonding wooden or plastic rods covered with fiberglass tape where needed.

Building Your Own Kayak

(The following section is not meant to provide you with detailed, step-by-step instructions on how to fabricate your own kayak. Rather, it purports simply to give you a general picture of how it can be done. As this book goes to press, the most authoritative book available on the subject is Charlie Walbridge's *Boat Builder's Manual* which gives comprehensive treatment of all phases of kayak building and repair.)

Three common ways suggest themselves to most people when they think of building their own kayaks. The easiest is to put together a kit. The kit, of course, is much cheaper than a finished boat. It usually consists of a deck, hull, seat, and some kind of bracing materials. It's your job to seam the hull and the deck together, install the seat, and fit the braces to your specifications. If you're a handy person, experienced in handling fiberglass and resin, and follow the manufacturer's instructions, you can realize substantial savings. For those inexperienced in fiberglass work, there are a few manufacturers who sell wood and canvas kits.

The second—and less popular—method for building a kayak is to design one of your own using wood or aluminum and rubberized or waterproof cloth construction. Here, of course, the sky's the limit in creative design. The technique is similar (on a much larger scale) to constructing a model airplane.

By far the most popular method of building a kayak is to do it by hand, using a mold and fiberglass. But first, three important points must be stressed:

1. *Ethics.* Home builders rarely have the time or talent to build a mold from scratch. The temptation is to pull a mold from a commercially manufactured boat. This is not only morally wrong, but it is illegal and can involve patent violations. Before such a mold is made you must have the written permission of the manufacturer—for your protection.

2. *Health.* Some people are allergic to fiberglass. The inhalation of the fumes of many chemicals is harmful, and skin contact with them can be irritating. **The toxic effects of fiberglass and resin are cumulative.** Therefore, if you're indoors, it is absolutely essential to provide excellent ventilation at all times. The use of face masks and gloves is also highly recommended.

3. *Partnership.* Although working with fiberglass is very easy and safe once you get the hang of it, the very best way to learn is to make friends with someone who has done it before. Get a partner. It is much better when two people work simultaneously on a boat, anyway. The work goes more smoothly, and there are two more hands available when needed.

A well-ventilated boat shed and the materials for building a kayak: bolts of fiberglass cloth, a barrel of resin lying on it side, a hipbrace and seat-coaming mold suspended from a hook on the wall, and molds for the hull and deck (foreground). (Robert F. George)

One of the best ways to find a partner is to join a kayak or canoe club. Perhaps you can act as an apprentice to someone making a kayak before you build your own.

The Process Itself

Having secured a mold legally and properly, you then should decide what kind of a "lay-up" you wish. Here's where your imagination comes into the picture, and a wide variety of options is available. Choose whatever combination of cloths you think will do the trick (six- or ten-ounce cloth and mat for example) and cut the material roughly to the dimensions of your hull and deck. Common lay-ups include three layers of fabric on the hull and two for the deck with reinforcements at bow, stern, and around the cockpit.

Next, prepare your mold with great care. It should be smooth with no traces of an earlier boat left. A mold release wax should be applied generously and carefully to the mold. Check to see that every square inch of the mold is covered by the release material. The smallest uncovered part will adhere to your boat, making its extraction from the mold difficult with serious damage to the mold.

The layers of cloth are then placed in the mold and saturated with activated resin using paint brushes, paint rollers, and squeegees. Too much resin will make the kayak heavy and brittle. Too little resin will prevent proper bonding between the cloth and the resin, creating tiny pin holes which reduce strength and allow water to enter the boat.

As the cloth cures, the waste around the edges is trimmed off. The hull and deck molds are clamped together and a seam of saturated fiberglass cloth is pressed out along the interior seams. Once everything is cured and the mold removed added strength can be created by placing an outside seam where the hull and deck join along the gunwale.

The seat and coaming unit, which was probably molded while you were waiting for the hull and deck to cure, can now be attached to the deck and the foot- and kneebraces installed to fit as you like.

Grabloops are drawn through a hole near the deck ends and then tightly wrapped to prevent seepage. A cup of activated resin is poured down to the point while the kayak is tipped up to a vertical position.

After everything has cured, you should examine your kayak for pin holes, sand all the rough edges, and test both the deck and hull to see if you need any structural support. Finally, be sure to place flotation bags at either end of your kayak before you try it in the water.

Repairs

One of the attractive features of fiberglass kayak construction is that it is so easy to repair. Should a minor break occur in the hull or deck it can be quickly and easily corrected—often from inside the kayak where it won't even show. For a more serious fracture you may wish to consider putting a patch both on the inside and on the outside of the boat.

The damaged area must be perfectly dry and well sanded. Usually two or more layers of cloth are used for a patch. Saturate the cloth and brush it on firmly over the affected area. If the crack goes all the way through, be sure to tape the back side to prevent the resin from draining through. After a couple of layers have been applied, thoroughly sand the cured patch for a smooth finish.

Having built a fiberglass kayak, chances are you'll have cloth, resin, and activator left over. Bundle them up and you'll have a handy emergency repair kit for the future. Another handy tip: carry a roll of gray duct tape (available at any hardware store) with you on boating trips.

Which Boat for You?

Although acquiring a kayak is not one of the major investments in a person's life, it still involves a commitment of several hundred dollars. So it's important to consider carefully what your needs might be. Here are a few tips.

An Inventory of Your Needs

If you're a beginner, you'll want a stable boat. If you plan to use your kayak for traveling distances on inland lakes and rivers, you'll want one that steers easily and has good speed. If you're thinking about overnight trips, you should look at kayaks that have a large volume so you can store your gear. Do you plan to paddle singly, or do you prefer a partner in the boat with you? Will more than one person in your family be using the craft, and each for different purposes? Spend some time asking yourself just what you might want to use your kayak for.

Kayaks, if well cared for, can last forever. But, don't neglect to consider the "trade-in" value before you purchase one. There are many facets to the sport; once you've mastered cruising, for example, you may wish to sell your boat and buy a hot racing model or a surf kayak. A boat in good condition is a marketable asset and obviously will sell better than a beat up old dog of a boat.

Basic Boat Characteristics

Generally speaking, the most common and popular type of boat is loosely called the *slalom kayak*. It is relatively short, very stable, yet extremely maneuverable. Most beginners in the sport naturally gravitate toward the slalom type kayak.

In a sense, the general slalom type craft stands in the middle of the kayak spectrum. To the right of it we find boats designed strictly for cruising. They will be longer, have a little more volume for storage, while they steer well, they are not as maneuverable as the slalom types. Further to the right you'll find the sleek, needle-nosed wildwater racing kayaks— fast, tippy, and not particularly maneuverable. At the extreme you'll find the flatwater racing kayaks. These are fast as greased lightning, unstable unless you're accustomed to them. They have no need for turning ability.

Toward the left of the spectrum from the general slalom type boat you'll find the forefront of slalom racing design. These are very low volume, extremely maneuverable and often are not very comfortable to sit in for any length of time. Still farther to the left you'll find some specialty boats designed specifically for surfing or for kayak polo. Each is maneuverable in the extreme—not fast at all, but very stable.

Surely, with so many exciting designs to choose from there will be a kayak just for you.

Your Comfort

Being able to sit comfortably in your boat over reasonably long periods of time is a prerequisite for pleasure in recreational kayaking; therefore, it's important to sit in the kayak before you buy it. Your hips should fit snugly, but not so tightly that circulation to your legs is cut off. If, on the other hand, you feel too loose in the seat, you can add pads to the hipbraces.

Special attention should be paid to the footbraces. They should be adjustable so that the ball of your foot rests comfortably against the surface of the footbrace. You shouldn't have to reach with your toes to touch them, neither should your feet be jammed up against them.

Kneebraces can be adjusted, if necessary, by taping an extra sponge rubber pad over the regular brace. The backbrace should give you firm support at the lower spine.

In summary, you should fit into your boat in a comfortably snug manner, snug enough that by rocking the kayak from side to side with your hips you can tip the craft on its side and comfortable enough so that your legs don't fall asleep as you sit there.

Purchasing a Kayak

Most sporting goods stores today sell kayaks, but you may have to look at their manufacturers' catalogues. Kayaks take up a lot of showroom space, so usually only a few are on display. Excellent commercially made kayaks are produced in Canada, Australia, Japan, England, and Western Europe, as well as in the United States.

Attending a kayak event can be an excellent way of finding the boat you want. Kayaks are often for sale at races, where people surf, and where clubs meet to go cruising on rivers.

For the beginner a secondhand kayak could be a logical choice. Its structural condition can be easily ascertained simply by looking at it carefully both inside and out. Next, you should sit in it. Don't be concerned about scratches on the hull, but check any patches that you see carefully. Most well used fiberglass kayaks will have patches. And, of course, float the craft in the water to see if it leaks.

Last, be cautious when purchasing a secondhand kayak. Since there is always the possibility of your purchasing a stolen boat, make sure you're really buying from the owner or his agent.

Shopping Tips

Here's a handy checklist to take with you when shopping for a kayak:
- Check the footbraces to see if they're adjustable.
- Test the grabloops for strength.
- Find out if flotation (air bags) is included in the purchase price.
- Check the boat for comfort while sitting in it.
- Check the stiffness of the hull. (It should give a little, but not be too flexible.)
- Check both the hull and deck carefully inside and outside for pinholes. (Pinholes leak.)
- Check the seams, particularly inside the kayak. (A rough edge will puncture an air bag.)
- Run your hands carefully over the coaming and kneebraces. (Sharp edges will scratch your skin.)
- Line the kayak up directly in front of you and examine carefully from both the bow and stern. (Is the boat warped?)
- Check the whole cockpit area for stiffness. (The coaming and seat should not be too flexible.)

2. Paddles, Lifejackets, and Helmets

The three most important accessories in kayaking are paddles, lifejackets, and helmets. Paddles are necessary for locomotion and boat control. Lifejackets are a necessity at sea, in the surf, in any kind of whitewater, and during cold weather. In fact, you are now *required by law to have a lifejacket with you* when you are in the kayak. Helmets are essential in whitewater and a comfort in cold or windy weather. They can also protect the boater from the sun's rays on large lakes and in the ocean.

Paddles

In kayaking you use a double-bladed paddle (a blade at each end of the shaft) to propel and control the boat. It is the paddler's most important asset: not only is it the tool by which the kayak is propelled and steered, but it is also used to right the paddler in case of a capsize.

The four basic parts of a kayak paddle are:

The Shaft. About 4 inches in circumference, 1⅛ inches in diameter and

Kayak blades are "feathered"—set at right angles—and slightly curved for more power in stroking. (Ledyard Canoe Club)

four to six feet long, it is fully rounded at the midpoint then gradually becomes oval shaped close to the paddle blade. The shaft must be very strong and light, and should not be too flexible.

Some shafts are made in two pieces with a ferrule joint at the midpoint. This is for ease in storing, but generally makes for a weaker paddle. It is not, therefore, as popular with paddlers in heavy whitewater. A two-piece folding paddle can, however, be excellent as a spare on a trip.

The Throat. The part of the paddle toward the end of the shaft as it joins the blade is called the throat. Some throats are perfectly round, but the better ones are oval shaped to give the paddler a better grip on the paddle.

The Blade. Attached to each end of the shaft at the throat, it is approximately 7 to 10 inches wide and 14 to 18 inches long. If the blade is too big—that is, if it presents too large a surface area to the water—it will quickly fatigue the paddler. One too small will not push enough water.

Most kayak paddles have *feathered* blades, blades set into the shaft at an angle to each other, somewhere between 75 to 90°. This decreases wind resistance when the upper blade slices through the air prior to dipping into the water again. Nonfeathered paddles are not efficient; they catch the wind. They are rarely seen now. The side of the blade that pushes against the water is called the *power side, power face,* or *face,* while the other side is called the *back.*

To increase the blade's effectiveness in the water, some blades are *spooned* (slightly concave on the power side). Spoon blades offset 90 degrees clockwise are for lefties, while right handers use a paddle feathered at 90 degrees counterclockwise. Sometimes left handers learn to use counterclockwise offset paddles and right handers the clockwise.

For the sake of simplicity, throughout this book we *assume that the paddler* is using a right hand controlled paddle. By right or left hand control we mean the hand that maintains a constant grip on the shaft throughout the complete forward stroke. The other hand grips the shaft firmly as the blade digs into the water then relaxes its hold to allow the shaft to twist a bit on the recovery stroke.

Feathered flat bladed paddles may be used with either right hand or left hand control. Flat bladed paddles, however, are considered not to be efficient.

The Tip. The extreme end of the blade, it often takes a lot of abuse and punishment. Therefore the tip must be of rugged construction. Some tips are made of a very tough, hard piece of wood, others of fiberglass or metal. This cap at the extreme end of the paddle helps to prevent the blade from cracking and from absorbing water.

A tip flat across the bottom of the blade is preferred in slalom racing because it puts the maximum surface area into the water. This gives the racer the best grip in the water. A more rounded tip is preferred by cruisers and by some wildwater racers because the blade enters and leaves the water at the end of the stroke with minimum resistance.

Types of Kayak Paddles

The slalom racing paddle is fairly short and square tipped. It must be very strong to withstand the extreme demands made upon it. The wildwater racing paddle is somewhat longer and lighter, with more rounded tips, slanted to permit a clean entry into the water. Flatwater racing paddles are a further refinement of wildwater paddles. Sleek, smooth, incredibly light, they are designed to enter and exit from the water cleanly. General, all-purpose paddles fall between the two extremes.

All paddles should weigh two to three pounds. Any paddle much under two pounds may not be strong enough. Those over three pounds can quickly tire the paddler's wrists and arms.

Although collapsible (folding) kayak paddles are not too commonly seen as mentioned earlier, they can be a welcome addition as a spare on a kayak trip. Pulled apart from an interlocking sleeve at the middle of the shaft, these paddles can be easily stored inside a kayak or taped to the outside deck for emergency use. Another interesting innovation in folding kayak paddles is the one that can be easily converted into two single bladed canoe paddles. A T-grip fits into the hollow end of each shaft.

What Paddles Are Made Of

By far the nicest looking paddles are made of wood. The ancient Eskimos would have appreciated fully the aesthetically pleasing appearance of an exquisitely laminated wooden paddle. Both shaft and blades are constructed of multiple laminations using different kinds of wood to assure the lightest yet strongest and most durable product. Knot-free maple, spruce, fir, cedar, basswood, and ash have all been used by paddle builders. Wooden paddles do, however, require an occasional touch-up if there are nicks in their varnished surfaces.

Kayak paddles are also made of fiberglass. The blades are fabricated with an intricate combination of fiberglass cloth and resin then molded to the design, size, and weight desired. The blades can be affixed to shafts of a variety of materials: wood, tubular aluminum or other light alloy, or even tubular fiberglass. Further shaft refinements include a light composition filler for the shaft tube to prevent water infiltration and to help the paddle float. The outside of the tube is wrapped in a plastic or epoxy material to make it feel warmer and to give a better grip.

Ingenious combinations of wood, metal, and fiberglass can create very sturdy paddles light enough to float, but not easily broken. They can be pleasing to touch and handle and need very little maintenance. They rarely warp if left out in the sun.

Which Paddle For You?

There are several options. A finely crafted wooden paddle is a masterpiece of construction, but like a good piece of expensive furniture it should receive loving care and attention. It feels warm to the touch. Thanks to modern laminating techniques, today's wooden paddle can be extremely strong and durable.

Combination paddles (those made from a combination of metal, fiberglass, and sometimes wood) are very serviceable and require practically no maintenance. They can be knocked around a bit and see heavy usage without much danger of damage.

Folding or take-apart paddles may be just what you need for the kind of kayaking you intend to do—especially if you are thinking of trips in the wilderness.

For the beginner, it really is not crucial to have a general, all-purpose paddle rather than one specifically for slalom or wildwater racing. Either of the latter two kinds is perfectly suitable for learning all the basic strokes. A paddle designed specifically for flatwater racing should probably not be used while you are learning the Eskimo roll. Junior paddles are shorter. They have smaller blade surfaces and are now available for pre-teenagers.

Some manufacturers sell paddle kits. The shaft and blades are supplied. You attach the blades to the shaft according to the type of hand control you wish.

The *length* of your paddle is important. Listed below is a suggested guide for suitable length:

Your Height	Slalom	Touring & Wildwater	Flatwater Racing
5'4"	78.8" (202 cm)	82.3" (211 cm)	85.0" (218 cm)
5'6"	79.1" (203 cm)	82.7" (212 cm)	85.4" (219 cm)
5'8"	79.5" (204 cm)	83.1" (213 cm)	85.8" (220 cm)
5'10"	80.3" (206 cm)	83.5" (214 cm)	86.2" (221 cm)
6'0"	81.1" (208 cm)	83.9" (215 cm)	86.6" (222 cm)
6'2"	82.0" (210 cm)	84.3" (216 cm)	87.0" (223 cm)

The chart should be used only as a general guide. Your effectiveness with the paddle (aside from your technique) may depend upon factors other than your height; for example, your body weight, how it is distributed, your arm length, etc. If you are 5 feet 8 inches tall, you might, for instance, wish at the start to try a paddle approximately 213 centimeters or 83 inches long for general cruising, using a slightly shorter paddle for slalom, or one a shade longer for wildwater or flatwater racing. With a little experience you'll soon find out if you're comfortable and effective with that particular length. The trend over the past few years is toward shorter paddles for *all* phases of kayaking.

Lifejackets

Your lifejacket or PFD (personal flotation device) is your greatest friend and protector in the water. A proper lifejacket will not only help to keep you warm and cut the wind, but will support you if you capsize and become separated from your boat in the water. That's its main function, of course, to keep you on the surface in a relatively upright position so you can breathe and not be obliged to tread water to stay afloat.

History of Lifejackets

Lifejackets manufactured before the turn of the century were made of cork and balsawood. The next flotation used was kapok, a vegetable fiber found in tropical tree pods—resembling milkweed. Kapok fiber had a waxy coating that provided the necessary buoyancy and was sealed in vinyl packets to prevent exposure to the water. Unfortunately these packets could be punctured, rendering the lifejackets useless. The use of kapok today is prohibited in most of Europe and in Canada.

In the 1960's a very light, flexible, body-fitting lifejacket came out of France. Called the *Flotherchoc* it featured small air-filled vinyl packets placed inside nylon chambers. The Flotherchoc resembled a vest rather than the older, more traditional horse-collar variety. It was an instant favorite, but, over time, even its vinyl air packets could puncture, losing buoyancy.

Space age plastics came to the rescue later in the decade, and now a closed cell foam encased in a nylon vest-like garment is used. Each tiny cell within the foam is a separate entity, unlike a sponge which has channels joining its various chambers. These closed cell foam pads could be punctured over and over again without losing very much buoyancy. Some of the better closed cell foam pads will not deteriorate even when they are compressed. The vest drapes comfortably over the paddler's chest, shoulders, and back. It can then be snugged up tight with a drawstring or a zipper.

Lifejacket Approval

The United States Coast Guard (USCG) and the Underwriters Laboratories have been monitoring lifejackets for many years. Under regulations established in the early 1970's, you are required to have at least one USCG-approved lifejacket for each person in your recreational boat. The regulations themselves are somewhat technical, but all you need to remember is that you should wear your USCG-approved lifejacket in a kayak and that your lifejacket must be the right size for you and marked with an approved USCG number.

The USCG has approved five different types of lifejackets, only three of which concern us in kayaking. The first, *Type I*, is a big and bulky vest-type jacket with enormous buoyancy and ability to keep you afloat. It is designed to turn even an unconscious person in the water from a face down position to a vertical or slightly head back position. Type I is shoulders, and back. It can then be snugged up tight with a drawstring suitable anywhere, but because of its bulk, it is unusually appropriate for paddlers exploring heavy whitewater rivers like the Colorado in the Grand Canyon. Type I was a favorite lifejacket of the late Dr. Walter Blackadar, who explored some of the greatest whitewater rivers in the world. Type I is less popular with racers and general recreational boaters because of its bulk.

Type II is designed to perform the same function as Type I except that it's smaller, has less buoyancy, and is more commonly shaped like a horse collar than a vest. Unfortunately the horse collar restricts a boater's twisting neck and head action and therefore is not very popular with most kayakers. The Type II's are the least expensive of the approved types and can often be found at boat livery rental places.

Type III is designed to keep a conscious person in a vertical or slightly head back position in the water. Type III comes in many styles, is the most comfortable of the three types, and therefore is a favorite with many paddlers. It's basically a nicely fitting closed cell foam-filled nylon vest.

Other Considerations

If you're thinking about racing, there are some things you should know. First of all, flatwater racing kayaks, for some reason, are exempt from the USCG regulations—no lifejackets needed. Second, to be eligible for whitewater competition, a racer must wear a lifejacket with a minimum buoyancy of 13.2 pounds.This may not seem like much protection, but it must be remembered that the weight of the human body in water is only a fraction of its weight on land. A lifejacket listed at 13.2 pounds of buoyancy will hold most people up easily. Incidentally, the Type III USCG-approved jacket satisfies this requirement nicely. Water ski belts are unacceptable for use in kayaking.

A new style of lifejacket introduced at the 1979 World Championships has the flotation located at the lower part of the paddler's torso and the underside of the spray cover. The idea was to reduce bulk around the upper chest and keep the racer's body as streamlined as possible to avoid touching slalom poles. Although the International Canoe Federation has approved this new style, the National Slalom and Wildwater Committee of the American Canoe Association, the U.S. governing body for kayak racing, has approved the style only for U.S. Team trials and National Championships (as of 1981). At all other races in America, competitors must have standard lifejackets.

Those adventuresome kayakers interested in cruising, camping, and exploring nature's waterways should consider a wilderness vest. It's a lifejacket with four pockets in front to store matches, compasses, and other wilderness necessities.

Choosing Your Lifejacket

Since there are well over a dozen manufacturers of Type III lifejackets, you will have a good variety to pick from whether you intend to go cruising, surfing, or racing. Keep in mind that USCG-approved lifejackets are available for children and infants, too.

Your best practical test for a lifejacket is to wear the top part of your paddling clothes into a store and try on Type III's while sitting in a kayak, if one is available at the store. Next, put on the spray cover and see if the lifejacket tends to ride up around your neck; you wish to avoid this if possible. Make sure your arms can move in all directions freely without chafing. Does the lifejacket move with your body as you twist and turn? (It should.) Make sure the zippers or clasps work freely and easily. Often a plastic zipper will catch less sand and dirt and thus work more smoothly than a metal zipper.

Check to see that the lifejacket is labeled USCG-approved with proper wording and type number. Check the seams for strength. If it feels comfortable and has met all the above-mentioned conditions, buy it. But your responsibility does not end there. Even if you find that it doesn't fit right after you've worn it a few times, *do not alter it*. An altered lifejacket loses its USCG approval. Get one that does fit. Inspect your lifejacket from time to time to see that it is free of rips, tears and holes, and that all the seams are firm. Never use your precious lifejacket as a boat fender, cushion, or kneeling pad.

Helmets

In a very real sense the helmet is the lifejacket for the head. It has a similar set of functions. Its primary purpose, of course, is to protect you against sharp blows to the head from rocks lurking in the rapids. It also provides warmth, protection from the sun and insects, as well as from the rain.

When should you wear one? Always, in every kind of whitewater. Just as you need a paddle and a lifejacket, you should also automatically reach for your helmet whenever a whitewater trip is planned. Although fast moving water creates cushions around rocks, you can still receive a stunning blow to the head if not protected. What's worse, especially in the rivers of the United States, people have used river beds as dumping grounds for old autos, refrigerators, and other large appliances. These create a hazard as well.

The weekend flatwater cruiser or oceangoing kayaker does not need a helmet to protect himself from rocks, but some kind of head covering is advisable to ward off insects and prevent sunstroke. Shade from a wide brimmed hat feels mighty good on a sunny day and makes kayaking much more pleasurable when the weather is inclement.

Some people wear helmets while surf kayaking and it's a good idea. Occasionally beaches have rocks protruding from them, and there is always the danger of being hit on the head by another surf kayak or paddle.

In the early days, once people recognized the need for head protection, bicycle helmets, rock climbers' helmets, hockey helmets, and even motorcycle and football helmets have been seen on the waterways. While these helmets were certainly better than nothing at all, fortunately manufacturers have now produced some interesting head protecting devices uniquely suited to kayaking needs.

Characteristics of a Good Helmet

The whitewater boater has specific needs: the helmet should be light (preferably a pound or less); the inner hat band (cradle) should be adjustable to the contours of the head; it must fit snugly; visibility should be good; vision should not be obstructed by the brow of the helmet reaching too close to the eyes; peripheral vision should be good but the temple area of the skull in front of the ears must also be protected; it should be reasonably waterproof, yet have good drainage for what little water does seep in; the helmet must provide for good hearing because recognizing the sound of rapids ahead is critical to safe boating. The chin strap should fit snugly so that the helmet does not get ripped off if you take an unexpected plunge into the water or get hit by a large, forceful wave. The helmet should float, of course, if you lose it in the water.

Kinds of Helmets

Solid shell helmets are made from hand lay-up fiberglass using a specially formulated high impact material. Although these helmets offer superb protection, they are somewhat heavier, weighing more than a pound.

Perforated shell helmets—those with narrow drainage holes—are made of injection molded high impact polycarbons and polypropylene plastics. Some are also made of Kevlar®—that extremely tough material used in the manufacture of bulletproof vests. These helmets are extremely light (under a pound) and are the favorites of racers. They will serve you well in most situations, but are not designed for unusually severe impact.

There are a few rock climbing helmets on the market today that can also be used safely in kayaking. They often have a thick molded plastic shell lined with a crushable foam for a snug fit around the head. These helmets weigh over a pound.

The interior fittings of a helmet are important. The inner cradle (hat band) should be adjustable and not absorb water. Adjustable sling suspensions are popular; others are built with closed cell foam padding. Still others come with a specially-fitted, interchangeable inner padding for different head sizes. The chin straps should not chafe and should be easily adjusted. They should fasten so the helmet will not wobble when you turn your head quickly.

Whitewater helmets have rapidly become a mark of individuality. Helmets have been seen on the waterways with the person's name or club insignia on them, even national flags. Others sport a high flying feather or are painted with a bright fluorescent color. Still others have bits of ribbon streaming behind them. To each his own. Kayaking is a sport that thrives on individuality.

3. Accessories for Kayaking

In this chapter we cover the major accessories used by kayakers. They include items for the kayak itself, personal gear, and tips on how to transport your kayak to the river, lake, or ocean.

Americans have been accused of being crazy for gimmicks and gadgets. Those who find themselves interested in the exciting sport of kayaking will not be disappointed. Many innovations and ingeniously designed accessories are available to increase your paddling comfort.

Kayak Accessories

Flotation Bags

The most important kayak accessory is flotation to make it unsinkable. A kayak filled with water, sinking slowly to the bottom of a river indicates a lack of foresight on the part of the owner and creates a potentially dangerous situation. Proper flotation keeps a swamped boat riding high in the water, decreasing the likelihood of collision with rocks as the boat is swept downstream, and facilitates rescue.

When fiberglass kayaks first became popular in Europe and in the United States, the need for flotation quickly became apparent. In plain words: fiberglass by itself simply doesn't float. Beach balls, inner tubes, and even lifejackets were stuffed into both ends to help keep a swamped kayak afloat. They had a way, however, of working free and popping out of the boat.

Eventually, more sophisticated means of flotation evolved. Float bags, air filled vinyl containers tapered to fit into the ends of a kayak, became popular. A smaller one was squeezed into the bow in front of the foot-braces and a larger one stuffed into the stern directly behind the cockpit. A further refinement involved split bags to be fitted into each side of the interior of a kayak with a supporting wall inside of the boat. Easy to reach hoses for inflation by mouth, similar to those used in inflatable camping air mattresses, are attached to the bags.

Some kayakers rely solely on a vertical ethafoam wall support system in the bow and stern of their kayaks. The ethafoam gives rigidity to the deck and hull, but provides a small measure of flotation as well. This arrangement is not recommended unless split bags are used on either side of the ethafoam.

33

The more flotation your kayak has, the higher it will ride in the water, making it safer, less prone to damage, and a lot easier to rescue. No kayak should ever be launched in any kind of water anywhere until it has an adequate means of flotation in the interior of *both* ends of the boat.

Spray Covers

The second most important accessory for a kayak is the *spray cover*. It serves a variety of purposes. In cold weather, a spray cover helps to keep your legs warm. It keeps waves from splashing into your cockpit on a windy lake, in the rapids, or in the ocean. In a capsize, it keeps the water out of your boat so you can execute the Eskimo roll. The spray cover is as important an accessory to your kayak as your paddle and flotation bags.

Spray covers have four basic parts: the tubular skirt that fits around the paddler's torso, the deck that flares out from the torso to stretch across and cover the cockpit, a special grabloop at the front of the cover for quick removal, and an elastic cord around the bottom of the cover to help seal it watertight under the coaming.

Spray covers are made either from a light rubberized waterproof cloth with elastic cords, or from nylaprene or neoprene rubber. Cloth spray covers are good for moderate whitewater and are very durable and less expensive. Suspenders can be attached to hold the skirt high up on the paddler's chest for greater protection against the waves.

Neoprene spray covers keep the water out better than cloth covers and keep you much warmer. Some neoprene rubber comes with a thin layer of nylon on one or both sides for added strength. Like the cloth spray cover, most neoprene ones use an elastic cord around the outer perimeter of the cover to seal it under the coaming. Nevertheless, some spray covers use a prestretched nylaprene rim band as the tension member around the coaming, instead of an elastic cord. It is knot free and wrinkle free, therefore more watertight.

One of the more recent designs combines a spray cover and a lifejacket in a one-piece unit. Described earlier as the new style lifejacket introduced at the 1979 World Whitewater Championships, its flotation is joined to the underneath of the spray cover thus keeping the racer's body as streamlined as possible.

Although spray covers can be purchased commercially, anyone handy with a sewing machine, a pair of scissors, and familiar with neoprene glue can fashion a personally fitted spray cover for himself. It is not a technically difficult procedure and can be done some winter evening before the boating season starts.

The Repair Kit

Another important item for the care of your kayak and equipment is the repair kit. It should accompany you in your boat on all wilderness trips and be readily available in your car at the races. An adequate repair kit (always housed in a waterproof container) consists of the following items:
- Resin, in a leak proof container,
- Hardener in a leak proof container,
- Swatches of 10-ounce cloth and mat,
- Mixing and measuring cups,
- Coarse and fine sandpaper,
- A pair of scissors,
- Mixing sticks, wax paper, a throw-away brush, and
- A tube of vinyl glue.

In the absence of a repair kit, the best single substitute is a full roll of two-inch wide silver/gray boat repair tape available in hardware stores. It is sometimes called duct tape. On a still structurally sound kayak, many a crack and hole in the hull can be made watertight with tape. The trick is to wipe off the section to be repaired very carefully so that it is clean and dry. Otherwise, the tape will not adhere.

Miscellaneous Items

The fastidious boater may wish to wax and polish the hull the way he would a prized automobile. Fiberglass boat waxes are available, and there are also a number of paste waxes that can help bring back the original color and shine of the boat and add a measure of protection as well.

Kayakers exploring ocean waterways out of sight of land and those encountering fog should have a compass in a waterproof case fastened securely to the deck in front of the cockpit where it is easy to read. Those traveling at sea would be smart to carry a flare and a waterproof flashlight as well. A ship-to-shore walkie-talkie would not be a bad idea either.

Expedition kayaks sometimes have footpedal operated detachable rudders to help with steering over a long expanse of water.

Accessories for Your Comfort

Nothing is more discouraging than sitting in a kayak cold, wet, and miserable. There really is no need for it. A judicious selection of clothing can bring you through the wildest waves, the highest surf, or the most inclement weather in comfort.

The Paddling Jacket

Let's start with the upper body. A lightweight uninsulated nylon jacket is usually ideal. The jacket should be one size too large for you, so there'll be no restriction of your arms and shoulders, even if you wear a sweater, underwear, or wet suit top underneath. A good paddling jacket has elasticized cuffs and a fully elasticized waistband to help keep out water and wind. It should fit snugly, but comfortably, around the neck. Velcro closures also work well for adjusting cuffs and neck openings.

Some nylon paddling jackets are lined with a thin layer of foam to help retain body heat, while still others have neoprene at the cuffs and neck for added warmth and protection against water. Look for zippers along the sleeves, and a pocket to keep small items like lip balm and sunscreen lotion handy.

Sweaters

Any old, ratty wool sweater can add much comfort worn under a paddling jacket. To keep you warm after it gets wet, the sweater had better be *all* wool. Wool "wicks" moisture away from the skin, drying from the inside out.

Paddling sweaters are also available commercially. They feature three-quarter-length sleeves and are made of a quick drying synthetic material. Wearing a sweater under a paddling jacket, you can paddle in comfort even on a cold, raw day. Some paddling sweaters are attractively designed for wear around the campsite as well.

Wet Suits

In the early spring or late fall when the water is below 50 degrees Fahrenheit, a wet suit is the best thing to wear while boating. Thanks to research, kayakers now have an interesting variety of choices.

A wet suit acts like another layer of skin to retain body heat and prevent penetration by the cold. The little water that seeps through to your skin is trapped and quickly warmed. You will not be perfectly dry in a wet suit, but if it fits properly you will be very comfortable. It's good protection from the rain and keeps you from being scratched by bushes along the river bank. It also helps prevent bruises from rocks.

Wet suits are made of neoprene rubber which fits the contours of the body. They are now available in a variety of color combinations and often come with a nylon skin on one or both sides for added strength. 3/8- and

¼-inch thick neoprene is a little heavy unless you plan to kayak in the polar regions. ⅛-inch thick neoprene is popular because it can provide enough protection and warmth while affording excellent flexibility. ¹⁄₁₆-inch thick neoprene is a favorite with racers since it is the lightest of all and is the most flexible.

Wet suits come in a variety of styles:

The Farmer John. Sometimes called *Long John,* this wet suit covers the legs and torso but is sleeveless. Worn with a paddling jacket this style is very popular because it affords unrestricted upper body movement. The ⅛-inch thick Farmer John is a general, all-purpose favorite.

The Standard Wet Suit. Consisting of a longsleeve jacket and pants, it covers the arms, legs and torso for total protection. Upper body movement is somewhat restricted depending upon which thickness you choose.

The Shorty. Cut off just above the knees and sleeveless, this wet suit keeps the torso warm and is popular with surf kayakers. Shorty or Farmer

Wet suits. From left to right: Shorty, Vest, Farmer John, Standard. (Evans Associates)

John wet suits, when combined with waterproof exterior rain pants, provide even greater warmth. Rain pants, made from a light rubberized material, usually come equipped with a waist drawcord and a snap closure for the ankles.

The Wet Suit Vest. This style is just what the name implies: it's simply a vest of neoprene. It's particularly effective at the start or end of the cold weather season.

The Combination Vest. A simple wet suit vest with waterproof nylon sleeves attached, its sleeves have neoprene cuffs to keep the water out. This combination vest is the best of both worlds. It makes obsolete the old long sleeved restrictive wet suit jacket while providing more protection for the arms than the Farmer John or the Shorty. A full length zipper down the front aids in ventilating your torso as it gets overheated while paddling. Wet suits can extend your paddling season significantly.

Protection for Your Feet. Booties are available from ⅛-inch thick neoprene reinforced by a molded hard rubber sole and heel. These can be worn with or without *wool* socks. The hard rubber sole has a tread that helps keep you from slipping on the rocks. In warm weather a pair of old "holy" sneakers do a fine job of protecting your feet. Plastic river sandals that attach firmly to the foot also offer good protection. Loose mocassins, loafers, and ordinary sandals quickly come off in the water and are unsuitable.

One-sixteenth-inch thick neoprene covered with nylon makes a good sock. You can wear these neoprene socks inside your old river sneakers or river sandals on the coldest day and remain comfortable.

Protection for Your Hands

It doesn't have to be a particularly cold day, if there's a raw wind blowing across the water, for your hands to lose their heat. Gripping the paddle will get tough, since cold, wet fingers soon become numb. Paddling or boating gloves are available in a variety of models. They go by several names: Pogies®, smittens, and wind gloves. They can be made of either neoprene or waterproof nylon cloth. A standard wet suit glove made of neoprene is too bulky for you to get the feel of the paddle.

A Pogie® consists of a piece of ⅛-inch thick neoprene/nylon that fits over the wrist like a sleeve. It is cut in such a way that, as you grip your paddle with your bare hand, the neoprene/nylon can be wrapped around your knuckles and fingers and be attached back to the sleeve with a Velcro fastener. The fastener will pull away easily and safely should you need to withdraw your hand from the paddle.

Pogie.® (Jay Evans)

If you cannot locate a pair of Pogies® and it's a cold day, water skiing gloves or thin leather driving gloves will do.

Miscellaneous Items

For kayakers paddling in cold conditions along the seacoast or on an open lake where a helmet is not required, a good all wool hat is highly recommended. It will resist rain and, when pulled down over your ears, it can provide plenty of warmth.

For those of you who wear glasses, don't forget to outfit them with an elastic strap around the back of your head to prevent them from being knocked away by a saucy splash of a wave. A defogging compound rubbed onto your lenses can help keep your glasses clear. Finally, a small first aid kit kept in a waterproof container can be a valuable asset to a kayak trip.

Protecting Your Gear

Storage Bags

Waterproof equipment storage bags come in many shapes, styles, and sizes. When purchasing a bag, look for lightness, waterproofness, and ease of access. The bag should be easy to open and close. A bag with shoulder straps comes in handy when you're carrying gear down to the river bank.

Net Bags

Some paddlers like to carry along net bags. Like onion sacks, these bags are perforated and make a handy receptacle for all your wet clothing. These bags breathe freely allowing your clothes to ventilate and prevent mildew.

Small Bags and Pouches

Small, individual vinyl bags, with Velcro or plastic zipper closures are good for carrying small articles, and your lunch or a snack. Waterproof pouches are important for other small items, such as matches and sunglasses.

Camera Bags

First of all, they must be waterproof, yet easy and quick to open in case a photographic possibility suddenly appears. Second, it's good to have a shoulder or neck strap on a camera bag. Third, some camera bags come with an inflatable chamber. This not only prevents your camera or binoculars from sinking to the bottom of the river in case of capsize, but also cushions your equipment to prevent abrasions and damage from rough handling.

Boat and Paddle Covers

Whitewater kayakers have never been known to baby their paddles or boats—they get such rough usage in the rapids anyway. However, flatwater kayakers have always been extremely cautious in the care of their boats and paddles. A nick or scratch on the hull of a whitewater boat is little cause for concern. For the flatwater racer it can mean the difference between winning and losing a race. Consequently, flatwater racers often keep their paddles (and sometimes their boats as well) in a protective cloth bag to prevent chafing during transport. The bag also protects the equipment from the elements and makes for handy storage.

No matter how carefully you stow your belongings inside a kayak, the chances are that, somehow, they'll get wet. Kayaking is a wet sport. Water gets into everything, but a little prudence and care will assure your arrival at the campsite with a dry packet of food and a dry sleeping bag.

Transporting Your Kayak

Owners of collapsible (folding) kayaks have it made. All they have to do is to pack their boats away in two duffle-like carrying bags, toss them into the trunk of the car, and away they go.

Car Top Racks

Owners of rigid kayaks need a little more ingenuity. Die-cast aluminum brackets are available that grip the rain gutter of your car securely. When bolted to a 2 x 4 or support member, you'll have a multi-purpose rack. There are also car top carriers for automobiles without rain gutters.

A further refinement is sometimes called a kayak stacker. It's a vertically upright post fastened part way along the cross bar. This allows you to stack several kayaks on edge, thereby increasing the capacity of the car top rack. Kayak paddles can be tied securely alongside each kayak.

Just as important as the car top rack itself is the tie-down system you use. Interstate highway speeds of 55 mph create considerable wind drag on kayaks stacked on top of your car, van, or camper. Therefore, you must secure the kayak to the rack, preferably with a tight fitting elasticized cord. Even more important, both bow and stern of the kayak must be securely fastened to the car's bumpers. This removes the risk of the kayak becoming airborne and flying off your car while you're cruising down the highway. Specially fitted tensioners and hooks can be used if you want to avoid having to knot your tie-down ropes. Plastic bumper hooks are handy because they simply fit over the edge of the bumper; but unless the tie-down rope remains very tight, the plastic hooks can slip loose. If this occurs at the rear of your car, you might not notice it right away. A safer system is to find some way of actually tying or fastening the rope around the bumper itself.

Always keep in mind that no rooftop car rack system for holding kayaks should ever be allowed to stand alone. The bow and stern of the kayak must be tied to the bumpers as well.

Trailers

Kayak trailers hauled behind a vehicle can carry up to two dozen boats if properly made. Trailers are ideal for college outing clubs and outfitters. The better ones are well balanced so that the trailer tongue can be lifted off the ground or unhooked from the trailer hitch even when the trailer is loaded. A storage area should be provided for paddles and other gear. A well built kayak trailer should have good vertical stability (not tip over

---

Caution

All kayaks and other gear must be securely fastened to the trailer, and the driver of the vehicle towing the trailer must know how to back the trailer up without jackknifing it. When passing another vehicle on the road, the driver must remember to pull at least three car lengths ahead before swinging back into the regular driving lane again. This will give plenty of clearance for the trailer behind it. Be sure that the turn signals and tail lights function properly on the trailer.

---

easily), a spare tire, complete wiring for lights, and a safety chain that attaches to the bumper or frame of the car.

Trolleys

In Western Europe and England small, folding two wheeled trolleys can be seen aiding in transporting kayaks, something like wheeled luggage carriers. These trolleys fit at the midpoint of the kayak and you simply pull the kayak along by the grabloop at the bow or stern.

It can sometimes be a long walk with your kayak to the river's edge from where your vehicle is parked. One easy way to carry your kayak is to team up with a partner. Place your two kayaks side by side. One of you takes the two bows, the other the two sterns, lift them off and away you go.

4. Safety

Kayaking looks more dangerous than it really is. Water is not, after all, man's natural medium, but statistically speaking kayaking is one of the safest sports around. Perhaps this is so because those who have taken part in the past have put a high premium on safety. Unlike some sports, kayaking has had a tradition of attracting cautious, conservative people. Perhaps it is the potential for danger in a water sport that at once attracts the adventurous person, but also makes him wary and careful.

Throughout this book aspects of safety are stressed where appropriate. Nevertheless safety in kayaking is so important to your enjoyment of the sport that it warrants a chapter of its own.

If your kayak is structurally sound, watertight, with grabloops and flotation at both ends, and you have a firm fitting but easily detachable spray cover, then you have gone a long way toward providing safe kayaking for yourself. If you have an inflatable kayak it should have multiple air chambers. Your paddle, of course, should be structurally sound.

If you are a strong swimmer in good physical condition, wear proper clothing and footgear, and have handy all the necessary accessories such as a first aid kit, lifejacket, and helmet, you have taken the next big step toward boating safety. The final steps involve human judgment and kayaking techniques.

Boat Control

Keep your kayak under control at all times. You must be able to stop by a rock, reach an eddy, or pull up on shore when necessary. You should never attempt rapids until you have scouted them thoroughly and feel that in case of capsizing you could swim to safety. Always be aware of other kayaks in your vicinity. Do not create a traffic jam on the river or on a surfing beach. Never attempt a lake crossing if the waves are too high for you.

While at sea, always be aware of the tide and time of day. Make the tide work for you rather than against you. Avoid busy harbors, shipping lanes, and channels. Stay well away from large seagoing or high speed craft.

River Hazards

Water reading and what to look for in rapids is discussed later in Chapter 9, but a few pointers here can be helpful. High water looks inviting to the adventurous, but higher than normal stream flow significantly raises the possibilities of danger on the water. As the flow rate increases so does the difficulty of making a rescue. Generally speaking, one should not go kayaking on a river in a flood. Brush, fallen trees, and other obstructions can pin a kayak and trap its occupant.

Dams along a river sometimes cannot be seen until the last minute, and the water below a dam often curls back on itself and can trap the unwary boater. On smaller streams in agricultural areas, fences and barbed wire are sometimes stretched across for the benefit of the farmer by keeping his cattle in, but not to the benefit of boaters.

In remote wooded areas, logs and pulpwood are floated downstream. In cold weather there is always the chance of ice accumulating along the river bank or on the surface of the water itself.

Beware of dam releases which cause a sudden rise in water levels. When kayaking at high altitudes, bear in mind that on hot sunny days snow melt from the mountain peaks can cause a significant rise in water levels.

One of the most insidious dangers in river travel is not what appears on the surface of the water, but what lies just under the water level. Sharp rocks, submerged logs, discarded autos, broken glass, and other menacing things dumped into the river create ever present possibilities for trouble. If you capsize and are swept down through rapids, always remember to keep your feet and legs as near as possible to the surface of the water, pointing downstream; float on your back. This will minimize the chances of a leg or foot getting caught under the water. Never kayak in bare feet; always wear sneakers or lightweight protective footgear.

The arrows indicate a "horizon line"—an immediate signal to pull to shore and inspect the hidden dam or weir that undoubtedly lies just below the line. (Ledyard Canoe Club)

Combating the Cold

In all outdoor travel away from shelter, a kayaker has a responsibility to his own body to make sure that it is warm and protected. Cold air, strong winds, and cold water will quickly lower your body temperature. This in turn reduces your ability to save yourself. It steals your strength and numbs your fingers so that even with people nearby to help you, your ability to help yourself is lessened. What's worse, the lowering of your body temperature (hypothermia) affects your reasoning ability; unfortunately, you will not realize that this is happening.

Wet suits should be worn when the water temperature drops below 50 degrees Fahrenheit, no matter how hot the sun is on that particular day. Windproof clothing and wool, as previously explained, are also good safeguards. The sensible kayaker always has a complete change of dry clothes in a waterproof package in the kayak or stored in his car at the take-out point at the end of a day's trip.

Soaking wet clothes lose about 90 percent of their insulating value; you lose heat from your body 240 times as fast in wet clothes as in dry clothes. If you cannot stay warm, then you must quickly get out of the wind or rain, go ashore, and get inside an automobile with the heater turned up to maximum. If no car is available, build a fire and make a secure, protected campsite. Never ignore shivering: your body is telling you to take whatever means are available to start restoring your body heat.

Removal of wet clothes and getting into a dry sleeping bag or wrapping yourself in an insulated blanket can help. Contrary to myth, the consumption of alcoholic beverages is not helpful: hot tea or hot soup is much better. A bath tub filled with water as hot as you can stand is better than a hot shower.

Self-rescue Techniques (See Chapter 11 for Sea Rescues)

As the old saying goes—"an ounce of prevention is worth a pound of cure." Self-rescue is the quickest and best safety measure of all. In light of this it is important to have a frank, unbiased knowledge of your boating ability. Resist peer pressure if necessary; get out of your boat and walk down the river bank if you are unsure of your ability to navigate the rapids safely. If the surf is coming in too high, head for the safety of the beach.

Going out in a kayak alone, of course, is never recommended. You're totally without help if you do. Never attempt whitewater alone.

There are certain basic skills that should be mastered right away. Train for capsizing. Practice exiting from your boat and swimming quickly to the bow or stern. Maintain the kayak's overturned position (this traps valuable air inside that helps buoyancy) and ferry it to shore. Remember always to remain on the upstream side of your overturned boat so you won't get wedged on a rock.

One of the most critically important skills for all kayakers to learn is the Eskimo roll (detailed in Chapter 6). It is no longer considered a stunt and really isn't hard to learn. If you capsize, in less than four seconds you can be right side up again. That's a lot safer than exiting from your boat and attempting to swim ashore.

If a member of your boating group capsizes and exits the kayak, go for the swimmer first. Let the swimmer hold on to your stern grabloop as you tow him/her to shore. You can always go back after the kayak and the paddle later.

Responsibilities of a Leader

Try to be familiar with the stretch of water to be covered. Knowledge of the area at high tide, low tide (or at high or low water levels) is essential. Knowing the abilities and limitations of all members of your party is also important. Are there any weak swimmers in the group? Do any of them have a history of convulsions or fainting spells?

One defective paddle or leaky kayak can spoil a trip for everyone. Make sure all equipment is in good repair. First aid kits, and repair kits should always be brought along.

Never encourage an inexperienced boater to try a stretch of the river beyond his ability. If the group is large (more than six kayaks), consider splitting into smaller groups. Each group should be of the same skill level; designate a leader and a "sweep," an experienced boater who brings up the rear. On the water, boats must be spread out enough for maneuverability, but all boats in each group should stay within sight of each other.

If your trip is an extended expedition into the wilderness, a daily trip schedule should be filed with appropriate authorities. Checkpoints should be established along the way, and preplanned exit routes selected in anticipation of an emergency.

Combating the Elements

Much emphasis was placed on taking adequate precautions against the cold in Chapter 3, and rightly so, but nature has other unpleasant surprises for the unwary. Beware of sunstroke and dehydration in the summer. Always wear some kind of a hat or helmet. Drink plenty of liquids—but never from the stream in which you are paddling. There are strange bacteria that would just love to get the chance to ravage your digestive tract. Carry your drinking fluids with you, or boil the water first.

Rescue Equipment

The kayak itself is a handy piece of rescue equipment. In a rescue mission paddle quickly over to a capsized boater and allow him to grab the point of your bow in order to right himself. An abandoned kayak floating downstream can be nudged over to shore by a kayaker pressing the bow firmly up against the side of the overturned boat.

On a large lake or at sea several kayaks can "raft up" by coming alongside each other and extending their paddles over each others' decks. This provides a stable platform for the one kayak or person that needs assistance.

A throw-line rescue bag is a very useful piece of rescue equipment. It consists of about 60 or 70 feet of ⅜-inch nonkinking yellow or orange polypropylene line that floats. The line passes through a grommet at the bottom of a nylon bag which contains a foam disc for flotation. The line is tied outside the bottom of the bag to form a large grabloop. The remainder of the line is stuffed into the bag with the free end sticking out.

To use it, hold the free end with one hand and with the other hand, toss the bag containing the grabloop with an underhanded motion. It is best to throw beyond the swimmer in the water rather than short of the swimmer. If thrown beyond the swimmer, the line can be quickly pulled back to where the swimmer can grab it. Aim slightly downstream of the swimmer, if he's floating down the river. If the swimmer is perched on a

Throw-line rescue bag.
(Charles Walbridge)

rock, aim slightly upstream so that the line will float to him. Once the swimmer has grabbed the line securely, make sure your feet are well braced with the line wrapped around your waist. If you have time, you may wish to place the line around a tree instead of around your waist. Mountaineers call this a belay; it acts as a brake.

Throw-line rescue bags are small enough so that they can fit into a kayak for ready use. When throw-line rescue bags are not available, ring buoys and heaving lines can be used, but should not be stored inside the kayak.

Some experts prefer a 70-foot length of ½-inch twisted polypropylene rope without an attached bag. It's thrown underhand or sidearm. The rescuer throws part of the coil out over the water, while the remaining part pays out of the nonthrowing hand as the rope becomes fully extended.

Boaters should experiment thoroughly with both kinds of rescue ropes, decide which system they prefer, then perfect their throwing techniques.

Breakaway Cockpits

It is possible for a kayak to become wedged between a couple of rocks in the rapids. This can happen even to expert boaters. When a kayak is pinned, the water creates an enormous force on the boat—enough to jackknife or buckle the craft. When this happens, the paddler, sitting in the chaise longue position, is vulnerable to having his legs pinned by the deformation of the boat. Deformation can happen almost instantly, although sometimes it takes a minute or two for the deck or hull to collapse. The paddler should forget about trying to pry the boat loose or about doing an Eskimo roll. The paddler should get out of the boat *immediately* and swim to safety.

Fortunately, manufacturers are beginning to recognize this potential hazard; they are building ever stronger boats. In some, nylon reinforcing around the cockpit has been discontinued, allowing the cockpit area to absorb stress only up to a point. After that, it breaks rather than bends. Once the kayak splits open, pressure on the legs is relieved, and the paddler can quickly and safely exit.

The result is a broken, but easily repairable kayak. More important, it means that the paddler is able to extricate himself from a potential hazard. When you're buying a kayak, consider one that has a breakaway cockpit.

PART II. BASIC KAYAK TECHNIQUES

5. Getting Acquainted With Your Boat

<hr>

Plan of Presentation

The purpose of this chapter is to present the basic kayaking procedures. These procedures are constant points of reference throughout the rest of the book, and any variations in method can be superimposed for special circumstances which are considered in later sections.

1. Throughout, it will be assumed that the paddler is a competent swimmer, and is ready to don sensible protective equipment after graduating from the shallow pool to deep and/or flowing water.

2. The sporty, ultra-maneuverable little slalom kayak is the "demonstration model" for the steps that follow. This choice is partly because it is the favorite all-purpose boat for whitewater, and partly because it requires the widest range of paddling technique. Owing to hull design, the cruising or touring kayak is much easier to track, and the wildwater racing kayak is hard to turn at all as the result of emphasis on forward speed. Therefore if newcomers to the sport learn how to control, stabilize and propel the tippy, mind-of-its-own slalom kayak, they can apply this acquired technique to managing the less recalcitrant boats.

3. Since every good paddler becomes virtually ambidextrous in the course of getting into the water and practicing, the matter of handedness and master-sidedness does not enter into basic kayaking techniques. The procedures described *start from the right.*

<hr>

Once upon a time Nathaniel Hawthorne remarked that his friend Henry Thoreau had told him it was necessary only to *will* a boat to go in any direction, and the boat would immediately assume the desired course as if imbued with the spirit of its pilot. Perhaps Thoreau was simply being a good salesman for the joys of boating on Walden Pond or the Concord River; certainly he wasn't talking about any craft that resembles the modern sporty kayak.

Anatomy of a Kayak

Grabloops: You use these to lift and carry a kayak, to haul a cap-sized kayak to shore, and also used to help tie down a kayak on a car rack.

Flotation bags: These are plastic bags filled with air to give a cap-sized kayak plenty of buoyancy.

Footbraces: Usually adjustable for short or tall people, the balls of your feet should rest comfortably against them.

Cockpit area:

Coaming: The lip around the cockpit over which the spray cover fits to keep out water.

Kneebraces: Foam pads for your knees to rest comfortably against.

Seat-hipbraces: Usually molded together as one unit, it hangs from the coaming about one inch off the bottom of the kayak.

Backbrace: An adjustable strap located behind the hipbraces.

Deck: The part of the kayak above water.

Hull: The bottom part of the kayak, most of which is under water or rests on the water.

Gunwale: The seam around the kayak that joins the hull to the deck.

My first kayak was named *Igluk* after the Eskimo god of mischief—and with good reason. One day during the early stages of my relationship with *Igluk* on a placid New Hampshire stream, a farmer haying close by noticed my predicament and called out: "You'll have to show 'er who's boss!"

So I was forced to learn kayaking technique. Which boils down to: (1) knowing how to get in and out of my boat; (2) knowing how to right myself when the kayak tips over; and (3) knowing how to paddle it so it will go precisely where I want it to go in any kind of water—in circles, sideways, forward, and backward. And I found out how much my back, hips, abdomen, and legs contribute to control and propulsion.

Dry Run: Adjustments

If you're new to kayaking, you must shed the notion that you sit in a kayak: what you really do is *wear* it, because the kayak feels almost like an extension of your body. Then, ideally, it will respond to a command from your brain.

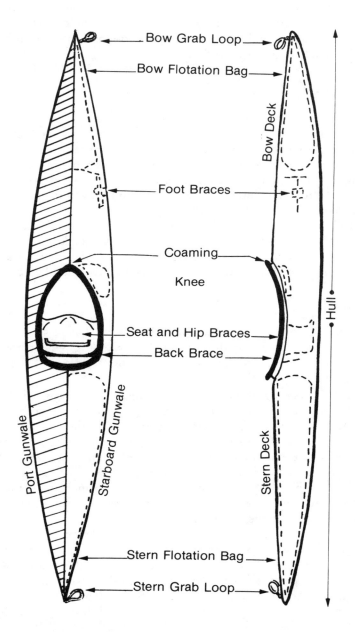

Anatomy of a kayak.

There are a few things, though, that you'll need to check out before you wear your kayak in the water, because if the fittings are too tight your legs will soon fall asleep, and if the fittings are too loose you'll rattle around inside the boat like a loose tie-rod.

For Legs, Back, and Knees

If you are tall, you may wish to move the footbraces forward toward the bow to be sure there'll be enough room for your legs to stretch out.

Some kayaks come equipped with a backbrace that can afford a measure of support to your lower back. This strap, which is often made of canvas webbing or rubber about 2 to 3 inches wide, stretches between the hipbraces just behind the seat. It can be adjusted to give you the firmness you need in order to feel comfortable yet snug in the seat.

Carefully run your fingers over the inside surface of the kneebraces just forward of the seat under the coaming. This is to make sure that there are no rough spots that might irritate your knees when you press them tightly against the braces. Any roughness should be smoothed out.

Now the Spray Cover

Because its purpose is to keep all water out of the kayak so your lower body will remain warm and dry when you're paddling, your spray cover must fit you and your boat snugly—*but not too tightly*, lest it constrict your movements.

Step into the spray cover and draw it up to your waist. Cloth spray covers often have an adjustable drawstring, which is a handy feature. Neoprene spray covers seldom need adjustment at the waist since they are so flexible. But if necessary, the waist opening can be made smaller by cutting out a 6-inch-long V at the waist, and gluing the two sides back together with wet-suit cement (in sewing, this would be called "making a dart"). Or if the waist is too small, simply cut a 6-inch slit at the waist, into which a slender, pie-shaped wedge of neoprene can then be cemented, enlarging the waist to the desired fit.

Once the waist is adjusted you're ready to try the spray cover on the coaming. Still on dry land, step into the kayak—being sure to "hike up your cover" on the backside before you lower yourself into the seat (if it is caught under your derrière it will be awkward to extricate after you're settled in the cockpit). Extend your legs forward until your feet touch the footbraces, and rest your knees against the kneebraces. If the seat and the foot-, hip- and kneebraces all fit properly, you'll begin to feel what it means to "wear a kayak."

Using both hands, tuck the skirt part of the spray cover under the outside of the rolled edge of the coaming, *always starting from the rear* and working your way forward. Some spray covers are supplied with a release loop or some other safety device that releases the cover immediately in case of emergency. If yours is, make sure the loop sticks out ready for use; then try it; to insure that it will slip the spray cover off the coaming.

The spray cover should fit snugly enough around the coaming to be watertight. It should also have enough flexibility so it will slip off the coaming if you draw your knees up and push yourself up and away from the kayak. Try this a couple of times to satisfy yourself that the spray cover will come away from the coaming when necessary.

Stepping In/Out When It's Afloat

Once you've discovered what it's like to wear a kayak on dry land, your next move is to locate a quiet, shallow pond, lake, or pool and learn how to enter a kayak while it is resting on the water.

Bobbing gently at the water's edge, your little craft with its rounded bottom and 23-inch width offers a tiny cockpit that seems hardly big enough to get into.

As you look down at it, your first inclination might be to place your foot somewhere in the middle of that cockpit.

Your next move might be to put some weight on that foot.

Your next—and final—move will be to hold your nose quickly as the kayak skitters away and you fall headfirst into the drink. (Don't laugh: this actually happened years ago in the most polluted section of the Potomac River to a first-time kayaker who eventually became a national champion.)

Stepping In

Here's what you *should* do. Place your kayak parallel to and against the bank or poolside in shallow water and, assuming that you are entering the kayak from the *right*, hold your paddle behind you with both hands. Squat down facing the bow. Reaching across the cockpit, hook the thumb of your left hand—which is still gripping the paddle shaft—under the coaming behind the seat. Next, place the right paddle blade so that it rests on the shore. Thus balanced by the paddle and crouched low next to the boat, step sideways into the boat, putting your left foot directly in front of the seat and slightly to the left of the centerline of the hull. Bring your right foot in next to the left foot, swing your fanny over the gunwale, and settle into the seat. Extend your legs forward until your feet touch the

Use your paddle as a brace to stabilize the kayak, and enter sideways, placing both feet in the cockpit before swinging your weight into the seat. (Ledyard Canoe Club)

footbraces. Swing your paddle around in front of you, and you are ready for business.

Sometimes more experienced paddlers grip the coaming of the foredeck with their left thumb while holding the paddle in front of them (instead of holding the paddle and gripping the coaming behind them) as they enter, but this method is a little less stable, and therefore takes a little more practice.

Stepping Out

To get out of your boat, first make sure that your spray cover is free of the coaming—if you had it on. Then draw both knees up toward your chest. Place the paddle behind you and—while holding it—grip the rear of the coaming with your left hand just as you did while entering the kayak. Your right hand should grip the shaft, providing you with a measure of stability as the right paddle blade rests along the shore. Carefully lift your right foot out of the boat and place it down on dry land next to the boat. Then do the same with your left foot and stand up.

You may want to practice your entry and exit several times to get them down pat before you try them with your spray cover on. And don't forget to hike up your cover in the back before you lower yourself into the cockpit.

The Wet Exit

As you begin to get the feel of what it's like to wear a kayak in the water, your first inclination may be to begin some forward strokes to see how neatly the little craft will skim across the pond. This would be like undertaking to drive on an ice-slick road without knowing how to keep from slewing out of control: you had better know the technique for getting out of a skid even though you hope no emergency will require you to use it.

Similarly, with a kayak you should *learn first what to do if your boat capsizes.* This is one of those things that every paddler has in his repertoire, whether he's on a seemingly placid tour or is racing through whitewater on a slalom course. A good kayaker will rely on the Eskimo roll, which will be described step-by-step in Chapter 6.

But first things first. So push away from the shore until you are in waist deep water. Place your hands on the gunwales—you're chicken if you reach for the spray cover instead—take a deep breath, then slowly capsize the kayak by leaning all the way over to your right.

Now you're upside down in the water, wearing a kayak. To prove that you don't feel uneasy about this new and unusual sensation, slowly slap the gunwales of the kayak three times before reaching for the coaming. Next, release your knees from the kneebraces and draw your feet up as you detach the skirt from the coaming. *All this should be done in slow motion.* Push the boat away gently with your feet as you slip out of the cockpit. If you are not wearing a mask or a nose plug, exhale slowly through your nostrils to keep water out of your nose until you have surfaced.

Later, practice the wet exit with a paddle, keeping in mind not to let your paddle get away from the kayak: catch it immediately as you swim toward the bow or stern grabloop. You can hold the paddle *and* grabloop in one hand as you use the other hand to help propel yourself and your boat toward shore.

Maintain Contact

Always maintain contact with your kayak.

The easiest way to do this is to keep one hand on the coaming as your head comes to the surface of the water, then swim quickly down to the bow or stern grabloop and begin to tow your boat to the nearest shore.

Keep It Upside Down . . .

Always keep the kayak upside down when you're towing it to shore after a wet exit: it will ride higher in the water that way, because of the air trapped inside.

Stay Upstream Yourself

Always *stay upstream of your boat* when you're swimming with it in moving current, and you'll never be pinned on a rock or other obstruction.

If you keep this point in mind whenever you practice—even in the gentlest of currents—it can become an almost automatic reflex when you're obliged to exit in whitewater.

Solo Kayak Recovery

Your companions have slipped around the bend of the river, just barely out of sight, and suddenly you capsize. Not yet knowing the Eskimo roll you do a wet exit, remembering to keep your kayak upside down as you head for the nearest shore. You also remember to keep your paddle at hand.

But help may be out of earshot, and you are on your own.

Now what?

First, while you stand in shallow water, run the bow or stern of the kayak as far as possible up on the shore, *still keeping the boat upside down.* Slowly lift the lower end of the boat—the end that is lying in the water—and allow all the remaining water to slosh toward the cockpit and drain out.

Quickly snap the kayak over, float it, and *Presto!* you're ready to get in, catch up with your companions, and remind them that kayakers should always stick together.

The solo kayak recovery is also helpful when, more experienced, you are practicing maneuvers and are tipping over rather frequently.

The Critical Point

In learning to drive a car you have to get the hang of what the gearing, brakes, and steering wheel do, before you head out into rush hour traffic. Likewise in kayaking, you must get used to your boat, its reactions, and its controls before you point your bow toward open water and its currents.

Start with exploring the stability of your boat and determining the

To empty the water from a capsized kayak, run the stern end up on shore or poolside while the boat is upside down, and lift the bow end to let water drain out of the cockpit. (Ledyard Canoe Club)

Supporting yourself with an extended Paddle Brace, lean as far as possible to one side to determine the critical point of capsize—often an angle as great as 90 degrees. (Ledyard Canoe Club)

critical point of capsize. The critical point is the maximum number of degrees you can lean to either side before you actually lose control and tip over. You'll be surprised what an extreme angle it is.

To find your critical point, position your kayak close to land in about a foot of water and extend your paddle until the blade rests on the shore: you are now using the blade as a support when you lean too far. This support is a stabilizer, and it's a rudimentary form of the *paddle brace*—which will be discussed in the next chapter under "Preliminary Exercises" to the Eskimo roll and will be discussed in full in "Stabilizing Strokes."

Now try first to lean at least 45 degrees without letting the boat slip out from under you. Then proceed to 90 degrees, where you wiggle back and forth with your hips just to show the kayak that you are in command. Recover, and repeat several times, on alternate sides, until you develop a good feel for the craft.

This exercise has an added importance because it gives you a sense of hip action and the power that the muscles of your abdomen and legs can exert on the kayak to make it react properly under you. This controlling action is the *hip snap*, and it is one of the most important components of kayaking.

Three Basic Control Strokes

The Sweep

The *sweep* is a turning stroke. It is too early to go into the fine points of paddle handling. These will be discussed in the section dealing with the *forward stroke*. For now it is enough simply to hold your paddle comfortably with both hands, keeping in mind that the scooped side—or face—is the business side of the paddle blade 99 percent of the time.

Try a sweep by placing the right blade in the water near the bow—at the 1 o'clock point—about 5 inches deep, then sweep out and around as far as you can without letting the blade sink deeper below the surface. In a slalom kayak one should be able to complete a round-the-clock turn in just three strong strokes.

Practice the sweep both to the right and to the left.

The Draw

The purpose of the *draw* stroke is to pull the kayak sideways in the water. What a great move this is to have in your bag of tricks when you're running the rapids and a rock suddenly looms in front of you!

To turn using a sweep stroke, bring the paddle around from 1 o'clock to 5 o'clock without letting the blade sink completely below the water's surface. (Robert F. George)

The draw stroke moves the kayak sideways. Insert the paddle as far as the throat on the side toward which you want to move, and pull steadily toward you. Lean toward the paddle to increase leverage. (Robert F. George)

To perform the *draw*, lean and reach out with the paddle to 3 o'clock. Lower the blade into the water as far as the throat, then pull the paddle steadily and evenly toward you, leaning strongly sideways toward the paddle to increase leverage and power. Remove the blade from the water as it approaches the gunwale.

It is also possible to draw while using your hips to hold the kayak on an absolutely even keel; that is, without leaning in the direction of the paddle.

Or, as an exercise to increase hip control, try holding a lean *away* from the direction of your paddle. You'll be surprised how easily the water slips under your kayak this way.

Practice drawing on either side for 50 yards at a stretch. At the Hampshire College pool we sometimes hold draw stroke races from one side of the pool to the other. Relay races can also be held in this manner for practice.

The Scull

Sometimes it is important to maintain a lean longer than a normal draw allows. This is where the *scull* stroke comes in.

Actually, the scull is not much more than a multiple draw stroke wherein the blade never leaves the water. It cuts a slight arc through the water as it is pulled toward the gunwale, then slices its way out again away from the boat in a motion rather like forming a figure 8. It is a graceful maneuver, and a very nice way of moving your kayak into a better position laterally.

After a long hard paddle on a hot day, a good sculler can refresh him-

The scull stroke enables you to maintain a lean or maneuver your kayak sideways. Move the paddle in a slow figure 8 from bow to stern. (Robert F. George)

self by leaning far enough over while sculling to duck his head in the water.

Practice sculling on both the right and left sides for 50-yard intervals.

Summary

You have now learned the parts of a kayak and how to get in and out of one safely and easily. You have learned how to attach your spray cover to the kayak and that it helps keep the boat dry inside. You may have been surprised to find out how stable a kayak really is. After getting it to capsize, you discovered you weren't trapped in the boat after all. Releasing the spray cover from around the coaming and then gently pushing away with your feet slips you out of the cockpit smoothly. Once the kayak has been emptied, you practiced the three basic control strokes: sweep, draw, and scull.

Don't be in a rush to go kayaking down the river or across the lake quite yet. May I urge you in the strongest possible terms to take time to master that exciting maneuver, the Eskimo roll (discussed in the next chapter) before you venture out on the water? It's the best safety insurance you can buy.

6. The Eskimo Roll

Eskimo kayaks first appeared in Western European annals on a map by a Danish cartographer drawn perhaps as early as 1425. But it was not until 1767 that there appeared written information available to Europeans about the Eskimo roll. David Crantz in his *History of Greenland* describes ten different methods Eskimos used to bring their fragile little skin boats back upright after tipping over. In 1927 the Austrian Hans Edi Pawlata learned to roll his kayak and began teaching others how to do it. This dramatic technique provided a springboard for the rise in popularity of kayaking in Europe. It stands as one of the major milestones in the history of modern kayaking.

After World War II, European kayakers like Paul Bruhin and Erich Seidel brought their skills to North America. Some of the first Americans to learn the Eskimo roll were from Colorado. One of them, Ron Bohlender, came East in the mid 1950's to the West River in Vermont. In front of a large, admiring crowd at a place on the river called the Salmon Hole he suddenly threw his paddle away and capsized. The crowd gasped. The kayak began to drift slowly downstream upside down. People ran down the river bank to rescue the boat. Suddenly a second paddle came out from under his boat and with it Bohlender completed an Eskimo roll. The crowd cheered. Bohlender had hidden a collapsible paddle under his deck. While head down, he had somehow drawn it out, fitted it together, and used it to roll.

Preparing for the Eskimo Roll

The *Eskimo roll*—"the complete capsize followed by a self-recovery full-circle to an upright position again"—is one of the most dramatic maneuvers in kayaking. It's something that anyone can learn with a little patience. There are people who can perform the full Eskimo roll without using a paddle at all: of these, some can bring themselves back upright with only one bare hand; and a real stunt man can do it with only his clenched fist.

Formerly, the roll was considered an advanced trick reserved for the expert. This attitude has undergone a change, though, and today the Eskimo roll is regarded as so essential to safety that the beginning kayaker must master it *before* he ventures out on a river or lake.

Mastery of the Eskimo roll not only assures an excellent margin of safety in most situations, but it also promotes psychological confidence and prepares the beginner for learning the other basics of handling a kayak. So what if you capsize? With a reliable roll you can come back up immediately, ready for anything.

In trying to teach the Eskimo roll to new kayakers, I have been both an astonishing success and a miserable failure: some people catch on to the idea faster than I can demonstrate, while others flop around for weeks, bewildered by the mystery of it all. There must be a direct relationship between a person's muscular coordination and the time it will take him to do a roll quickly and confidently, for the well coordinated kayaker can learn it in a very short time even with poor instruction, while someone with less physical harmony will simply have to be more patient. But the roll, truly mastered, is like riding a bicycle: you never forget how to do it.

A person with only average coordination, therefore, should not be disheartened. One national champion took an entire month to learn how to roll.

The following sequence for the roll has evolved over the years, and is designed specifically for the average person who has no special athletic ability.

First—Observe

If possible, watch an expert perform the roll several times in slow motion. Stand in shallow water, and with each of his revolutions concentrate your attention on a different aspect of the maneuver: notice where and how he grips his paddle; note the sweeping motion of his arms, then the motion of his upper body; pay particular attention to the blade angle. Study him in action from the front, from both sides, from the rear. Next, take a pair of goggles and watch his roll from several underwater positions.

As you watch from all angles, this is what you see: A deliberate full capsize until he is completely upside down in the water; the placing of the paddle in the correct position and then the arc of his stroke sideways just under the surface; a hip snap—and he's brought himself upright again, on the side opposite from the one he went down on.

Preliminary Exercises

Now that you have the overall picture in mind, you're ready to get in your boat and perform in sequence the following exercises that build up to your own Eskimo roll.

Note: All the procedures described are accomplished in water *no more than 3 feet deep*—which will give ample clearance for even a tall person upside down in a kayak. The photographs to demonstrate the sequences were taken of paddlers in the shallow end of a regulation swimming pool, but the kayakers could just as easily have been practicing at the shallow edge of a pond if they had established that there were no obstructions underwater. Of course in open or unfamiliar water each would have been wearing a helmet, as every capable boater does.

Exercise No. 1: The Eskimo Rescue

This first exercise starts with a partial capsize and recovery back up on the same side, and it is designed to give the new kayaker confidence in his ability to control his boat and himself, and to demonstrate the value of the hip snap in his recovery to an upright position.

Aside from your own boat, the only thing you need for the *Eskimo rescue* is another kayaker stationed at 3 o'clock with the bow of his boat pointing directly at you and only a foot or so away from your right elbow.

Reach over and grab his bow with both hands, and slowly lower yourself to your right into the water, allowing your kayak to capsize while you maintain your grip on the bow of the helping boat.

Then, still hanging on to his bow, use a hip snap to see if you can get your kayak back upright again without having to chin yourself too much on the rescue boat. Exerting pressure on your kneebraces will help your hip snap immensely, so here you press your right knee strongly in against its brace to add power to your hip snap and force your kayak to slide back under you again.

The idea of this exercise is to rely chiefly on the hip snap, and to use your arms and hands only to a minimum extent as you pull yourself upright.

Repeat, alternating the side you capsize on, until the procedure of re-

In the Eskimo rescue, first allow your boat to capsize while you hold on to the bow of a friend's boat which is positioned perpendicular to yours. To right yourself, combine hip snap with a minimal pull on the rescue boat. (Jay Evans)

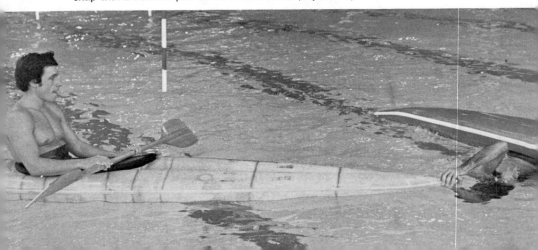

This kayaker, practicing an assisted recovery to the opposite side, had capsized to his left side and is recovering on his right side, using a friend's paddle to help pull himself upright. His head and shoulders should emerge last. (Ledyard Canoe Club)

covery becomes second nature. Increase your lean as you practice, so you can go over with confidence the full 180 degrees, until you and your kayak are completely upside down, before you come back up with the help of the other boat.

Now you're ready to go all the way over *without using the stand-by craft to help you tip over.*

Bend forward at the waist—any capsize is smoother if your trunk is positioned low—lean to the right, and ease yourself into the water as your hands rest lightly on the gunwales.

Pause there upside down for a moment to let things settle. Then slap your hands on your hull as it lies above water to draw your partner's attention. He will quickly bring his boat over to you until his bow nudges your near hand. Grab his bow with both hands, give a good hip snap to do most of the work, and bring yourself back up again.

The Eskimo rescue sure beats having to wet exit, to tow your boat to shore, and to bail it out before you can get going again. And the rescue is particularly useful when a bunch of beginners are together practicing, or are training in an indoor pool.

Exercise No. 2: Assisted Recovery to the Opposite Side

This exercise is similar to what you did in the Eskimo rescue, except that here you make a 360-degree turnover, coming up on the *opposite* side in your recovery. You're getting closer to the actual Eskimo roll, even though you rely on a helper to recover.

In Exercise No. 1 you got the hang of a controlled capsize to the right without assistance. Now, though, you will use the same method but you will *capsize to your left.* And the important part will be how you recover on the second half of the revolution—through the remaining 180 degrees—and come up on the right as before.

First, have a helper stand in waist deep water on your right side just behind your cockpit. There he will position your paddle steadily on the surface of the water parallel to your boat and about 6 inches away from it.

Then, when he is ready, you will capsize to your left.

After you complete the capsize, reach across your body until you grasp the paddle shaft that is being held for you (your helper must maintain firm control of the paddle, keeping it immovable).

Finally, pull yourself up toward the paddle and, at the same time, use your hips to make the kayak slide under you until you are completely upright again. However, *your head and shoulders must emerge from the water after the kayak has begun to assume an upright position.*

Try capsizing several times on either side until the recovery becomes a very natural and relaxed motion—and always with your head and shoulders coming up *last,* for this point is highly important to a successful Eskimo roll. If you let your head and shoulders emerge first, your assistant can remind you by rapping his knuckles on your unsuspecting head as it comes up. A couple of sharp raps and you'll remember to keep your head down.

Exercise No. 3: The Little Fingers Technique

The necessity of a good hip snap in executing the roll is the point of this one.

Ask a helper to stand in waist deep water next to your cockpit facing you. Interlock the little finger of your left hand with the little finger of his right hand; interlock the little finger of your right hand with the little finger of his left.

Now gently capsize toward him, keeping your fingers interlocked with his. No fair grabbing his whole hand! You are now upside down but still connected to your helper.

You will need herculean strength if you attempt to right yourself solely by pulling with your fingers in order to get your head and shoulders above water. Instead, exert pressure on your hip- and kneebraces in an effort to force the kayak to slide under you. You'll be surprised how easily the kayak does this, and how quickly you see daylight. The more hip and knee pressure, the less effort will be needed with your fingers.

Don't forget to practice the little fingers exercise capsized to the other side.

Exercise No. 4: The Paddle Brace Recovery

By now you are at ease in the controlled capsize, and you can employ good hip snap to help get yourself topside again. Therefore with this exercise you are advancing to the self-recovery aspect of the Eskimo roll: here you will begin to *paddle yourself upright.*

You have come far since you used a dry land paddle brace in discovering your critical point of capsize when you were getting used to wearing a kayak. This time, though, it will be a real brace, which uses leverage on the water instead of on solid ground.

But before you start, let's take a look at your paddle again to see how it will function in this maneuver.

Get set in water no more than 3 feet deep, and have an assistant close by to effect an Eskimo rescue if your efforts get a bit scrambled before you get the knack of this new maneuver.

Lean to the right almost to the critical point of capsize. Next—still leaning—slap the face of your righthand paddle-blade *flat on the surface of the water* near your bow at 1 o'clock. Then swing your blade—still holding it flat on the water—in an arc until it's about at 3 o'clock, and you will automatically resume an upright position.

Now lean a little farther, and right yourself with your paddle brace as before. Repeat, leaning more each time, until you can go well *beyond* the critical point, each time swinging the blade around to 3 o'clock in order to recover.

Eventually you'll be able to brace for several seconds while your shoulder and even part of your head are in the water, *and still recover.* At the end of your swing you may want to draw or scull a little to assist your recovery.

The paddle brace recovery should be practiced many times on both

Your Blade Angle in the Brace

The blades at each end of your kayak paddle are feathered, which means that they are set at a right angle to each other. Thus when one blade is flat on the water the other blade is standing up like a fin.

In addition, the chances are 10–to–1 that the blades are scooped— i.e., they have a slightly concave face, or business side, and a slightly rounded back. This spooned design makes your pull through the water more effective. However, it also means that your blade can "dive" when you swing it flat along the surface of the water in a paddle brace unless you *keep the leading edge slightly raised.*

Nonscooped blades will dive too, of course, if their leading edge is not slightly raised during a brace.

sides. And it is a good general warm-up exercise when you first get into your kayak before attempting rapids.

Exercise No. 5: The Half Roll to the Right

This *half roll* contains the key maneuver for self-recovery in any Eskimo roll, and it is the final exercise before you proceed to the full roll itself.

The half roll is a controlled 180-degree capsize and recovery back up on the same side by initiating a paddle brace while you're upside down in the water, and by using "body English" mainly in the form of a strong hip snap.

You will recover without help from anybody else—but do have someone standing by in the water to assist you the first few times in case you can use a helping hand. And it would be a good idea to wear goggles or a face mask: you'll welcome a clear underwater view of the pitch of your paddle blade until you can bring off the recovery by feel alone.

Throughout the maneuver you will be using an *extended paddle grip*—which increases the effective radius of your paddle, as you will see—and you *must maintain your blade angle by keeping its leading edge slightly raised*.

So start by holding your paddle alongside the left gunwale with your right hand somewhere comfortably near the middle of the shaft, palm down and thumb toward you. This is where the "extended" part comes in: with your hand moved back on the shaft instead of its normal grip nearer the forward blade, you're adding about 18 inches to your paddle's range.

A kayaker prepares for a half roll to the right. Note the correct hand and paddle positions along the left gunwale. (Ledyard Canoe Club)

Lay your forward blade flat on the water near your bow, *face up* (so it will be business side *down* when you get completely capsized), and with its leading edge slightly raised. To maintain it at the correct angle and increase its leverage, reach your left hand back and, thumb down, grasp the tip of the rear blade to insure that it stands up like a fin and thus maintains your forward blade approximately flat.

With your paddle set, bend forward for a smooth capsize and turn completely over to your right.

Upside down in the water, keep your paddle close to your left gunwale and at the surface of the water in the same position it was before you capsized. You're now ready to use the pressure of a paddle brace to initiate your recovery.

Swing the forward blade in a quarter circle away from your bow, watching your leading edge through your goggles to insure that it is slightly raised and thus will skim along the surface without diving. As you bring your blade around from your bow, give a good hip snap to help get yourself upright again. Remember that the more pressure you exert against your right kneebrace, the more effective your hip snap will be, and the more readily your kayak will slide under you as you come back up again.

If you can recover successfully on your very first try at the half roll you're some kind of athlete!

The rest of us, though, can probably use a little outside assistance. Thus:

1. Station a helper so he will be standing near the tip of your forward blade after you have capsized to the right.

Go completely over, and allow your friend to guide your blade lightly in the proper arc on the surface of the water. Immediately, you will feel the torsion produced by your upside-down paddle brace; at the same time you'll sense the effectiveness of the pressure exerted by your right knee in aiding the hip snap portion of your recovery.

2. Move your helper to a position just behind your cockpit on your left. When you capsize to the right, he will reach across the bottom of your hull, take hold of your left gunwale, and gently pull it back up as you work with paddle and hip snap to get yourself upright again.

As you become more proficient, he will help less and less—until, at some point unknown to you, you are accomplishing your recovery without any help from him at all.

3. In the course of your practice with a helper you will get so accustomed to the feel of the correct angle of your forward blade that you no longer need the extra control derived from holding your rear blade by its tip. At this stage you may wish to move your left hand up to the throat of the rear blade and control the pitch of your forward blade from there.

After capsizing in a half roll to the right, have a friend guide your blade in a paddle brace arc on the surface of the water. This pressure, plus the force of a hip snap, brings you upright. (Ledyard Canoe Club)

For extra help in the half roll, have your helper move behind the cockpit and gently pull on the kayak to help you roll back up. (Ledyard Canoe Club)

Exercise No. 6: Half Roll to the Left

In many cases, people learning to roll will wish to continue working on one side until their roll is perfected. However, the "compleat kayaker" is one who eventually masters the Eskimo roll on *both* sides, and thus can recover from a capsize at will, righting himself from either side as it suits his fancy at the moment.

Therefore those paddlers whose goal is to be ambidextrous in the water will want to take some time out to practice the half roll to the left. The procedure is simply a reversal of the exercise used for the half roll to the right.

With your left hand at mid shaft and your right hand behind you holding the tip of your rear blade, place your forward blade on the water face up, just to the right of your bow and with its leading edge slightly raised. Capsize to the left and, when you're 180 degrees upside down, arc your forward blade back from the bow, give a strong hip snap with good pressure on your left kneebrace, and recover to an upright position.

Repeat the maneuver with the aid of a helper until you have it down pat, and can recover confidently on your own.

Master-sidedness may be a slight factor here. Occasionally a paddler who has cinched self-recovery on one side will take longer to perform the exercise well on the opposite side. The answer of course is to practice half rolls until there are no hang-ups with recovery on either side.

The Full Eskimo Roll

When you have nailed down the half roll and recovery, it is a simple matter to complete the full 360-degree *Eskimo roll.*

You merely capsize to the opposite side from the one on which you initiated the half roll, and, when you're in position to start your self-recovery, you execute exactly the same paddle movement and hip snap that brought you up from the half roll.

Thus if you're going to recover on your right, you place your paddle on your left and capsize to your left.

If you're going to recover on your left, then position your paddle correctly on your right and capsize to your right.

On the first couple of tries you may want a helper standing by as in the half roll practices—but the partner will be there mainly for moral support. Actually, you are likely to find the full 360-degree roll easier, because you have momentum going for you as you reach the 180-degree mark in your capsize.

And remember: *How you capsize is far less important than WHAT YOU DO ONCE YOU'RE UPSIDE DOWN to get yourself topside to daylight again.*

The complete sequence of steps in the Eskimo roll takes you full circle from the initial upright position (top of drawing) through the capsize and recovery. (Walter Richardson)

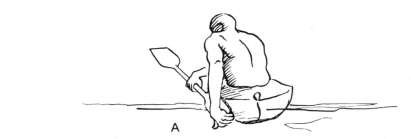

A

B

C

G

F

E

D

Summing Up Other Key Points in the Eskimo Roll

1. Hold your paddle in an extended grip and have the forward blade positioned perfectly, then capsize.

2. Keeping the leading edge of your forward blade slightly raised—lest it dive when you swing it around in the brace movement—bring your blade flat in an arc from bow to side.

3. Exert pressure against your recovery side kneebrace to give added strength to your hip snap.

4. Synchronize your brace and hip snap so your boat slides under you *before* your shoulders and head emerge from the water.

The Eskimo Roll in Current

Every newcomer to the sport who has gained confidence in the roll as the result of honing his technique in pool or pond will be doubly pleased with the maneuver when it is executed with a gentle assist from flowing water.

Therefore the next step is to find a safe place in a river. "Safe" means a spot that is near the bank, is about 3 feet deep, has been thoroughly checked to be free of underwater obstructions, and has a modest current.

Which bank you choose to take off from is up to you: you are going to capsize in the current while leaning *upstream*, and recover on the *downstream* side. Therefore do your very first "river reading" to decide how you will point your boat upstream initially to get broadside to the current.

Are you more comfortable in a recovery to the right? Then plan to have your left side upstream. If you're more proficient at recovering on the left, plan to get in position with your right side upstream.

Then put on your helmet and lifejacket and have a helper in the water standing by (these are rudimentary safety measures that show you have common water sense), paddle your kayak a few strokes to the chosen place—and try your roll.

You will be pleasantly surprised at how much easier it is to roll as the current gives you added momentum, but in the excitement of moving water you may temporarily lose your skill in completing the roll. Don't be disheartened. This is only natural, and it happens to most of us. Simply withdraw from the moving current and practice the roll in calm water or in a pool for awhile.

When you feel completely confident about handling the roll from an upstream capsize, practice rolling from a variety of positions in the river. You might even try recovering on the upstream side: it really isn't all that difficult.

. . . Then the "Wild" Roll

Before you tackle the roll in actual rapids, simulate whitewater conditions by sprinting for at least 20 yards in relatively flatwater, then capsize suddenly without taking time to set your paddle angle or otherwise position yourself correctly before you go over. Once underwater in a full capsize, get organized for a correct recovery—and roll back up.

Practice capsizing at full speed on both sides, with correct recovery. Be sure to sprint long enough so you're slightly out of breath—as you would be if paddling hard in demanding whitewater. And as you gain confidence, capsize while holding your paddle with only one hand.

. . . At Last, in Whitewater

Later, when you have truly learned to "read the river," will come the ultimate phase of this maneuver: the Eskimo roll in whitewater.

When practicing your roll in rapids it is more important than ever before to make sure the water is deep enough—the usual 3 feet is plenty—and that there is a quiet pool or "catch basin" just below your practice spot to give you a welcome parking place.

The difference here is that *you* chose the place and time to roll rather than having the river dictate that choice for you. Therefore, you should practice rolling from different angles in whitewater from completely sideways to heading directly up or down stream. Always remember to assume a protective tucked forward position as you capsize. This will provide you with maximum protection should you bump against a submerged rock. Don't be in too much of a hurry when you're upside down in whitewater—you can hold your breath long enough to do 10 consecutive Eskimo rolls. It's important to set your paddle properly in the right position before you commence the roll. Slap the paddle blade a couple times on the surface of the water just to make sure it's at the right angle and that it's at the surface—not below.

Sometimes the water around you will appear frothy and foamy, without much substance to it. If so, just relax for a moment. You'll soon drift down the river into heavier water.

If your first attempt doesn't succeed, simply take a deep breath, go under, and carefully set up again. I have seen people make as many as ten attempts before succeeding. That's OK; it's a lot better than swimming. Your first accidental capsize in really big water, followed by a successful roll, will be the highlight of your day. What a feeling of confidence it gives you! If in the future the rapids get sassy and pitch you around a bit, even tossing you over—so what? Simply roll back up and continue on your way. You may not have mastered the river, but you have mastered yourself.

The Broken Paddle Roll

Most of today's paddles are strong enough to withstand all but the worst treatment, but there's still the chance that a blade will get wedged between submerged rocks and break—possibly causing a capsize as well. A simple exercise like the following is worth the time spent in practice: it could come in handy some day.

First, get a paddle that has one blade broken and thus is useless as a lever for performing the Eskimo roll. This shouldn't be a problem, because paddles break either at the throat or somewhere on the blade itself. If you can't find a broken kayak paddle, use a canoe paddle; since it has only one blade, it will serve your purpose.

Second, pretend you don't know your paddle is broken, then capsize in the first stage of the roll, and try to recover with the broken end. You'll feel immediately, as you swing the paddle around in its accustomed arc, that you are getting little or no leverage.

Third, slip back again into a fully capsized position, and simply *switch your paddle around in your hands* so you are now working with the good blade. Carefully set its angle with the leading edge slightly raised, sweep it out and around, using good hip snap, and you will roll back up with the good half of the paddle.

The Hands Only Roll

Once you have become proficient in the Eskimo roll you'll feel a great sense of accomplishment and achievement. You have mastered the ancient art of the Eskimos. This new skill is your best bet against getting into difficulty in the water.

Some of you, however, will want to take it one step farther. Suppose in a capsize you lose your grip on the paddle. It floats away out of reach. Never fear. With some practice you can actually learn to roll your kayak back to an upright position without using the paddle at all!

Here's how it is done. First you should be totally secure with your roll with a paddle, preferably on *both* sides. You should have a good hip snap, and the roll must be very reliable. Once you've achieved that through practice, you're ready to advance to the next step.

Discard your kayak paddle and replace it with a small canoe paddle; practice your roll with it. The sweeping motion is the same as you learned for the kayak paddle assisted roll. Once this is mastered, cut yourself two 1-inch boards about 10 inches wide and 2 feet long. Holding one in each hand, capsize and perform the roll. You'll notice with each progressive step you are relying less and less on the "paddle" and more and more on your hip snap. Again, sweep the two boards around in that now familiar arc to complete the roll.

At this stage it is essential that the boat slips under you first, then your shoulders emerge, and finally your head. If your head pops up first, stop right there and go back to your paddle. Practice rolling with your head coming out of the water last.

The next step is to try it with a pair of ping-pong paddles. Then with only one ping-pong paddle, using the flat palm of your hand in place of the other paddle.

Now, cast aside the remaining crutch, the ping-pong paddle. Capsize, link your thumbs with your palms out flat, sweep around in the familiar arc, give it a strong hip snap, and—presto—you're seeing daylight again.

Now try it with only one hand. Tuck the other into the top of your spray cover. In each of these steps, once you have learned it on one side, you should then take time to master it on the other before moving on to the last step.

You are now ready for moving current. Head diagonally upstream and toss your paddle to a nearby companion, after making sure that the water is deep enough and that there are no underwater obstructions in the area. Allow the upstream gunwale to become caught. Over you go. Using both hands (ping-pong paddles are certainly acceptable for the first few times you try it), you'll discover to your surprise how easy it really is. The secret, of course, is that when you roll over upstream and then recover on the downstream side, *you are making the current work for you.* The force of the water against your boat helps the hip snap in righting the kayak again.

Summary

Learning the Eskimo roll is essential to your becoming a competent and safe kayaker. Don't leapfrog over the exercises provided in this chapter unless you're a great athlete. For most of us, it's like learning long division in mathematics: you must first learn to add, subtract, and multiply. So it is with the Eskimo roll. Master each exercise thoroughly—on both sides of your boat before moving on to the next skill. You'll be glad you did.

7. Driving, Stabilizing, and Turning Strokes

The Driving Strokes

Having got the wet exit and the Eskimo roll under our belts, we can now concentrate on getting from here to there in a kayak. Let's start with the forward stroke, examining its components and seeing how the paddle will work in our hands.

The Forward Stroke

The *forward stroke* can be one of the most beautiful movements in all sport, exhilarating for the spectator and paddler alike. Knowledge and many hours of practice are required to perfect it.

In flatwater kayak racing an efficient and powerful forward stroke is absolutely vital to success.

In whitewater races a smooth-flowing forward stroke, properly executed, does wonders toward positioning the boater properly as he negotiates the gates.

And, last, a quiet day's cruise across a lake or down a stream for several miles is done in a greater degree of comfort, with less fatigue, if a good, efficient forward stroke is learned beforehand.

How it Works

Basically the forward stroke is a cycling movement of arms and shoulders. It is similar in principle to pedaling a bicycle, and it must be executed with great precision and smoothness in order to be efficient. It is the economic application of effort properly done that permits the paddler to attain a greater sustained speed at less expenditure of energy.

Such a prolonged effort can be maintained only if the muscles relax in the course of the stroke. Fortunately, in kayaking the business of alternating your arms between the dip and the recovery will ensure this relaxation.

Body Position

As you settle into your kayak, maintain a naturally comfortable position with your feet firmly against the footbraces and knees against the kneebraces. Now lean forward slightly—but not too far. And don't slouch: keep your head up and look forward.

With both hands palms down grasp the paddle in front of you so that it is parallel to the water level. Your hands should be about 3 feet apart and approximately 6 inches up the paddle shaft from the throat. This position will make your arms create an angle of about 90 degrees at the elbows.

How the Paddle Will Turn

Virtually all kayak paddles today are feathered, and the majority of these are spooned in such a way as to require right control or left control—with right-control paddles being by far the most common.

Therefore as you make a stroke on the right side with a right-control paddle, you will rotate the shaft a quarter turn with your right hand so the blade will enter the water in the correct position. Simultaneously, your left hand relaxes a bit to allow the shaft to rotate.

To stroke on your left side, again rotate the shaft with your right hand so the left blade will enter the water properly, and then grip the shaft firmly with your left hand as you pull the left blade through the water.

The turning of the shaft with each individual stroke makes certain that the other blade just removed from the water will slice neatly through the air, offering little or no wind resistance.

If you find that your paddle is left-control (as mentioned earlier, this is determined by the spoon of each blade), then your left hand always turns the shaft while your right hand relaxes.

Components of the Forward Stroke

We can divide the forward stroke into three closely interrelated parts—the dip, the draw back through the water, and the withdraw/recovery.

1. *The dip.* Lean slightly forward—but not too far. Extend your right arm forward as far as you can toward the bow and insert the right blade completely in the water. Meanwhile your left wrist should be at ear level, your left elbow pointed down and slightly away from the kayak to provide maximum leverage. The fingers of your left hand may be fairly relaxed on the shaft at this point.

2. *The draw.* With full muscular effort, draw the blade straight back to the midpoint of the kayak *but not beyond.* Your right wrist is straight, but your right elbow flexes as the blade comes directly back alongside the kayak. To apply more power, don't hesitate to turn your body and shoulders a little to the right as you draw the blade back. Put your body into the stroke, because if you let your arms do all the work, they'll soon tire.

While your right hand was dipping and drawing back, your left hand (which controlled the other half of the paddle) pressed straight forward toward the center line of the kayak at eye level. This movement of the left arm and hand is not unlike putting the shot in track, or delivering a straight left to the jaw of your opponent in boxing.

A

B

C   The forward stroke is basically a cycling motion of your arms and shoulders. The feathered kayak paddle is rotated during the stroke so that each blade enters the water in the correct position. The stroke includes three steps: the dip on the right side (A), the draw back to the midpoint of the kayak (B), and the recovery of the blade from the water (C). The paddle is then set to begin the same sequence on the left side (D, E, F). (Robert F. George)

D

E

F

Don't allow the dip-and-draw arm to do all the work in each cycle of strokes: if you paddle this way you'll soon be fatigued (maybe after only a quarter-mile of paddling). Instead, think of the power of the forward stroke as coming from two distinct sources: about 65 percent from your dip and draw, and about 35 percent from your forward punch with the other hand—while rhythmically moving your body and shoulders at the waist to the right and left to complement both draw and push. Both power sources working in harmony together not only produce an amazingly efficient forward stroke with which you can paddle for miles, but they also create a graceful movement that is completely satisfying aesthetically.

3. *Withdraw/recovery.* Your right hand smoothly lifts the paddle from the water in a natural upward movement after the right blade passes the cockpit. Your left hand is now in a position to begin the dip of the left blade near the bow of your kayak to complete the stroke cycle.

Practicing the movement of the forward stroke doesn't have to be limited to sitting in a kayak. After you're through experimenting on the water take your paddle home with you for the evening. Sit in an ordinary straight chair with your feet on a footstool. Then follow through the cyclical movement carefully. (Beware of chandeliers.) Have a friend observe and criticize your motions. If you have a large mirror in your house, practice in front of it. You'll be surprised at what you see.

Breathing

Even when you are in pretty good physical condition, if you're a beginning kayaker, you may suddenly find yourself out of breath after a fast spurt of forward strokes. Why? Simple: maybe you forgot to breathe!

You've been careful to keep your head up to give those air passages to your lungs a chance to work for you. Now try taking one full breath for each right-left cycle of strokes. Faster breathing will rarely permit a full exchange of used air, but a steady and rhythmic movement of the diaphragm contributes to proper circulation and helps to prevent an oxygen deficiency. A good rule to remember is: *INHALE as your right hand dips, EXHALE as your left hand dips.*

Paddling on a full stomach impairs your breathing. Not to mention ruining your digestion. Don't talk unnecessarily while paddling: it disturbs the rhythm of your breathing. Remember to keep your head up at all times, although you are leaning forward for added power.

Keeping on Track

Proper tracking—keeping a kayak running in a straight line—requires a subtlety of paddle angle and delicate paddle pressure that come only from experience. What this boils down to is making tiny corrections with each paddle stroke in order to keep the boat going straight, rather than employing one or two big forceful corrections on one side after the kayak has begun to turn off course.

Now that you have your kayak moving along in one direction by using the forward stroke, don't leave it at that. Keep paddling for a mile or more each day until you begin to feel your two power sources working together smoothly. Don't be discouraged—it will take time. Don't be alarmed if your craft occasionally acts like a spooked horse and veers off in some unlikely direction quite different from where you wish to go. Your kayak is merely displaying a "tracking syndrome." However, with a few miles of paddling under your keel, your kayak will recognize you as master and begin to behave.

Balancing Exercises

Give yourself a change in practicing your forward strokes by leaning to the right with each dip to the right, and leaning to the left with each left dip. Lean far enough with each stroke so your gunwale is awash.

Practice leaning for a hundred yards at a stretch without losing your rhythm. On a long paddle across a lake this can help give you a change of pace.

When you are proficient at maintaining rhythm while leaning on your dip side, lean on the side opposite from each stroke for a hundred yards at a clip. This is a great exercise for loosening up your hips and for practicing general boat control and stability.

The Back Stroke

Normally you'll want to use forward strokes to get you where you want to go. But occasionally you'll find yourself in a situation where a good, hard *back stroke* can help you get in a desired position. (You'll also use this stroke in *backferrying*—which we'll get to when we start to practice in a current.)

Lean back a little, instead of bending forward at the waist. Without changing the basic forward stroke position of the spooned side of the blade, dip your right paddle into the water slightly behind you. The back of the blade is now your "business side" as you *push* it forward in the water, using a lot of body pressure. Meanwhile your left hand is *pulling* the left blade back in the air.

Follow the same procedure on the other side if you need to take more than one back stroke to get yourself positioned advantageously.

Even though you'll seldom need to keep backstroking, it's worthwhile

A

For the back stroke, dip the paddle into the water behind you (A), then push it forward through the water (B). (Robert F. George)

B

to practice the cycle: then you'll have the skill to bring off a strong, precise back stroke when you want it.

The dip and push of each back stroke form a perfectly natural and easy motion, and are a cinch to learn. But after you think you're pretty good at it, try leaning toward your stroking side; then try leaning away from each back stroke.

If you are honest about leaning, some interesting things can happen—including a capsize. But as a kayaker you don't mind getting wet. And it offers a chance to practice your Eskimo roll.

A more extreme form of back stroke occurs when you twist your shoulders and head around so far that you are almost facing backward. You can twist your wrists to dig the business side of the paddle blade into the water near the stern and literally *pull* it back toward you as your body slowly uncoils. When your blade reaches the cockpit, you pivot the blade back to its proper forward position and then continue to *push* it forward toward the bow. This stroke is sometimes used by slalom racers who are in a hurry to get through a reverse gate in a race.

Ferrying

The *ferry* is a controlled sideslip across a current, the paddler using the power of the water against his partially angled kayak to carry his boat where he wants it to go—instead of pointing his bow directly toward his objective and stepping on the gas. It is most effective in whitewater, where the strong swirl of water can be the initial propellant, aiding the boater to go crabwise across the current. In a good ferry you never have to fight your way across the river; you let the river do most of the work for you.

We have not yet graduated fully to whitewater, however, so the beginner must settle for a stream that has moving current and is clear of obstacles in which to practice ferrying. There he can learn how the forces of paddle, current, and weight distribution combine with his boat angle to bring off the exercise successfully. The fine points of the maneuver will be honed later on when he plays in real rapids.

There are two kinds of ferrying; the *backferry* (or *ferry glide*) uses back strokes to place and keep the boat in an advantageous position to sideslip as it points downstream roughly in the same direction as the current. The upstream or *forward ferry* uses forward strokes to maintain a proper angle against the current and help propel the boat across the current.

When learning to ferry, there are two basic principles to keep in mind: Always *angle your boat* slightly away from the direction of the current; *always lean downstream,* regardless of the direction you are traveling:

if you lean upstream, the current will come down on your lowered gunwale and flip you over in an unplanned capsize. In addition, the downstream lean offers a larger surface area for the current to work on in helping you sideslip across the river.

By putting these principles together in a coordinated action you *and* the river join in a unique partnership to propel your kayak in the desired direction with little effort.

Pinpointing Direction

Up till now we have used clock numbers to designate the position of your paddle in relation to the bow of your kayak. Here, though, let's use the clock to show the direction your bow is pointing, and therefore your boat's angle in ferrying.

Because there are no obstructions in the water where we are practicing, we will assume that the current flows straight down the river rather than changing direction, as it does when rounding an obstacle in whitewater. Thus "downstream" and "current" will mean the same direction for simplicity's sake, and your bow will be at 12 o'clock as you go directly downstream with the current.

In the same way, when you point upstream straight into the current, your bow will stay at 12 o'clock.

Backferry (Ferry Glide)

In a *backferry* to the right while paddling downstream apply a couple of back strokes on your left side to angle your bow toward 11 o'clock downcurrent. Then lean to the right (downstream) and apply a series of back strokes on both sides of your boat to help maintain the correct angle as you sideslip across the current. You may have to paddle a bit harder on your right side in order to maintain correct boat angle. If you are required to paddle too hard on your right side, it simply means that your ferry angle is too extreme. To correct this you must turn your bow back toward the 11 o'clock position.

In a backferry to the left, first angle your bow toward 1 o'clock downcurrent with a couple of firm back strokes on the right side. Then lean to the left (downstream) and backpaddle briskly on both sides as you sideslip over to the left side of the river. Again, if your bow slips much past 1 o'clock on the way to 2, this will force you to paddle harder. Your ferry angle has become too extreme. Readjust your bow back to 1 o'clock.

In an *upstream ferry* your boat must be headed roughly upstream, either because you are simply drifting downstream backward or you have just emerged from an eddy with your boat pointed upriver.

To ferry toward your right, first angle your bow toward 1 o'clock upcurrent, then lean to the right (downstream) and use several firm forward strokes on both sides of your boat to maintain your correct angle to help propel your boat across the current. Again as in the backferry, you may be required to paddle a bit harder on your right side in order to maintain correct boat angle.

In an upstream ferry to the left, you simply angle your bow toward 11 o'clock upcurrent, lean downstream to your left, and use several forward strokes to initiate and maintain your sideslip toward the other side of the river.

Remember, a well executed ferry (unless it's done in water above Class III—these classifications are covered in Chapter 13) is smooth and almost effortless. You are applying the laws of physics to your kayak, and it responds as if it were self-propelled.

Stabilizing Strokes: The Paddle Braces

Having learned the *half roll* via the *paddle brace recovery* and then the Eskimo roll, you are well acquainted with the powerful leverage your paddle blade can exert on the water. Now we're going to review the brace on its own merits, and then see how it works forward, backward and to either side.

Braces are used not for propelling, but rather to help you stabilize your boat and to make subtle directional changes. As your skill increases, you will rely more and more on your paddle blade, extended way out from the boat, to give you more and more stability.

Forward Brace

In the *forward brace* on your way to the roll you leaned to one side and slapped the face of the blade on the water near the bow. Then, as you began to tip over, you swung the blade out sideways and around from 1 o'clock to 3 o'clock. The leading edge of the blade is slightly raised at all times, preventing the blade from slicing downward through the water, thus losing its stabilizing "outrigger" effect.

In practicing the forward brace, keep leaning farther and farther each time until your head is immersed in the water and you can still recover.

Back Brace and Stern Rudder

The *back brace* stabilizes a kayak, and is also used quite naturally and without any formal training by neophytes who are simply trying to steer their boats by holding their paddles on the water behind them.

In the back brace—a stabilizing stroke—lean backward and slowly slide the rear blade in a short arc away from the boat on the surface of the water. (Robert F. George)

The stroke consists of leaning backward and slowly pressing the rear blade—normally backside down—in a short arc on the surface of the water. By leaning to the right and sliding the blade from 5 o'clock to 3 o'clock, the back brace is completed on the right side. Sliding the left rear blade from about 7 o'clock to 9 o'clock on the left side will complete a back brace on that side.

The back brace becomes a *stern rudder* stroke if you change the paddle angle from a flat to a vertical position in the water to help steer the boat.

The brace and the stern rudder are highly useful strokes to have in your repertoire (particularly when coming in for a landing on shore), but they do slow your forward momentum. Therefore experienced paddlers soon wean themselves from the stern rudder and back brace, and use any number of forward stroke combinations to make the kayak go in the desired direction without loss of speed.

The Side Brace

This stroke is used almost entirely as a means of stabilizing your boat rather than as a steering mechanism. If you feel unexpectedly unstable while moving forward, extend your right blade out on the water face down at 3 o'clock. Place the blade as far from the kayak as possible, with the leading edge slightly raised. Lean hard to your right, with your left hand holding the rest of the paddle above your head. Surprisingly enough, you'll find that you're very stable in this position—just as much as when you are sitting quietly in a kayak in still water.

From the beginning of a *side brace* it is natural to move into a draw by digging the blade into the water and pulling it in toward the boat. From a side brace you can also swing the blade forward in an arc toward the bow and then pull directly back, thus converting your brace into a standard forward stroke. You can also swing the blade back toward the rear of the kayak and transform your side brace into a stern rudder or back stroke.

Slipping into a variety of strokes from the basic side brace can be an exhilarating complement to your kayaking style.

The High Paddle Brace Position

The braces previously described are called *low braces* because the paddle shaft and both wrists are held well below eye level. A *high brace* is a more daring and powerful maneuver.

Let's start with a *high side brace* to the right. It's easier to do this while the kayak is moving, so take a dozen or so energetic forward strokes. Then, with your right hand reach way out to the right at 3 o'clock. Hold your left hand at eye level or a little above. Simultaneously *lean* to the right.

Your first few tries may be a bit hesitant, but with practice you can learn to lean far enough over to get your ear wet. Try the high brace position for the forward brace and for the back brace on the right side and then on the left side.

Caution

Avoid allowing your wrists to drift too far behind your head. Wrists behind your head may look fancy, but in powerful water the extreme position invites a dislocated shoulder. Therefore, never let your wrists get behind your head.

Two Great Turning Strokes

The proficient kayaker will often find good use for the spectacular *Duffek stroke* and the *cross bow draw*. Both are turning maneuvers that use forward momentum and the paddle as a pivot. Both are unusually effective in whitewater.

The Duffek

This great stroke revolutionized the sport of kayaking. It was developed by Milovan Duffek, a Czech kayaker who first demonstrated the move at the 1953 World Championships in Geneva. Ever since his innovation,

A Duffek turn into a gate. (Evans Associates)

kayakers have not had to rely on the boat itself for stability: the paddle becomes the primary means not only of support but also for *turning the kayak while in brace position.*

What a nifty stroke it is—particularly in whitewater! But first learn the basic idea in flatwater; otherwise you'll spend a good share of the time upside down wondering what went wrong.

To simulate moving current in flatwater it is best to get going very fast—almost full speed in a forward direction. Then lean out as far as you can to the right. With the face of the blade at an angle of about 45 degrees to the forward direction of the boat, insert the blade at about 2 o'clock or approximately 3 feet away from the bow. Without stroking at all, hold your blade right there while your left hand is held high above your head. Presto!—the kayak will spin around to the right with the paddle acting as a pivot. Remember: never allow your hand/wrist to extend behind your head. In extreme cases this could cause a shoulder separation.

The exact blade angle to use depends upon your speed, how far you lean, and how abruptly you wish to turn. The Duffek stroke can often be finished with a firm but short draw stroke to correct your balance.

If you wish to perform a *Duffek turn* to your left, simply hold your right hand high above but not behind your head and use your left hand to insert the left blade properly.

This is one of the most exciting moves in kayaking, but get the idea of it in flatwater, then try your luck in moving current, and then advance into eddies. As an added bonus you will be pleased that a Duffek properly done does not cut down your speed appreciably.

In flatwater—on a lake or gentle river—you can come steaming up to a dock or other chosen point on the shore, pull a Duffek, and bring your kayak into a snappy landing right on the button. You will have earned the right to hotdog it for the folks on shore.

Cross Bow Draw

If the Duffek pales with you, here's another move that is as stimulating as it is effective and abrupt.

While paddling forward hard, quickly swing the right blade over the bow and place it in on the *left* side in a draw position about a foot away from the boat. This requires quite a bit of body twist at the waist. The blade enters the water almost in a vertical position—way forward at about 11 o'clock. Your left wrist will be slightly above your left ear, with your left elbow pointed comfortably out about 45 degrees. Your right elbow should be directly in front of you slightly below eye level.

Lean hard on the left, and pull the blade toward you; quickly the kayak will respond and snap around for you. The more you dare to lean, the more effective the *cross bow draw* stroke will be for you. Once the kayak has turned you can lift the paddle back across the forward deck and then smoothly execute a forward stroke.

In order to do the cross bow draw stroke to the right, simply extend your left blade over the deck to the right and go from there.

A paddler uses a cross bow draw to whip his boat around to the left. Note the excellent placement of the paddle. In this case, the kayaker is heading upstream; the current is moving from left to right. (Ledyard Canoe Club)

Using the Extended Paddle

In automobiles we have a passing gear, which, when you press the accelerator to the floor, will give you an added surge of power; in a jet aircraft the afterburners are fired to boost the plane over the clouds or out of the enemy's reach. In kayaking we have the extended paddle technique, which, if used judiciously, can increase your quickness and maneuverability just when you need it the most. One of the most renowned practitioners of this art is former World Champion Jürgen Bremmer from the German Democratic Republic. Bremmer most often employed the *extended blade* in his sweep strokes and Duffek turns.

Quite simply, the maneuver involves quickly sliding your hands along the paddle shaft until one hand is at the throat of the paddle. The other hand remains halfway along the shaft, and the far end of the paddle will be the one in the water. This increases your leverage considerably. The net effect is to provide a temporary advantage of having a much longer paddle. Once the sweep stroke or Duffek is completed, quickly slide the paddle back to its normal position in your hands.

One of the prettiest sights in kayaking is to watch a former *Weltmeister* (World Champion) like Bremmer weave his way smoothly through a slalom course subtly employing the extended paddle to increase his power and mastery over the rapids.

Other paddle and stroke techniques for other kinds of whitewater craft will be discussed by themselves before the whitewater techniques are covered.

8. Handling Other Closed-Deck Craft

The techniques learned in a single-seater, slalom-style kayak can also be applied to other closed-deck craft. Let us first consider the two-seater kayak (K-2), found more often on lakes, gentle streams, and in the ocean than in rapids.

The K-2

Years ago the K-2 was sometimes used for whitewater competition, but it has all but vanished now from the whitewater racing scene. There is probably not more than one K-2 for every 300 or so K-1's available in the United States, although it is popular in Europe as a Sunday outing craft and in the British Isles. A highly specialized K-2, long and sleek and very tippy, is a legitimate flatwater racing class. In flatwater competition there is even a K-4—a magnificent boat to watch when all four paddlers synchronize their strokes.

For general recreational paddling purposes there are a couple of companies that manufacture the K-2 both in rigid fiberglass and also as a folding boat that can be dismantled in about 20 minutes and packed into two medium-large duffel bags for easy transport.

Applying Technique to the K-2

Whether the K-2 has one large cockpit accommodating two paddlers or separate cockpits fore and aft, and whether it is a collapsible folding boat or made of fiberglass, the same paddling principles apply. Using the basic maneuvers we have learned, the bow and stern paddlers simply have to put these techniques together and synchronize their movements.

For the most part these K-2's are far more stable than the sassy little K-1's; designed for cruising, they therefore are not particularly fast or maneuverable boats. Because a K-2's main function is to go from here to there in a comfortable and pleasurable fashion—no quick turns in rough water, no standing on your ear to pivot around a rock—spray covers are not often used except while crossing windy lakes or in the ocean.

The Trim

Since two people paddle a K-2, it is important to consider the craft's trim. A stern heavy boat wallows through the water and is sluggish to handle;

Synchronizing their strokes, two kayakers paddle their wooden K-2 in the inland passage between Alaska and Seattle. These men are using spray covers, which are not always necessary in the stable K-2. (Chris Knight)

a bow heavy boat plows through the water and makes steering difficult. Therefore a K-2 when fully loaded should rest evenly on the water, neither bow nor stern heavy. If the heavier partner is in the bow, his seat should be moved back a little to compensate, just as one moves the heavier partner closer to the fulcrum of a seesaw to redress the balance. If the heavier partner happens to be the sternman, then either the bow seat or the stern seat (possibly both) should be moved forward a bit. Only a couple of inches can make a big difference in the trim.

In a K-2 one person should be designated as "commander" before either paddler steps into the boat. It can be either the bowman or the sternman, but it usually turns out to be the more experienced boater of the two, or the owner of the boat. Customarily the bowman steps in first while the sternman holds the boat in position for him. Then, while the bowman maintains the boat steady, the sternman slips into the rear seat and announces that the K-2 is ready to get underway. In disembarking, the bowman will step on shore first.

Bow and Stern Duties

Most of the strokes that are used in the K-1 are also applicable to the K-2. Because the K-2 is a stable craft, it more commonly calls for the traditional forward, backward, and the simpler turning strokes, rather than relying so much on hanging (stabilizing) strokes.

As a general arrangement the paddling duties between the bow and stern divide themselves logically between forward power and steering, respectively. This does not mean, however, that the bowman only provides power and the sternman simply sits back and steers. It is logical for the bowman to set and maintain the stroke rate since the sternman can always see him, but he cannot always see the sternman.

The sternman, meanwhile, is the chief helmsman, and he will make frequent use of the stern rudder, the draw, and the sweep, always being careful to coordinate his strokes so he stays in rhythm with his partner in the bow. The stern paddler will provide his share of driving power with firm forward strokes in rhythm with his partner.

A K-2 is rarely put into reverse, but when the need occurs both paddlers contribute toward backing up.

A good K-2 team must practice together conscientiously in order to combine their strokes for maximum effectiveness. For example, combining a bow sweep on the right with a sharp stern rudder or stern sweep on the left side will greatly aid spinning a K-2 toward the left.

Because K-2 paddlers often do not use spray covers, the Eskimo roll is only rarely performed in a K-2. But if they do use spray covers, they follow K-1 procedures for wet exits or rolls. Both paddlers should take care to synchronize the swing of their recovery braces (and of course do them on the same side!).

The C-1

For whitewater racing, the International Canoe Federation recognizes two other kinds of boats: the single-seater covered canoe (C-1); and the two-seater covered canoe (C-2), with either two men aboard (C-2) or paddled by a man and a woman (C-2M). (The "M" stands for mixed.) Although not yet officially recognized for World Championship competition, there are two other boats, the C-1W (a single-seater covered canoe paddled by a woman) and a C-2W (two women).

Information about open-decked canoes may be found in the American Red Cross manual on canoeing. The American Canoe Association sanctions open-decked canoe races, but these are justifiably restricted to gentler whitewater of a nature more suitable to open boats. They are far less maneuverable and could easily be swamped in big rapids.

Years ago, open-decked canoes had a waterproof covering stretched across their decks to keep the water out. From that primitive start there has been an exciting evolution in the design of decked canoes. Both the single-seater (C-1) and the two-seater (C-2) are now shaped much like kayaks, although technically speaking they are *not* kayaks.

C-1/K-1 Comparison

A kayaker (K-1) sits in his boat and uses a double-bladed paddle, while the C-1 paddler kneels in his boat and uses a single-bladed paddle. The C-1 is wider, and has a round cockpit hole, whereas the K-1's cockpit hole is shaped more like a pear or a teardrop.

The C-1 has the following advantages: it is more stable, will turn faster, and the paddler can reach out farther to put more power into each stroke. In the kneeling position the paddler's head is at least a foot higher than that of a paddler seated in a kayak; and, therefore, the C-1 paddler has better forward visibility. The kneeling position also allows the paddler to rotate more of his body.

K-1's are more comfortable to sit in for any length of time, and theoretically they are faster boats. In recent years, however, C-1 scores in slalom races have often equaled, and in some cases have surpassed, the best K-1 scores.

The C-1 is really designed for racing in flatwater and whitewater; the K-1 has a wider variety of hull and deck styles to accommodate a greater number of water activities.

C-1 Paddling Position

To keep his legs from becoming fatigued in kneeling, the paddler in a C-1 has a wooden crossbar (thwart) slung from just under each gunwale to rest his butt on.

To prevent his feet from slipping around, a couple of foam or wooden blocks are fastened to the floor of the canoe directly behind the thwart. These toebraces give the paddler something to push against and they act as chocks to keep his feet in place.

Even more important than the toebraces in keeping the paddler in efficient and comfortable position are the thighbraces, which prevent him from lurching forward. These thighbraces are usually straps whose lower ends are attached to the floor of the canoe on either side of the centerline and just in front of the thwart. Each upper end is attached to a gunwale to provide firm support for the inside of his thighs as he kneels.

Wet Exit and Roll in a C-1

For a wet exit simply release the spray cover from around the coaming as you did in a K-1, and untuck your legs from the thigh straps by lifting your feet up and away from the toebraces. As you drop clear, remember to keep one hand on your boat and the other on your paddle.

The Eskimo roll in a C-1 is very similar to the broken paddle roll that we practiced in the K-1. Capsized (and kneeling), you reach for the surface with your paddle and make sure that the blade rests flat on the surface. In the brace recovery, there is more emphasis on the bracing aspect and less emphasis on the sweep of the blade as it arcs along the water.

Don't forget the importance of hip snap, and the fact that your head and shoulders should come up last.

Canoe Strokes

The Driving Strokes

The basic parts of the forward stroke—dip, draw, recovery—in the canoe are similar to what we have already learned in the K-1. In flatwater competition for C-1's the forward stroke is of such overwhelming importance compared with other strokes that thousands of words have been written by experts dissecting all aspects of it. However, this book is focused more on kayaks and whitewater, so the fine points of an appropriate racing stroke for flatwater can be found elsewhere.

INDIAN STROKE

This stroke is a legacy from the Indians and was used to give them a silent approach to wild game or an enemy.

Instead of lifting your paddle out of the water at the end of a forward stroke, you simply feather the blade so it will be parallel to the gunwale— its edge thus offering little resistance to the water—and draw the blade back through the water to the bow, where it is rotated back to its correct working position. You cannot get such a high stroke rate this way as is possible in the conventional recovery of the blade through the air, but there is no sound of water dripping from the blade as it swings through the air, and no splash as it dips into the water to start the stroke. It is a silent, restful, and smooth way to paddle.

BACK STROKE

For the simplest kind of back stroke, place your blade behind you in the water and push it forward alongside your boat, using the back of the blade as the business side.

A second effective kind of back stroke is the twist-pull-rotate-and-push combination that is spectacular to watch when done well. First, twist your body around so you are facing the rear of the boat. Insert the blade into the water with its face forward and pull it toward you alongside the boat. When it reaches your hip, rotate the paddle 180 degrees and in one smooth motion finish your back stroke in the conventional way.

The Correcting Strokes

Since you stroke only on one side of the boat at a time, you must eventually compensate for the boat's natural desire to veer off-course away from the paddling side. Therefore there are two correcting strokes: the J stroke and the *pry*. Both are unique to the canoe, thanks to the single-bladed paddle. Its short shaft and top hand grip let the kneeling paddler exert power where it is needed. The double-bladed kayak paddle is simply not as efficient in the J and pry strokes, although some expert kayakers may use a modified form of the pry.

THE J STROKE

The J *stroke* gets its name from the design the blade traces in the water as it completes a forward stroke. On the left side of the boat it forms a conventional J, on the right side a J that has been flopped over.

If you look down on a canoe from above, the forward stroke creates the upright part of the letter as the paddle moves alongside. Just prior to recovery, twist your blade a quarter turn outward and push away as you remove the blade from the water. It is this outward curl of the J that brings the canoe back on course. When used best, it is a subtle motion, sometimes only for a couple of inches to keep the bow pointed straight ahead. It doesn't take much practice to determine how much of a curl you want on the J or to see that this stroke, used often, will prevent you from being forced to make big correcting strokes on the other side. The J stroke steers the boat without slowing it down as much as the pry stroke.

THE PRY

The *pry* is a more vigorous version of the J stroke and can be thought of as tracing a smart right angle in the water.

At the end of the forward stroke you give your blade a *brisk* quarter turn outward (instead of a gentle outcurl); as you turn the shaft, press it hard against the gunwale—which acts as a fulcrum—and in one sharp motion use the blade to pry the boat sideways.

There are subtle variations to the pry stroke: a stern pry, a midships pry, a bow pry, and even a sliding pry. In some cases the pry is better than the J because it is more powerful and can be turned into a bracing stroke very quickly. However, it is a slower stroke than the J; most experts J more often than they pry.

The forward stroke in a C-1 is similar to that stroke in a K-1: The dip (A), the draw (B), and the recovery (C). (Robert F. George)

THE MINNESOTA SWITCH

Many North American paddlers use the *Minnesota switch* to keep their boats on course, instead of repeated J and pry strokes. In simplified terms it involves a series of strong, powerful forward strokes on one side followed by an equal series of forward strokes on the other side. This is accomplished by swapping your hand grips as you switch the paddle in your hands from side to side.

Europeans have been slow to pick up on the switch, but since Al Button—a genuine Minnesota switcher—won a bronze medal in the World Championships in 1975 interest has increased. Al and other Minnesotans, like former national champion and Olympic Team member Angus Morrison, lent the name "Minnesota" to this technique.

The C-2

The marvelously orchestrated teamwork of the whitewater C-2 is a joy to behold. Designed for rapids running and whitewater racing, it has an entirely covered deck and is paddled by two people, one in the bow and one in the stern. Like the C-1, it has toe- and thighbraces for the kneeling paddlers; its relatively flat, keel-less hull makes for quick turning. Flatwater C-2's, sometimes called *Tandem Canadians*, likewise call for precision teamwork, superb conditioning, and great balance.

Becoming a member of a C-2 team requires a very special kind of temperament. Like Siamese twins, you go where your partner goes whether you like it or not. The failure of one paddler's stroke in a C-2 can be critical.

One of the most exciting things to watch in all of sports is a well coordinated whitewater C-2 team weaving its way through a slalom course. Each man knows his job, and each man knows what his partner is doing. Every stroke and movement have been practiced and planned ahead of time. By combining their efforts—with a minimum of shouting and instructions—they make the canoe respond beautifully between them, spinning and pirouetting its way toward the finish line.

C-2 Technique

You can think of a C-2 as a long, slender rectangle having four corners at which the paddle can be applied to make the canoe respond to the will of its masters. At the bow there will be a right corner and a left corner as the bowman kneels in position. Although the bowman will choose whether he will paddle most of the time on the right or left side of the

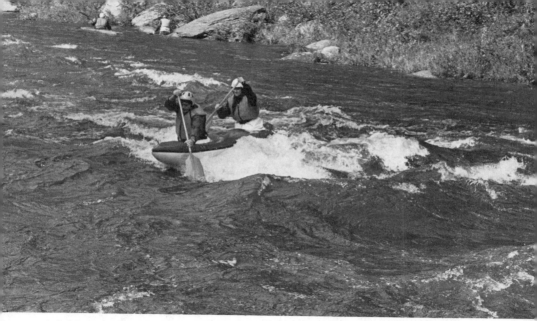

A C-2 ferries across a stretch of whitewater. Precise teamwork between the two paddlers is the key. The C-2 is second only to the K-1 for speed in whitewater. (Robert F. George)

canoe, he must also have as part of his repertoire the spectacular cross bow draw and similar movements that are performed on his off-side.

The stern provides two more corners. The sternman normally will paddle opposite from the side the bowman paddles on. Thus a symmetry of power and motion is provided, which helps to keep the boat going in a straight line. Occasionally the sternman may also feel the need to switch over to his off-side in case extra power is needed there.

Older C-2's literally had the bow and stern paddlers at each end of the boat. Under the new rules the paddlers are allowed to station themselves much closer to the center of the boat, making turning much easier. The boats also have much less volume now.

Bow and Stern Duties

The division of duties in a C-2 is not quite the same as for a K-2, where the sternman was primarily the helmsman and the bowman the power source. The sternman is also concerned with using draw, sweep, and pry strokes whenever the need arises.

Since both paddlers kneel so closely to each other, both are responsible for initiating turns. By using powerful sweep, draw, and pry strokes both paddlers, working in unison, can make the C-2 extraordinarily responsive to their touch. It is only natural that a good C-2 team is often made up of two top-flight C-1 paddlers. Their strokes form a continuous and integrated pattern, creating a steady power flow that seems to come from a single source.

PART III. ADVANCED TECHNIQUES

9. Moving Water

Water on the move is nimble as well as subtle. It is apparently made up of an infinite series of layers that seem to slip over each other with very little friction. Running water is a truly dynamic medium, especially when temporarily obstructed by irregularities in the riverbed, by rocks in the way of its flow, or by unexpected twists and turns in the river. Water that makes up the oceans of the world, when affected by wind and tide, can be among the most awesome forces of nature.

A kayaker needs to know and become familiar with all the idiosyncrasies of water on the move. Then will come the application of basic technique suited to each circumstance—and the exhilaration of paddling on moving water.

Reading the River

Water, in its headlong course toward the sea, carves for itself a highway that tries to take the path of least resistance across the surface of the land.

Basically there are three forces at work here: (1) gravity—which constantly lures water downward; (2) centrifugal force—which greatly affects a river as it swings around a bend and changes direction; and (3) power—water while moving creates one of the strongest and most irresistible forces in all of nature.

If we could cut a riverbed crossways and examine the cut end of either section, generally speaking we would notice the deepest portion of the river in the middle, with the water becoming more shallow as the sides of the riverbed slope up to meet the shore. Also, the fastest current can be found at the surface of the water in the middle part of the river. Toward the edges of the river, where the water becomes more shallow, there is greater friction for the volume of water, and the current slows down. Of course, this description is true only where the river bed runs along evenly and in a straight line.

102

Around the Bend

There are notable exceptions to the above rule for current, and they are dictated by the terrain through and over which the river flows. The river paddler, however, heading smoothly down a slow moving current, has little with which to concern himself. If he stays roughly in the middle of the river, he'll get the benefit of the strongest current and deepest water the stream can offer.

The simplest variation to deal with occurs when the river swings around a corner to head in a different direction. It is here that centrifugal force acts upon the water to create a lopsided river bottom, for here the deepest water will invariably be found near the *outside* edge of the river's bend. Novice river-runners will be tempted to "cut the corner" and thus save several yards, but the experienced paddler will swing wide, stay with the fastest water, and will beat the novice around the bend.

Sectional view of the river depicting differential flow of water along a straight bed.

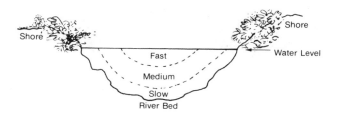

A bird's-eye view of the same river.

Sectional view of a river seen from the upstream side at the beginning of a left turn.

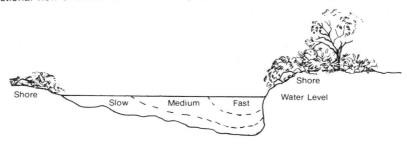

A bird's-eye view of the same turn in the river.

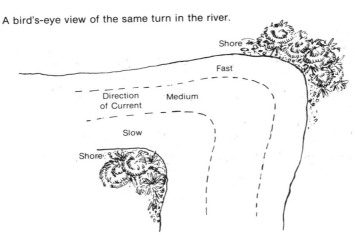

Classification

Most traditional whitewater rivers are babbling and shallow bottom-scratchers much of the year. Such streams depend for whitewater on the spring runoff from melting snow. They rise and fall annually, earlier in the south and later in the north; the rivers that have substantial snow bases where they rise stay higher longer. Toward the end of the white-water season a good rainfall will restore the water level of these rivers and temporarily prolong the season.

Whitewater rivers are classified in six general categories (see Chapter 13 for details), with several factors determining classification: the complexity of the riverbed, the elevation drop per mile, the river's course, and the volume of water. The last factor—the volume of water—is the greatest variable and can alter a river's category dramatically.

Most beginning kayakers will be content with Class I and Class II water. Good whitewater touring is found in Class II and Class III. Rivers with stretches of rapids that fall into classes IV, V and VI—such as the great western rivers—are for experts.

Heavy Water

Paddlers often use the expression "heavy water," "big water," or "hair" when describing a stretch of rapids that looks awesome. It would be misleading to define heavy water simply as anything over a certain number of cubic feet of water per second in a river, for there are at least three other variables to consider: The size of the riverbed, the degree of vertical drop, and the experience of the boater all must be taken into account.

In terms of the riverbed and water flow, it is reasonable to classify the Olympic slalom course at Augsburg, Bavaria, as a heavy water rapids, yet there is rarely more than 900 cubic feet per second pouring through its small, narrow bed. With a wider and bigger riverbed like that of the Housatonic in Connecticut, 900 cubic feet per second is barely enough to cover the rocks and float a boat.

For the novice, a Class III rapids may appear to be heavy water, whereas the expert might almost be bored by a "mere" Class III. As the rate of water flow increases, however, more boaters will agree that it is, indeed, heavy water. Few would deny that the Mackenzie River in Canada or the Colorado River in the Grand Canyon is heavy water.

Faster Water and Its Obstructions

As a river quickens its pace, the fun begins. So watch sharply ahead and by observing carefully you will find that the water before you will form an inverted V in which the wide part is upstream and the pointed end, through which the current funnels, is downstream. Generally speaking, this inverted V in the water is a guide indicating where the main current is flowing, and where you want to go. A gentle yet perceptible descent can be felt at this point.

Riffles

When you pick up a little speed in the V as it narrows to its point, you'll notice ahead some small waves in the surface of the water. If the waves are not over a foot high, they indicate a stretch of shallow water underneath. Such small waves are called *riffles*, and they are caused by an unevenness—submerged rocks, ledges, or sunken logs—in the riverbed below.

This is what kayaking is all about: high water on a fine spring day, and a kayaker heading toward the V in a rapids. (Ledyard Canoe Club)

Haystacks

Much larger standing waves—2 or more feet high—are often caused by huge submerged boulders, or they occur at the end of the chute of water from a V. These waves are called *haystacks,* and usually three or more come in succession. Haystacks in certain parts of the world on giant-sized rivers are so large that they appear to be hills of water in themselves.

Rock Gardens and Staircases

If the water level is low and the gradient fairly steep, the water will be churned up a bit and lots of little rocks will barely show their heads above the surface. Boaters will often call a section like this a *rock garden.* Navigation through a rock garden is tricky, and a paddler is lucky to get through one without at least once scratching the hull of his boat.

Another common river phenomenon is the *staircase*—a series of ledges or descending shelves over which the current spills. Again, the cautious paddler will search out the inverted V and follow, sometimes in a zigzag course, the flow of the greatest amount of current. Parts of the beautiful Shenandoah River in Virginia are famous for their staircase-like appearance.

A series of haystacks promises a challenging ride downstream (current flows away from the viewer). Haystacks are often caused by huge submerged boulders. (Ledyard Canoe Club)

Eddies

Pockets of relatively still water can sometimes be found near either bank
of the river or downstream of large exposed boulders or logs out in midstream. These pockets are called *eddies,* and they can be either benign
or malicious.

The ones with relatively little current and which contain quiet water
are great places to park and take a breather, and they are fine vantage
points from which a camera buff can photograph oncoming paddlers as
they plunge toward him down the rapids.

However, not all eddies can be considered friendly or as places to linger
for long. Owing to complex hydraulic phenomena working on the irregularities of a riverbed, an eddy can provide some nasty water for the unsuspecting kayaker. Often water will boil up, swirl and twist about—
even forming whirlpools—making such an eddy unpredictable as well as
unpleasant as a rest stop. You feel as if some underwater monster had
reached up and grabbed the hull of your boat, taking fiendish delight in

The current (flowing from left to right) creates a giant eddy (dark water) where it flows
around a rock outcrop (at left of picture). Strong, frothing jets pour past on either side, but
the kayaker can sit quietly in the protected eddy. (Ledyard Canoe Club)

yanking you from one side to another. This type of eddy is no place to relax or loiter, but well-executed braces will stabilize your boat, and several strong forward strokes will take you out into the mainstream again.

One of the most famous of malicious eddies was the one just below the formidable Avery Brundage Rock on the upper part of the 1972 Olympic whitewater slalom course in Augsburg, Bavaria. This notorious eddy was redesigned, the concrete boulder which created it pared to a smaller size for safety. Another eddy well known to paddlers lies just below the Dumplings on the West River in Vermont. Such unstable water lures photographers, because it is here that the unsuspecting boater will provide the camera with spectacular happenings.

The Anatomy of an Eddy

In general, as the current diverges around an obstacle, it forms a very fast and powerful chute, or jet, that skirts past the head of the eddy, which lies immediately below the obstruction. The characteristic circular motion of the eddy is created in part by the passage of the jet: this milder countercurrent in the surface water of the eddy curves inward and upstream; then, when it meets the obstacle at the eddy's head, it peels off and heads downstream.

A sharp delineation can be seen between the chute roaring downstream and the more placid eddy water. This is called the *eddy line*.

A short eddy wall is sometimes formed at the top of an eddy right on the eddy line if the chute (jet) of downstream water is of unusually heavy volume and force. There can be a difference of a foot or more in this wall between the eddy water and the chute next to it.

A couple of boat lengths downstream is an area often called the eddy tail. Here the chute fans out and loses some of its force, which causes the eddy water itself to lose its upstream momentum; and the river water merges again.

A midstream eddy offers you a choice of moving out either from the right or the left as you proceed down the rapids, and a careful examination of the next 100 yards or so below the eddy from a position of safety in the eddy itself will give you a clue as to which side you may wish to leave the eddy from.

Eddies at the Side of a River

All kinds of interesting things are happening near the river bank as a river picks up speed and descends more sharply. Quite common is the *side eddy*, caused by the jut of a large boulder or point of land into the main

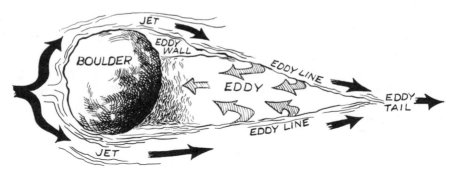

This drawing illustrates the characteristic circular motion of water in a mainstream eddy. (Walter Richardson)

stream, leaving a space downstream of it where water can swirl back and return in an upstream circular motion.

A side eddy can be a welcome haven. It is an automatic "parking place" while you plan your next move downstream; it can provide ready access to shore and a chance to get out to stretch; and it's a very good place for putting-in at the start of a river journey.

A side eddy offers many opportunities to practice precision boating or just a chance to play around. And it is also a likely place to find lost paddles or other debris. The most feasible way to search for lost gear is to scout out each side eddy carefully as you proceed downriver.

Rollers, Souseholes, and Reversals

Among the other demanding obstructions to watch for in rapids are *rollers* (also called stoppers or keepers), *souseholes* (suckholes), *reversals*, or just plain *holes*.

Although there may be some technical differences in these terms, they are used somewhat interchangeably according to the section of North America you happen to be paddling in. No really precise definitions are necessary because Nature can, in her own way, provide an almost infinite variety of challenges in a stretch of rapids.

Regardless of what you call them, however, they all share one basic characteristic: water at the downstream base of the obstacle recirculates back toward the obstacle in apparent total defiance of the natural downstream flow of the current. It is enough to be able to recognize that these things do exist in turbulent waters and, after recognizing them for what they are, to know what to do about them.

Rollers

The recirculating water (or turbulence) called a roller or stopper is a tricky wave that remains in the same place athwart the river, and is formed (see diagram) by water pouring over a large obstacle in the riverbed and plunging down into a trough below it. The term stopper has been applied to roller because that is exactly what it is likely to do to your boat if you linger too long in its vicinity: If you get stuck sideways down in the trough, the roller can actually stop your forward motion downstream. If it is a giant roller with a steep wave downstream of it, it can even stop your boat if you are pointed directly downstream.

A roller or stopper is studied much more easily if you look upstream at it from the safety of the river bank rather than from the cockpit of a kayak heading downstream. It can be fairly small and localized or it can extend most of the way across the river.

At the Quarter Mile Rapids on the White River in Vermont during unusually high water, a truly delightful roller extends diagonally all the way across the river. Another famous and challenging roller is located on the River aux Sables in the northern part of Quebec in Canada, about halfway down the slalom practice area near Jonquière.

Souseholes

Souseholes, suckholes, or reversals are formed in nearly the same way as a roller or stopper, except that they are often concentrated in one central spot in the river rather than extending across the stream. They too are formed by a huge boulder or ledge, but can also be formed by a weir or dam.

Bird's-eye view of an eddy on each side of a river.

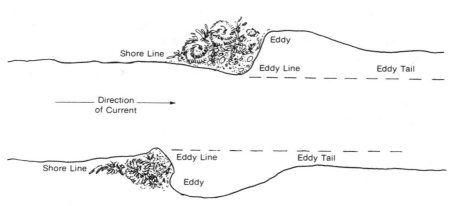

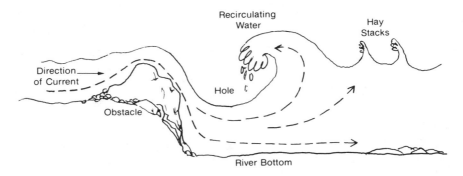

Cross-sectional view of a hole.

The water, as it plunges over the obstacle, divides itself into two main components: (1) the water that goes deep and continues on downstream, and (2) the part that is deflected back upstream toward the obstacle, creating a foaming, boiling backlash. To the unwary it looks like the jaws of a water monster—and a sousehole deserves respect from every paddler.

A sousehole may contain a roller as part of its composition, depending upon the river's configuration at the moment, and a roller can have as part of its repertoire the makings of a sousehole.

Weirs and Dams

There are very few rivers within easy reach of civilization that are not obstructed by at least one dam or weir, and this is one of the reasons why every competent paddler scouts an unfamiliar stream before undertaking to travel it.

A weir is a small dam up to about 5 feet in height, and sometimes it has a sluiceway at one side to conduct the water to a mill or pond. In both dams and weirs, the water spills over almost vertically and usually creates immediately downstream a roller or sousehole, which in turn tends to toss back toward the barrier any debris that has floated over it.

When you look downstream at a dam or weir you see a "horizon line" ahead on the surface of the water. This occurs because the water usually is backed up against the barrier and the water is likely to be calm there without much current. Then, as the water goes over the dam, it creates a straight horizontal line across the river—as if the river simply stops and drops off the earth. Larger dams, of course, have superstructures on either side of the river—and sometimes all the way over the river—making identification easier.

A small sousehole.

Direction of Current

Obstacle Under Water Here

The Trough

White foam is the water recirculating back on itself

Every boater should always be on the lookout for these horizon lines across the river ahead, and should pull over to shore immediately to scout out the dam *before* running it. And then, run it only with the greatest of caution, and preferably with a rescue party to assist you from shore.

The Ocean

The behavior of water in the ocean can be quite unlike that of a river. The sea can develop currents as the tide works its timeless way up and down a coastline. It is a constantly changing medium, appearing the same for only a few moments.

Ocean waves and swells are most often caused by the action of wind on the broad surface of ocean water. When waves run against the upward sloping floor of the ocean toward dry land, the action of water against seabed creates a force which makes each incoming wave unstable. The wave is gradually forced up, slowed down, and finally crests in white frothy foam, while the water from an earlier wave that has played itself out on shore recedes quickly back under the incoming surf.

Proper handling of a kayak in ocean water is discussed in Chapter 11.

10. Running Rapids

Some sports are designed mainly for one purpose: competition. Kayaking, however, is a versatile pastime, offering plenty of chances for self-expression. Compete if you wish, or just go out with a few friends and run the rapids on a beautiful day. What's even better is to combine these activities. It is a common sight to see a group of slalomists practice hard on a certain stretch of the rapids for an hour or so, then suddenly peel off down the rapids in wild abandon, shouting to each other as they automatically size up what is approaching and then making the appropriate moves for the occasion.

Up until now your technique has been polished in flatwater, and you have learned what a nimble little craft you have under you. Now with the Eskimo roll and basic strokes mastered, you are ready to enter the exciting world of whitewater.

But kayaking through the rapids should be much more than a simple, bouncy ride interspersed with a few unexpected thrills. Sunday afternoon thrill-seekers who are ill-equipped and ill-prepared can be a menace to the sport as well as to themselves. Such people's inability to read the river is measured in their perplexed expressions as they emerge spouting water after their kayaks have capsized.

On the other hand, instead of "shooting" the rapids mindlessly just for an instant's worth of thrill, the true paddler will study the rapids carefully and then weave his way down, following a plan more well thought out than merely hoping to stay upright and dry.

Working over a stretch of whitewater with a sporty little kayak can be a very fulfilling experience. It's a real thrill to *know* a river well enough to use its currents, eddies, and waves to choreograph pivots, spins and glides as your boat dances through the water.

Safety Measures

To save yourself embarrassment and possible loss of your boat, paddle, or even your life, adhere to the following without fail:

1. You must be a strong, competent swimmer; you should never go river running with anyone who is not a good swimmer too.

2. If you value your life as well as your boat, you'll never kayak alone in rapids. Two boats are a *minimum* for safety; three or more are better.

3. No unknown rapids should ever be run without being scouted beforehand, and maps should be studied with care. Know what you are getting into: there are bound to be stretches where it's mighty difficult, even for experts, to reach the haven of an emergency take-out spot on the river bank.

4. In addition to the lifejacket and helmet that you should always wear, in cold weather it is smart to wear at least part of a wet suit too, lest you find yourself helpless in the grip of cold water. Water below 50 degrees Fahrenheit will soon sap the energy of the strongest.

5. Have adequate flotation in *both* bow and stern so your boat will ride high in the water in case of a capsize. This means flotation bags: half-inflated beach balls, casually stuffed inside your boat, are not enough.

6. Grabloops at each end of the boat are also essential. With them your boat can be quickly controlled and pulled to shore in case of a capsize.

7. Resist temptation to attempt any rapids beyond your ability. Be an accurate judge of your own skill and never be teased, coaxed, or bullied into running a stretch of rapids you have serious doubts about successfully completing.

8. *Warm up.* Never attempt a rapids unless you are fully warmed up and physically loose. A warm-up can be as simple as jogging up and down the road while waiting for the car shuttle to return; or it can consist of a few exercises while sitting in your boat in a quiet eddy. Try a few bracing strokes, an Eskimo roll or two, twist and stretch your shoulders and arms. Ferry out into the stream a little way to get the feel of the moving current. Work up at least a little sweat before you take on the rapids below.

Rules-of-Thumb

Intelligent rapids running involves a continuous mental exercise to interpret the demands of the water as the river unfolds in front of you.

Actually "playing the river" involves two distinct things: (1) recognizing what it is you are approaching in the rapids, and (2) anticipating the appropriate move for the occasion.

Lean Downstream

When playing in the rapids always remember to *lean downstream*. This is probably the single most important rule in all of rapids running.

It is highly unlikely that you will ever capsize if you remember always to lean downstream while maneuvering in rapids. However, the moment you get careless and allow your upstream gunwale to dip, the force of the water will grab your gunwale—and over you'll go.

Experienced boaters often refer to this phenomenon in terms of mythology. Old river runners will tell you about an underwater creature called the "Muncher" that lurks in the rapids and likes to punish boaters who disobey the basic fundamentals of river reading. The Muncher will spin your boat around if you don't pay strict attention to the currents; and if the Muncher is unusually hungry, he might even tip your boat over in the rapids, but you can always foil the critter by careful water reading, by leaning downstream, and by having a reliable Eskimo roll.

Deep Water

Generally speaking, the deepest water will lie in the middle of the now familiar inverted V of glassy water where the main current is flowing.

When the river is going around a bend, however, the water will be deepest on the *outside* of the turn.

Keep Going

When in doubt or startled, it is best to paddle hard *forward* rather than to try to back off with backward strokes. Never hoist your paddle above your head in despair: an "air brace" provides no stability.

Dealing with Anxiety and Fear

It is the brave person who admits fear. Only a fool tries to hide it. A certain amount of anxiety is not only natural—it can be healthy. It keeps one wide awake, sharp, and alert.

Try to bear in mind that during your very first run down a set of rapids you probably will be frightened. After all, this is a brand new experience, in a foreign medium (water); and it is simply you, your boat, and the river. You're on your own. Your paddling companions should be sensitive to your situation and be supportive.

Anxiety is often caused by ignorance—or fear—of the unknown. Anxiety can be overcome by intelligence, skill, practice, and exposure to the river at first hand. The big, unanswerable question is—how much fear is too much? If you are paralyzed by fear, then you have obviously gone too far. Back off and try a less demanding section of the river. Work your way up more slowly. Never hesitate to pick up your boat and walk past any rapids beyond your skill level.

In many cases, though, when people are put into an anxiety-creating situation, they react well. Better yet, soon comes that tremendous feeling of accomplishment when you spin into an eddy at the foot of a rapids and look back to see what you've just passed through. Basic paddle strokes and maneuvers recently learned came into play automatically as you negotiated the rapids. You have just won a great victory—not over the river, but over yourself.

Very shortly your anxiety can be put into proper perspective. Was it simply inexperience and lack of familiarity with the situation? In a small

way you have joined the ranks of the world's great explorers and ad-
venturers—like the first person to fly or the first person to set foot on
the moon.

Experience builds confidence, but in kayaking confidence should never
turn to brashness. Always try to draw the line between being confident
and being foolhardy. Don't overdo it. Reckless boaters are a danger to
themselves and to their boating companions.

In summary, face up to the fact you're frightened. Analyze your fear
objectively and take whatever constructive steps you can. In this way the
sport of kayaking can become a tremendously important learning process
for you.

Haystacks

At some point in a rapids you are likely to encounter a series of those
large standing waves called "Haystacks." They are formed, as described
in Chapter 9, when a fast jet of water passing over submerged rocks
slows down in a rapids. Haystacks are also formed when two currents
within the same river meet at an angle as at a bend in the river where the
main current hits the outside wall hard enough to be deflected back on
itself.

Quite often haystacks are found toward the bottom of rapids. If they
are not too large for your taste, you may wish to smash straight through
them for a real roller coaster ride downriver.

If they appear more ominous than hospitable, steer slightly to one side
using a draw or sweep stroke or even a stern rudder, and skirt the heavier
haystacks lurking in the middle.

Haystacks don't have to be confronted from a straightforward position either. It is perfectly acceptable to approach them broadside—just
so long as you always remember to lean and brace downstream.

Riding haystacks backwards can also provide a thrill, but you'd better
know what lies downstream of them, or you'll be in for a surprise.

Using Eddies

Your greatest ally in the rapids is an upcoming eddy. Let's say that you
have spotted a side-eddy to your right a hundred yards ahead downstream. From the configuration of the land or a boulder, you can anticipate
the location of an eddy before it is clearly visible from your boat. Head
toward it, driving hard with firm forward strokes, always bearing in mind
that the jet (chute) just alongside the eddy will tend to carry you downstream farther than you expect. Therefore aim for a point higher upstream
in the eddy than you really plan to go.

Keep paddling hard forward toward the eddy line and into the eddy water itself. As the eddy line extends under your boat about halfway to your cockpit, you will begin to feel the upstream eddy water begin to grab your bow and force your boat around to the right so that it is pointing upstream in the eddy.

Strokes for Entering an Eddy

A combination of strong forward strokes, coupled at the last minute with a strong sweep, will propel your boat into an eddy. A favorite stroke to use here is the Duffek. The most common error, though, is to begin the Duffek stroke too soon. If you perform the Duffek too far away from the eddy proper, or in the jet itself, your boat will simply wash downstream and miss the eddy entirely. Resist beginning the Duffek until you can practically lean over and place your paddle blade in the calmer water, *beyond* the eddy line. This takes skill and good timing.

At the precise moment your boat leaves the downstream jet and actually enters the eddy, you should shift your weight so as to lean *away* from the eddy. Centrifugal force plus the upstream current in the eddy will tend to pull you over to the left, so counteract this by leaning back toward the main current of the river. A little practice will give you the feel for what to do. Don't get discouraged if you tip over several times while entering an eddy, because proper anticipation and timing take a lot of experience. Once learned, this maneuver is a pleasurable one.

Leaving the Eddy

Once in the eddy you'll have time to gather your wits and decide how to proceed out of the eddy and get on your way down the rapids.

First, look downstream and decide where you want to go, then choose which of three possible exits from the eddy is best for you. One way is simply to drift below the eddy tail as you slowly turn to head downstream; if there are no obstructions directly downstream of the eddy tail, this is probably the easiest way to leave an eddy. Or you can choose to peel off from about halfway up the eddy; or you can continue up the eddy and peel off dramatically just inches below the rock at the head of the eddy.

The Peel-off

The *peel-off* is a spectacular maneuver that can be done forward or backward.

To get ready to peel off to the right, you consider directly upstream as

12 o'clock. Back down the eddy as far as you can, to get a running start; then charge full steam ahead up the eddy with your *bow pointing between 1 and 2 o'clock*. The moment your bow crosses the eddy line into the jet of fast-moving current you should continue to paddle hard and at the same time *lean hard downstream*. (It is at this point that one of the cardinal rules of whitewater kayaking will be driven home to you: *lean downstream*. Otherwise, the moment your bow hits that fast water you'll be upside down as quick as a wink.) The closer your bow points toward 2 o'clock the greater the chances that you'll spin quickly out of the current in an exhilarating manner and head down the river again.

For a left side peel-off, back down for a running start, then paddle forward fast with your bow somewhere *between 10 and 11 o'clock*. Lean downstream as you hit the jet, and let the current complete your turn to the left.

Peel-offs can be done backward as well as forward. Simply turn your boat around and, by using several firm back strokes, move out of the eddy with your stern pointing between 1 and 2 o'clock if you're intending to peel off to the right (or pointing between 10 and 11 o'clock if you're peeling off to the left). Either way, you'll spin around and find yourself out in the current facing upstream. And in certain situations it could be more desirable to be facing upstream.

The Cartwheel

It is fun as well as good practice to leave and then re-enter the same eddy at almost the same spot. This is called *cartwheeling*. For a cartwheel to the right, take off from the top of an eddy forward at about 2 o'clock (considering 12 o'clock as directly upstream), lean hard downstream and then, with a couple of sweep strokes on the left side, guide the bow of your kayak back across the eddy line into the eddy again. The main force of the current in the jet will then catch your stern and swing it around until you find yourself safely parked in the same eddy again facing upstream.

For a cartwheel to the left, point your bow at 10 o'clock; continue as above. Cartwheels can very quickly become a game between two kayaks to see which can make the tightest turn and lose the least amount of downstream position. It is also fun to see who can do a cartwheel with the least number of sweep strokes.

Trying cartwheels both forward and backward out of eddies from both right and left can work wonders in improving your skill in boating. What's more, it will give you a real feel for the eddy line, the power of the jet, and for the eddy itself. Good cartwheelers can spin out of an eddy, sweep quickly around and cut back into the eddy at almost the same place, all with very little loss of position.

Ferrying

Ferrying is basic to safe navigation in whitewater, and the trick is to get the massive forces of nature to do the work for you. I once saw former World Champion Jürgen Bremmer peel off out of a side eddy on the Passer River in Italy and ferry across the entire river using only one stroke. A clever ferryer can actually work his way upstream in the rapids by judicious use of ferry techniques and eddy hopping.

Backferry (Ferry Glide)

If you want to move laterally across at least part of the river while moving downstream in strong current you can use the backferry sometimes also called the ferry glide.

Suppose you are heading down through rapids and see an obstruction ahead that you'd like to avoid—for example, a rock dead ahead with a clear passage to the right at 1 o'clock.

Your first and natural inclination is to point your bow to the right at 1 o'clock and paddle hard toward the clear passage.

However, the current may be stronger than you think, and your defensive efforts too late. So stop paddling forward, point your bow to 11 o'clock diagonally away from the direction you want to go, and then employ several strong back strokes while leaning downstream. The angle you have created with the boat and the water, plus the force of the current against the slowed boat, will work wonders for you.

After you have sideslipped over as far as you want, you can straighten your boat out with a forward sweep stroke so you are pointing straight downstream again. Ferry glides both to the right and to the left are standard moves all good kayakers use in picking their way down rapids.

The Upstream Ferry

Equally challenging is the upstream ferry. This is usually begun by driving hard out of an eddy upstream at an angle of not more than 1 o'clock if you are heading out to the right into the river, or 11 o'clock if you are heading out to the left into the river. Continue to paddle forward hard and remember to lean downstream when you hit the eddy line.

Getting the right angle and thrust so you'll slip across the river will take a bit of patience and practice. Here are two likely mistakes and how to avoid them:

First, if your boat keeps turning downstream like an unmanageable horse, your angle of exit from the eddy is too close to 3 o'clock if you are moving out to the right, or too close to 9 o'clock if you are moving out to the left. Make sure your bow is pointed *not more* than 1 o'clock for a ferry to the right, or 11 o'clock for a ferry to the left.

Second, if your boat ferries out nicely about halfway and then stops moving laterally across the river, the chances are your bow has crept back toward 12 o'clock. Allow it to fall off *slightly* toward 11 or 1 o'clock while paddling forward, and your ferry will begin again.

Eddy Hopping Upstream

Most people think of rapids as something for a boat to go *down* through. Yet salmon go up very swift streams in search of spawning grounds, and by borrowing a few ideas from these denizens of the river we too can work our way upstream. If the rapids are not too severe and a variety of eddies abound, it is great fun to test your skill in eddy hopping *up* the river.

Start from one eddy and move up to its head, then charge hard out of it and ferry, maintaining strong forward strokes, over to the tail of an eddy on the other side of the river. Work your way up from the tail of this eddy to its top—where you look for the next eddy upstream.

In a way, eddy hopping can be compared to crossing from the head of one ski lift to the bottom of another farther up the mountain as you hitch to the topmost run of an alpine ski area. In this case the eddy acts as your ski lift—with the added bonus of having no lift lines or tickets.

Playing in Rollers

A roller can flip you over quickly if you're unprepared—as explained earlier—but a roller can also provide some wonderful opportunities for exciting whitewater boating. An entire afternoon can be spent at one single place in whitewater that has a good roller with accessible eddies on either side.

If you turn around and back slowly down into a roller, you'll soon feel the exciting sensation of having your stern rise high behind you as your bow disappears underwater at the bottom of the trough below the roller. At this moment you may start to swerve right or left, but with a good paddle brace you can correct your position nicely to avoid getting broadside. However, if you *do* become broadside in a roller, follow your natural tendency to do a high paddle brace—that is, bracing with an extended blade—on the downstream side, and you'll be perfectly OK.

Sometimes the roller will shoot you straight back into the air. In other cases you will do a modest loop-the-loop or "ender," winding up upside down. In any event simply be patient when you find yourself capsized, and Eskimo roll back up.

Some stretches of rivers are already well known where enders can be done like the Endo Rapids in Westwater Canyon on the Colorado River, and the Nose Stand Rapids on the American River in California. Near the Nation's Capital, people can watch kayakers doing enders at Observation Deck Rapids near Great Falls on the Potomac.

A roller enjoys keeping kayaks broadside to the current so they can be bounced around a bit. If it is a worthy roller, it will challenge your ability to get out of its clutches. In small rollers the high downstream side paddle brace is enough to pull you out. If not, then you should combine the side paddle brace with a couple of strong forward or back strokes: these will force you to the side of the roller. At this point, as if in disgust, the roller quite likely will spit you out into an eddy or into the main portion of the river.

More daring is coasting forward downstream into a roller—but meanwhile back paddling strongly, so your boat slowly sinks into the roller itself. Then lean back until you feel your stern go deep into the trough and finally get caught by the strongest downstream current, which moves you straight downstream standing on your tail.

Modest end-over-ends can be done this way as your stern literally goes under while your bow sticks high into the air. Again, when this happens, simply wait a moment or two underwater, then complete your Eskimo roll to right yourself again.

With a handy eddy on either side of a roller it is fun to head upstream from one eddy toward another by skimming across the top of the roller with your bow just missing the trough. Usually this creates one of the fastest upstream ferries imaginable.

Rollers with no dangerous rocks underneath can be places to strut your stuff with an Eskimo roll. Better yet, I've seen some experts on the Farmington River at Tariffville Gorge in Connecticut do numerous Eskimo rolls while broadside in that roller—hand-only rolls at that, because they have thrown away their paddles!

On many of the really big rivers large rolling waves will be seen. Try an upstream ferry out to the top of such a wave, then keep your bow pointed toward 1 or 11 o'clock while facing upstream. Lean slightly downstream and the big current forcing up against your hull will slide your kayak neatly across the surface of the wave. By shifting his weight and controlling his boat, a good paddler can glide back and forth several times on the same wave.

Playing in Souseholes

Souseholes (suckholes or reversals)—even though they may be part of the roller complex in a stretch of rapids—should always be approached with great caution. The smaller, safe ones are fun to play in, but large souseholes should be avoided by everyone except the most expert boaters. For souseholes such as those found on the Colorado River in the Grand Canyon or the Bull Sluice on the Chattooga River, even top-notch paddlers wear—just in case—the big 33-pound buoyancy lifejacket rather than the lighter racing vest, which does not provide nearly as much flotation.

Of course every competent boater wears a helmet in rapids, and the importance of this protective headgear is demonstrated in souseholes. The "jaws" of a sousehole can catch you quickly, making for a very speedy capsize in all that frothy foam, which can conceal a variety of lurking obstructions.

Good boating sense dictates that you stay away from big souseholes in general, and start with the smallest ones before working your way up to larger holes as you gain knowledge of the powerful hydraulics involved.

Entering a Hole

If you wish to play in the smaller souseholes, try nosing down into the hole in a forward position, meanwhile making back strokes in order to travel slower than the rate of the current.

Another approach is to sneak from an eddy on either side into a sousehole. Move diagonally upstream out of the eddy with strong forward strokes, and dive into the sousehole. More daring boaters may wish to drop down into a sousehole backward or sideways.

Once into the hole your boat will be buffeted and bounced around a bit and will very likely turn diagonally one way or another: *At this point always remember to lean and brace downstream.*

Small or reasonably-sized souseholes offer splendid opportunities to learn boat control. A truly expert boater can stick his bow or stern directly into the center of a sousehole and force the onrushing water to spit his boat straight back—sometimes even into the air. Or, if driven in deep enough, the bow or stern will be caught by the powerful water beneath the surface and the kayak will be forced to go end-over-end, which can be one of the greatest thrills in kayaking.

A more constructive procedure is to use several firm forward strokes to augment a downstream brace when you are ready to exit from a sousehole. Or, sometimes it is more convenient to blend that downstream brace with several firm back strokes to back your boat out of the hole.

Dealing with Larger Holes

In really heavy water (anything over 2,000 cubic feet per second) that offers the likelihood of powerful souseholes, there are basically two schools of thought concerning procedure. The first emphasizes that a boater should—contrary to his natural instincts—paddle *hard* right through the hole itself. Here you'll have to make yourself keep paddling, but the force of your momentum augmented by the power of your strokes will see you through.

A second school of thought believes that you should relax and take it easy. Allow your boat to float along the downstream current and do not take any aggressive action at all *until* you are in the very heart of the sousehole: at that point lean and brace on your downstream side. Practitioners of this art love to drop into souseholes or ride giant haystacks in a sideways or even backward position. It really doesn't make much difference in what direction the boat is heading as it drops into the hole, because you then can play or exit, as you wish.

About Running Weirs and Dams

It is a common thing these days to see photographs of kayaks actually airborne as they sail over weirs and dams.

To the unwary thrill-seeker this may look like the ultimate in boating. It is more likely to be an invitation to trouble.

Running a weir or a dam will inevitably cause undue stress to your boat—one that it was never designed to take. In addition, the impact of hitting the water below the dam at an awkward angle can create a physical shock to the person in the boat, possibly injuring his spine or neck. And, finally, the backwash of water just downstream can pin the paddler and his boat in its grip. He then must be rescued from shore with his boat perhaps abandoned and battered to pieces against the foot of the barrier.

Don't be fooled by the innocent appearance of a weir or dam. It may not look particularly large or ferocious, but never underestimate the power of water. The infamous Brookmont Dam across the Potomac River just above Washington, D.C., is such a place. Because it looks so benign, each year boaters have come to grief trying to run it, tragedy being the sad ending to a trip.

In general, therefore, do not run dams and weirs unless there is a sluiceway provided. Portage instead. The momentary thrill of going over the steep pitch of water is negated by the variety of dangers involved.

11. Kayaks in the Ocean

Boats and Equipment

You could put to sea in almost any kind of a kayak. If your purpose is simply to explore a small harbor or an inlet, a slalom or general touring boat might do. But if you venture out into a larger estuary or poke your nose around a headland into the open sea, then a boat designed specifically for that purpose must be used.

The general touring or slalom kayak tends to plane even at slow speed, making it useless in fast tidal streams. Its bow is not meant to cope with ocean waves, and its rockered hull is not suited for straight running at sea.

For sea kayaking, a boat must have a sharply pointed bow to part the waves, followed by a flared forward section to provide substantial lift to keep the boat on the surface of the water. Some designs compromise on the flare and attempt to get the necessary lift with extra width amidships, but this causes a bouncy "dancing" response in steep, confused seas.

Other designs ignore flare and width amidships and depend entirely on the sharp vertical entry at the bow, coupled with a raised foredeck. These designs, however, are suitable only for paddling in relatively calm water. The best designs use a sharp bow (technically called a "narrow entry") followed by a forward flare that develops gradually. The result is a boat that stays well on top of the water and always climbs dependably up and over waves rather than slicing through them. The resulting bow or stern lift is quite gentle and predictable, no matter what the angle is between wave and boat.

Oceangoing kayak.

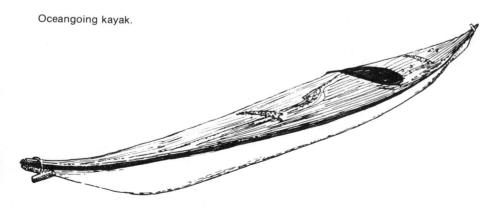

Stability in a sea kayak is a two-edged sword: high initial stability may result in low secondary stability, the analogy being a sailing catamaran. The natural tendency is to design for width to provide the feeling of stability. Such a boat may pitch and toss as it conforms to the surface of the sea in rough weather. Under very rough conditions, the boat may actually "trip" over its own width, particularly if the hull is more flat than rounded.

In contrast, a narrow, long boat with a rounded bilge feels very tippy *at first*. In other words it has low initial stability but higher *secondary* stability. The narrower width reduces the rocking and pitching around, while the boat remains upright even in steep pitching seas. The result is a genuine feeling of stability, with that low initial feeling of stability being only temporary.

It is this stability factor which has produced major departures in recent boat design and prevented any one design theme from emerging. As a result, sea kayaks can be classified into four basic groups, each of which tries to solve needs for speed, strength, paddling efficiency, and storage capacity:

The West Greenland Eskimo Kayak Design. These designs display long, narrow, low decks, rudderless, round-bilged, gently sweeping bow and stern, hull flare fore and aft.

The West Greenland Compromise Design. These are similar to the design above except they are shorter and wider.

Ocean Touring Kayaks. Quite often these are modifications of high volume touring kayaks. They can be either long or short, about 25 inches wide, high decked, very little rocker, a U-shaped hull, sharp vertical entry at the bow, and fitted with a rudder.

Large Cruising Kayaks. These are very high volume open ocean tourers.

The speed and paddling efficiency of the West Greenland Eskimo Kayak design has been well documented, especially in England. The trick is to get adjusted to its initial sense of instability.

Accessories

Although regular whitewater-style paddles can be used at sea, lengthier paddles with longer and narrower blades are better. When they're used correctly, it's like paddling in low gear. The propulsion is about the same, but the effort seems less. The returning blade in the air offers less resistance to the wind.

Asymmetrical flatwater paddles are popular since they are light, flutter free, and feel comfortable. Whether the paddle is feathered or not is a matter of personal choice. It is helpful to have a sea paddle painted a bright fluorescent color to make it easy for a boater to be seen. Better yet, a bright colored deck, hat, or lifejacket will increase chances of being spotted.

In regard to clothing, one must remember that for the most part ocean water is cold—very cold. Therefore some sort of a wet suit is *de rigueur*. The Farmer John is preferred because it provides the most protection with the least amount of chafing and restriction. Also, pile clothing is beginning to make inroads. A Gore-tex jacket in combination with pile can be suitable boating gear. Helmets, which are so important in white-water, give way to an imaginative mélange of headgear—bush hats, straw hats, and fancy sailing caps have all been seen on oceangoing kayakers. A good hat should keep your head warm, dry, protect it from the sun, and stay on in heavy wind or a capsize.

A lifejacket must be worn at sea, ALWAYS. It must have lots of buoy-ancy, help to retain body heat, contain pockets to carry things in, be comfortable to wear, and easy to swim in. Compasses with luminous pointers can be fastened to the deck, ingeniously set into a visible pocket in the spray cover, or attached with a cord around the wearer's neck. When using a compass, make sure you keep it away from your walkie-talkie or other metal objects. Other important safety items for a venture at sea include flares, an automatic electronic signalling device, a flash-light or caver's headlamp, sunglasses, a whistle, and a waterproof watch.

Bulkheads and watertight hatches are better for kayaking in the ocean because in case of capsize only the cockpit fills with water and can be bailed out using a deck pump. A good pump cannot only bail out the cockpit but its hose can also be placed into a companion's boat or into a flooded bulkhead or storage compartment with hatch failure to empty them. A pump provides a new and wider margin of safety for paddling at sea.

Deck-mounted shock cords can be useful for holding charts, extra gear, and spare paddles. For ocean paddling, anything on the deck stands the risk of being washed overboard if the cords are not very tight. Recessed fittings, integral parts of the deck, are the best. These fittings can even be rigged with full deck lines to provide a grab point for anyone trying to hold on to the kayak while in the water—and this includes you in a capsize and wet exit.

Some Paddling Hints

Most of the basic kayak strokes are also useful in propelling and steer-ing a kayak in the ocean. The forward, backward, draw, and sweep strokes are the same. The Duffek stroke can be modified to become a bow rudder. The longer paddle used in ocean travel facilitates dipping the blade far forward at 10 o'clock or 2 o'clock to draw the bow to port or starboard.

The standard rear brace or rudder turn is called a *telemark* by sea kayakers. The paddle blade is placed in the water at the stern with the power face angled slightly inward. The kayaker then leans on the paddle to carve a graceful arc with his boat in the same direction as the lean.

With long paddles, slower stroke rates are more common. Bracing strokes timed with the approaching waves become very important to smooth paddling when a heavy sea is running. A paddler must forget his whitewater instincts and always lean *into* a wave, especially if the wave is breaking. The bigger the breaking wave, the harder the lean and brace.

Launching and Landing

Launching from a beach can be simple. Watch how far the waves roll up on the sand, then hurry your kayak down as close as possible in between waves and get in. (On the West Coast of the United States there are commonly 8 seconds between waves, on the East Coast about six seconds.) When the next large wave washes up on shore this may be enough to enable you to push off and paddle firmly out to deeper water. If not, position an upright paddle on one side of your boat. Bend forward and place your other hand down on the sand along the other side of the boat. Push down on both sides and inch your way forward toward the water. A partner on shore can also help push you out quickly into deeper water when the next waves roll up on the beach.

Launching from a rocky shore is similar to launching in a river (see Chapter 5). Be careful not to slip on the rocks; beware that a surge of incoming water doesn't lift you up and settle you down on a sharp rock. With a partner or without, you can do a "seal" launch when rocks are covered with seaweed. Simply get into your boat; use paddle on one side and your hand on the other side to slide your boat down into the water. A partner can help by lifting your stern and giving you a shove seaward.

Landing a kayak can be a rough or smooth experience depending upon how well the kayaker can read the pattern of ingoing waves. The surf should be studied carefully. Sometimes there will be 5 to 7 large waves rolling in followed by a pause with a couple of smaller waves. This phenomenon results from wave interference between two sets of waves arriving simultaneously from two separate and distant storm sites. This is not necessarily a regular occurrence, so don't count on its happening every time you wish to land. In any event, study the waves until you can sense some kind of pattern; then sprint to shore just ahead of the smallest wave. As soon as you touch bottom, leap out and quickly drag your kayak up the beach out of the way of the next incoming wave.

Landing on a rocky shore is more difficult, but the principle is the same. Carefully choose a sheltered spot where you can make it in. Wait for a pause in the wave pattern and go in. Jump out of your kayak and move it quickly away from the next incoming wave. On seaweed covered ledges, ride a surging wave onto the ledge. As the water recedes leaving the boat high and dry, jump out of the boat and move the boat and yourself to higher ground. On a rocky shore or island there are many small coves with some protection from winds and waves for landing.

Wind

Beam Gales

In a *beam gale* (a 35 mile per hour or more wind blowing at you from 9 o'clock or 3 o'clock), while making forward strokes, keep your blade low on the windward side as it returns to take another stroke on that side. For example, with a wind coming from 3 o'clock when you finish your forward stroke on the right side, simply let the right blade skim the water on its way back forward, rather than lifting it so it is in danger of being caught by the wind. When paddling in a beam gale, always lean into the wind and time the strokes to allow paddle entry and drive as the wave crest arrives. Otherwise, the boat may be tipped if the paddler's weight has shifted downwind and the windward blade is caught by a gust of wind. If a strong gust of wind does hit your raised blade, don't fight it. Relax the grip of your upper hand and allow the paddle to flip over. This will prevent a capsize.

Weathercocking

While paddling parallel to the wind and waves with any degree of forward speed, you will notice a phenomenon called *weathercocking*. In spite of your best efforts, your kayak will tend to turn into the wind. This can be exasperating because you are forced to paddle constantly on one side just to stay on course. This phenomenon can occur when the wind is coming at you broadside or diagonally both fore and aft. Generally speaking, the longer and narrower the kayak the less there is of a tendency to weathercock.

Weathercocking is caused by an imbalance of two forces acting on your boat. The wind pushing up against the exposed deck area of a kayak

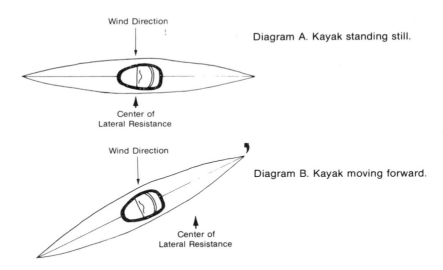

Wind Direction

Diagram A. Kayak standing still.

Center of
Lateral Resistance

Wind Direction

Diagram B. Kayak moving forward.

Center of
Lateral Resistance

is called *windage*. This force must be perfectly counterbalanced by a second force—the *lateral resistance* of the area of the kayak below water line (see Diagram A). However, as the kayak moves forward (sideways to the wind direction), the center of lateral resistance also moves forward thus forcing the kayak to turn into the wind (Diagram B).

Weathercocking can be counterbalanced in a number of ways. As mentioned earlier you can simply make strong corrective forward strokes on one side. Second, a rudder can help correct the situation, but a rudder creates drag and can be damaged in launching and landing. Kayaks with low deck profiles leaving very little exposed to the wind are not affected quite so much by weathercocking. The Eskimos moved forward or backward in their cockpits, because by shifting their weight fore or aft as needed they did not have to make those exhaustive correcting strokes constantly on one side.

Some modern seagoing kayaks have a sliding seat and footbrace arrangement that can be adjusted while underway. Thus, if your kayak tends to turn into the wind, simply slide your seat forward or backward until that motion stops. What you have done is to bring back into balance windage and your boat's lateral resistance to it. (Technically, it is called having a balanced wind-water couple.) If you significantly alter the forward speed of the kayak, you must also adjust your seat accordingly. If the force of the wind changes, you must also compensate for it by repositioning your seat. Finally, it is assumed that your spray cover and cockpit are ample enough to allow you to move your seat forward or backward.

A sliding seat may not be the complete answer, however, because such an arrangement requires a larger cockpit. The larger the cockpit the greater the danger of having a heavy sea pound your spray cover down into your lap, filling your boat with water. In the open ocean this is more than disconcerting—it can be dangerous.

Some kayaks have an extended keel or a removable skeg that helps to keep a kayak on course. Paul Coffyn, in his circumnavigation of New Zealand, used a removable skeg to combat weathercocking.

If you lack both a rudder and a sliding seat, the "one-knee hang" is a technique that can be used. When a beam wind is blowing, simply press your knee on the leeward side hard up against the kneebrace allowing your other (windward) knee to straighten out. This will cause the kayak to tilt toward the wind and will compensate for weathercocking. Another solution is to use an extended paddle on the windward side and transform your forward stroke on that side into more of a sweep stroke. As you can see, there are a variety of ways to attack the problem of weathercocking.

Winds from Other Directions

In a headwind you should develop a steady paddling rhythm, try to keep the spray out of your face, and be patient. It may seem that you are not making much headway, but you are.

If the wind is coming at you diagonally, either from bow or stern, you have a couple choices. One alternative is to turn about 45 degrees so that the wind is now coming from either 9 or 3 o'clock and proceed to paddle parallel to the waves making adjustments for weathercocking. In so doing, you will not head directly toward your destination, but will complete a dogleg. For instance, if you wish to cross a channel but face a beam wind at 9 o'clock, by paddling parallel to the waves your crossing will take you downwind of your destination. As soon as you reach the leeward side of the channel, you must then turn back toward 9 o'clock and head straight up along the coast to your goal. Close to shore those waves won't be as troublesome.

Waves

Waves will be your constant companion when you paddle on the ocean. Waves, their style, character, size, and ferocity should be well known to you.

Waves consist of three basic parts: the *crest* which is the top or highest part of the wave, the *trough* which is the lowest part of the wave, and the *soup*, the name given to a wave after it breaks. The length of a wave is the distance from one crest to another, and its height is the distance vertically from trough to crest. The time required for two wave crests to move past a reference point is called the *wave period*. Counting the seconds between successive breaking waves on the shore also gives you the wave period.

Wind blowing against a tidal current will produce steep, choppy waves. Wind blowing across water flowing at exactly the same speed will produce no waves at all. Wind blowing in the same direction and faster than the speed of the current will produce smooth, rounded waves.

Seas and Swells

As you paddle on the sea, you will soon become aware of two broad classifications of waves: *sea* and *swell*. Seas are generated locally by wind. They appear confused and irregular in pattern. They tend to have sharp, angular crests, and no regular wave period; and the wind whipped crests often spill forward.

Swells have often travelled thousands of miles across the broad expanse of the sea. As seas move away from their point of origin, they smooth out into long, regular crests of definite wave lengths and wave periods.

Whitecaps

When the wind blows strongly enough to whip up a deep water wave higher than one-seventh of the distance between crests, then the tops of the waves fall over, forming whitecaps. As waves move toward shore, they change some of their characteristics. As waves encounter the rising ocean bottom, their period may remain the same, but their velocity and length decrease while their wave height increases. Eventually, as with a deep water wave, they will begin to break when their ratio exceeds 1:7. When the wave gets close to shore in water only about $1\frac{1}{4}$ times its height, the crest topples over in a breaking wave.

Reflected Waves

Unfortunately for the kayaker, waves can be reflected into the ocean after striking piers, headlands, or even islands. Thus incoming and reflected wave patterns interfere with one another to create a very confused and choppy pattern. Sometimes the reflected wave crest is perfectly timed to meet an incoming wave, and they collide explosively. This can be dangerous, and kayaks should avoid areas where this occurs.

Plunging Waves

A plunging (or dumping) wave should be avoided by kayakers. Steep waves approaching a steep beach tend to plunge. This kind of wave has an overhanging curl of water that comes crashing down with tremendous impact. Launching and landing should not be attempted through plunging or dumping waves.

Spilling Waves

Spilling waves are steep waves that approach a gently sloping beach. They are good surfing waves which break smoothly with the water tumbling down the forward slope. They lack the violence of a plunging wave and are better waves in which to surf or safely launch and land boats.

Rip Currents

While observing waves breaking and rolling up on the shore, look for strong, narrow currents of water carrying the excess water back out to sea. These are called rip currents. The water accumulates and disperses to either side eventually to exit seaward in narrow and swift currents with waves not nearly so high. These currents can be quite strong; at high tide they can be very pronounced. Rip channels can be found along the sides of bays and can provide a fast way of getting out into the sea.

Turning in Waves

To change direction in big waves, wait until your kayak rises to the top (crest) of a wave; then, using a sweep stroke, quickly turn your boat in the proper direction. The crest of the wave passing under the kayak clears the bow and stern providing an easy pivot for turning since both ends are in the air above water. It is much more difficult to turn a kayak when it is down in the trough of a wave.

Tides

No one should ever launch a kayak for a trip in the ocean without being fully aware of what the tide is doing and of tidal streams and currents, if any, that will be encountered on the voyage. If you plan carefully, the tide and current can work for you and make your journey pleasant and easy. Fighting tides and current is useless.

Fortunately charts and maritime booklets are available for most inhabited and mapped coastal areas of the world. To make use of the tide, it is important to keep a couple things in mind: First, from low tide (when the tide is way out), the current gradually increases in speed until about half way through the first tidal cycle, about 3 hours. After the midpoint of this first cycle is reached, the current slowly decreases until high tide is reached in about another 3 hours, a total of a little more than six hours from low to high tide. The same thing occurs in reverse from high tide back to low tide. To make it more complicated there can be a lag between the position of a tide out at the mouth of an estuary and that farther up the estuary.

Crossing from the mainland to an island one must bear in mind that the tidal stream flows faster, the narrower the gap between the two pieces of land.

Tidal streams which appear in channels and straits should not be confused with true ocean currents. For example, the famous Gulf Stream in the Atlantic Ocean is not a tidal stream, but a current. It travels toward the British Isles at a constant rate of about 3 miles per hour.

Navigating By Kayak

Poets have extolled the wonders as well as the dangers at sea. It has often been said that the sea doesn't care. The sea can be tantalizingly deceptive. For example, you can be duped into believing that the direction you aim your kayak in is the direction you actually go in. Far from it. Nature, in the form of wind, tidal streams, and ocean currents, will conspire to send you way off course. Then, if fog descends, you won't even be able to see your destination.

The purpose of this section is not to provide complete information on navigation at sea. That is a science that has been studied for centuries, and many valuable books are available on the subject. Suffice to say, it is a complex subject that deserves the complete respect of anyone venturing out from the mainland in a small boat. Perhaps one brief example will give you an idea how to proceed.

On your ocean trip you plan to leave the mainland and paddle straight out to a lighthouse on a small island 4 miles from shore. You already know that you can comfortably cruise at an average rate of 4 miles per hour. Therefore, discounting wind, tide, and currents, it should take you approximately one hour to make the trip.

First, consider the tidal current at your proposed place and time of crossing. Let's say it is 3 miles per hour from 3 o'clock. Draw two sides of a triangle (A and B) as in Diagram C. Line A represents the actual track

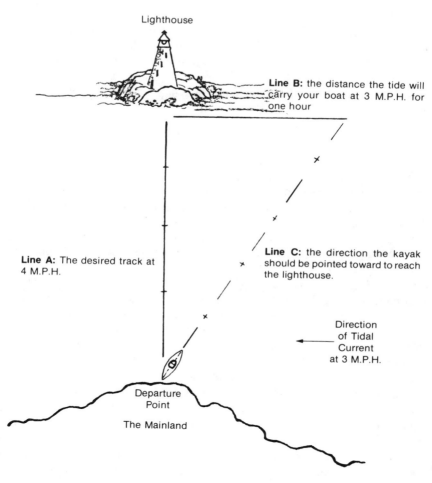

Lighthouse

Line B: the distance the tide will carry your boat at 3 M.P.H. for one hour

Line A: The desired track at 4 M.P.H.

Line C: the direction the kayak should be pointed toward to reach the lighthouse.

Direction of Tidal Current at 3 M.P.H.

Departure Point

The Mainland

Diagram C.

you wish to follow. Line B represents the distance the tidal current will carry you at 3 miles per hour if no course correction is made. (Be sure— for purposes of finding the proper course angle—to lay out line B *upstream* from the tidal current.) Line C (the hypotenuse of the triangle thus formed) reveals to you not only the direction your kayak should be pointed, but will indicate that you will either have to travel at 5 miles per hour in order to reach the lighthouse in an hour; or at your average rate of 4 miles per hour, it will take you longer than an hour to get there.

Navigation Aids at Sea

Fortunately, most harbors and estuaries are well marked with buoys and other navigational aids. You should be familiar with all of them, so if you paddle up to one in a dense fog, you'll know exactly where you are. Since kayaks are not the only craft to ply the oceans, a kayaker should be aware of the meaning of the various ships' signals and always stay away from large vessels.

Fog

Generally speaking, do not venture out to sea on a foggy day, or even if fog is predicted in the weather forecast. Keep in mind that fog is caused by warm air blowing off the land over a cool sea which chills the air down to its dew point. In parts of the world where warm air blows across a warm ocean current (the Gulf Stream, for example) and then encounters cold water, fog will form.

Should fog suddenly envelop you at sea, don't panic. Simply follow your compass and charts. As soon as you *feel* you are close to your destination (since you can't see it), stop paddling and start to rely on your ears. All land emits sound of some kind. It may be waves breaking against a rocky shore, dogs barking, or even the noise of birds, a chain saw, or an automobile.

I recall an embarrassing moment in the middle of the Connecticut River on the border between Vermont and New Hampshire, just south of Ledyard Bridge, near Hanover, N.H. Fog so thick descended I couldn't see either river bank. I had paddled long enough to get where I was going but nothing showed up on the limited horizon. Apparently I had paddled in a circle. It was enormously frustrating until, far away, I heard the sound of an automobile crossing the bridge. I headed in that direction and soon the bridge loomed up in front of me.

Transit Markers

One of the oldest navigational techniques in the world is the use of transit markers. Simply line up two identifiable objects on land that stand in the direction you wish to head. Keep one object in view directly in front of the other and you'll be on course. Two headlands kept in line can accomplish the same purpose. Sometimes you can use two sets of transit markers at right angles to each other to pinpoint your position exactly.

On the Sea at Night

As with fog, generally speaking, it is not wise to paddle a kayak in the ocean after dark. In addition to the normal challenges of navigation, you have two additional disadvantages: you can see very little, and nobody can see you. Even if you have a headlamp or strong flashlight, most large vessels will not see you. Even if they did, they could not steer away in time to miss you. Paddling at night should be done only by the most competent kayaker who is totally familiar with the route, can identify the available shore lights—and then only under favorable weather conditions. An easily readable, illuminated compass attached to your deck is also an important accessory.

Sea Rescues

The river bank is never too far away when you are paddling down a rapids and something goes wrong. At sea, however, you are likely to be far from shore. Your kayak, lifejacket, and your companions are your sole means of survival and rescue. Nevertheless, if you take appropriate precautions and master a variety of rescue techniques, kayaking at sea can be a safe venture.

Each of the following rescue techniques should be thoroughly practiced with your trip companions in a swimming pool or lake before you, as a group, head out for the ocean. It should also be understood that, although some of the following rescue techniques seem somewhat complicated or involved, each one should be accomplished within 60 seconds by a well trained party.

The Eskimo Roll (See Chapter 6)

This is by far the quickest and safest means of rescue. It is your first line of defense. Any kayaker aspiring to paddle at sea must have a totally reliable roll on both sides.

Caution

For the sea rescue techniques described, bear in mind even after you have thoroughly mastered them in an unloaded boat in calm water, doing it for real in a choppy sea with a fully loaded kayak, can be much more difficult. If possible, all of these rescue techniques should be mastered eventually with *loaded* boats before embarking on an ocean trip.

Solo Re-entry

If you inadvertently fall out of your kayak in a capsize, it is possible to get back in and complete the Eskimo roll. Face to the rear of your overturned boat, grab the coaming, and do a reverse somersault to get your legs back into the cockpit and fit into the kneebraces. Then place your paddle into the correct position and roll back up.

This is not as difficult a technique as it appears. After you roll back up your cockpit will be full of water, but at least you *and* the boat are right side up and you are safely back in the boat. You can then take your time and bail out the cockpit before replacing the spray cover.

The Eskimo Rescue (See Chapter 6)

If you capsize and remain in your boat but cannot roll it back up, simply slap your hands hard on the exposed hull over your overturned craft. One of your companions will nudge the nose of his kayak up against your hand. Grab the bow of the kayak and pull yourself up. Be prepared to hold your breath for at least a minute. You can do it.

Eskimo Side Rescue

The rescuer paddles quickly alongside the overturned boat and places his paddle across the capsized craft while the kayaker is still in the boat. The rescuer grabs the kayaker's wrist and places it on the paddle shaft. The overturned kayaker can now pull himself up to an upright position while the rescuer holds the paddle firmly at a 90 degree angle across the overturned hull.

The H-I Rescue

So-called because of the position of the kayaks, for this rescue two kayaks raft up by crossing their paddles in front of them on their cockpits as they position themselves alongside each other. This forms the figure H. Next, the overturned kayak, the I, is drawn up over the paddles between the rescuers' boats, emptied out, flipped over to an upright position, and then wedged between the two rescuing kayaks. The swimmer mounts and straddles the rear deck of the kayak and wriggles into the cockpit.

Kayak Over Kayak Rescue

Sometimes called the *T Rescue* (because of the position of the kayaks). In this rescue the rescuing kayak approaches the overturned boat at 90 degrees. With some help from the swimmer, the rescuer slides the overturned bow up over the foredeck enough to allow water to drain out of the cockpit. The rescuing kayaker flips the boat upright, slides it back into the water, and then pulls it alongside and holds it steady so the swimmer can mount and straddle the rear deck and wriggle into the cockpit.

Double T Rescue employs two rescue kayaks located at the cross of the T. The capsized craft makes up the shaft of the T. It is much easier to haul the overturned boat up on to the foredeck with two rescuers working side by side.

The All In Rescue

In the worst possible case, all kayaks have capsized and all paddlers have come out of their boats. Make sure that all boats, paddles, and swimmers are connected by holding on to each other's boats and paddles. Do not allow one boat or swimmer to drift away. Then empty one kayak by drawing it perpendicularly up over a second overturned boat, making sure that this pivot boat remains upside down to keep air trapped inside the cockpit for as much buoyancy as possible. With a swimmer on either side of the pivot boat, empty the water out of the first boat, flip it over, and drop it alongside the pivot boat right side up.

Extend a paddle amidships across both boats. The second swimmer on the outside of the overturned pivot boat holds the paddle firmly, while the first swimmer uses the other end of the paddle as a firm brace to assist his crawling over the side and into the emptied boat.

Once the first swimmer is back in his boat, he performs a T rescue for the second swimmer and boat. Then both of them perform an H-I rescue for other overturned boats and swimmers.

Summary

The kayaker who challenges the sea will find adventure galore. In one of the most efficient and seaworthy crafts in the world, kayakers can travel where few other boaters dare to go. They can hop from one bay or island to another and avoid the roughest water by slipping in close to shore. They can ride beam to a breaking sea that is many times their own height. They can even capsize and be brought right side up again in a moment.

However, anyone who chooses to follow the path to ocean adventure must abide by the following rules:

- Use a kayak designed specifically for ocean travel; other kinds of kayaks are not suitable.
- Bring along all the appropriate equipment and know how to use it.
- Be totally skilled in all forms of rescue.
- Never venture forth with fewer than three kayaks in a group.
- Take weather, tide, wind, and currents into account before launching a kayak in the ocean.

With the above rules scrupulously adhered to, a whole new world of sport awaits the kayaker. Sea kayaking is truly the new frontier for recreational muscle-powered watercraft.

12. Surfing

Running rapids, crossing a wilderness pond at twilight, or island hopping along the ocean shore are activities for which kayaks are ideally suited. There is, however, another form of water that has attracted the attention of adventuresome people in small boats. It is the waves that ceaselessly roll off the ocean's surface and crash against the great masses of the continents. This endless activity and motion where the sea meets land have always been a source of fascination.

For years outdoor enthusiasts have used a flat board to ride these waves as they roll up on the beach. Surfboarding is well-established as a respectable sport in most industrial nations fortunate enough to have one or more good seacoasts.

It was inevitable that someone, someday, would try the same thing in a kayak. At first, whitewater kayaks were used, but their pointed ends occasionally dug into the sand. Soon kayaks were designed more like surfboards with a flat bottom and the seat well aft of center. Double-bladed paddles were used to get these "surfyaks" quickly back into position to take advantage of the incoming waves.

As with surfboarding, the West Coast of the United States, at least 25 years ago, became a center for kayak surfing. Both the British Isles and the wonderful beaches of Australia have become havens for the sport as well.

A slalom kayak slides down the face of a wave. However, flat-bottomed surf kayaks made expressly for surfing are easiest to control as you ride in on a large wave. (Old Town Canoe Company)

Equipment

It is possible to run almost any kayak in on the surf and enjoy an invigorating ride toward the beach. Nevertheless, thanks to modern ingenuity, the prospective kayak surfer can do better.

At first the early kayaks designed specifically for surfing were shortened and flattened slalom boats with squared off ends. They had a tapered flat stern, and a pronouncedly upswept bow. They looked something like a slipper. More recently *surfskis* or *waveskis*™ have emerged. These look something like a surfboard complete with a seat, seat belt, and a place to secure your feet (known as foot wells). There is really no cockpit at all. In these racy new craft a paddle is used and therefore they go beyond the traditional surfboard in the mastery of waves.

A helmet should be worn while surfing. This is not so much to prevent the head from hitting a rock or the ocean floor as it is to protect against riderless surfboards, other surf kayakers, and stray paddles.

A lifejacket, of course, must be worn while surf kayaking. After a capsize, it can be a long swim back to shore. Or, if you are knocked away from your boat and catch a mouthful of ocean water at the same time, it is mighty nice not having to worry about struggling back to the surface and swimming energetically just to stay afloat.

Footrests or foot wells should be designed so they cannot trap your feet and the seat belt on a *surfski*, must have a reliable instant release mechanism that is not adversely affected by sand or salt water.

Where to Find Surf

Playing in ocean surf means that you are entering a potentially violent environment. Surf is the whitewater of the sea. Seawater is much heavier than the freshwater found in lakes, ponds, and rivers. You will notice the difference the minute you attempt to empty ocean water out of a swamped kayak. Seawater can pack quite a wallop and should always be treated with respect.

Most beaches popular with board surfers will also be suitable for kayak surfing. Those beaches known for very gradual sloping bottoms usually make excellent spots for surfing. The best surfing conditions exist when there is little or no wind, a warm, sunny day, and large, even swells providing regular, open ended waves in predictable patterns. Beaches where the waves wash up against a cliff or large rock formations obviously should be avoided, as should any beach that tends to produce high, dumping waves.

Beach Courtesy

Respect for the rights of others in the enjoyment of nature is something all surf kayakers should observe. Others enjoy the surf besides you. Family groups with little children, swimmers, people fishing from the shore, and surfboarders all have a right to enjoy the surf.

Be sure to check with the local park service, land owner, or life guards on duty to make sure that you may surf your kayak in an area, that it is safe, and that you will not become a danger to others. Never kayak close to swimmers, fishermen, or surfboarders. Always leave plenty of room. Never kayak alone in the surf.

Riding Waves

First of all (if you are a beginner), choose a day when the waves are not too high. Anything over 2½ to 3 feet can be intimidating. Second, recall how to launch a kayak off a beach (see Chapter 11). Place your boat close to the water's edge pointing seaward. Get in, put your spray cover on and shove your boat along the sand by leaning forward and using an upright paddle on one side and your other hand on the opposite side of your boat. Inch your boat along and when the next wave comes rolling in, you'll be waterborne. Keep heading directly out, paddling swiftly toward the incoming waves in deep water.

Forward Running

Paddle straight out for several yards until the first breaking wave comes along. Before it reaches you, turn and point your boat directly toward shore, perpendicular to the oncoming wave. When the soup (the white, frothy part) is a few feet behind you and gaining fast, start to paddle forward briskly. The wave will soon catch up to you, and you'll feel that magic sensation of power in the wave that hurtles you toward the beach.

Place your paddle in the stern rudder position and try to maintain a straight course. When the wave plays itself out, turn around and head back for the next one. This time, however, allow yourself to be caught sideways—parallel—to the wave. NOW, THE MOST IMPORTANT THING TO REMEMBER—lean *into* the oncoming wave and hang a high side brace over the soup. On small waves you can actually place the paddle on the back side of the wave. Contrary to what you learned in whitewater kayaking about always leaning downstream and away from the current, in the surf you lean *into* the soup. This prevents a capsize. If you lean away from a wave, the force of the water will work to overturn your boat.

After you've played around a bit getting used to the feel of the surf, sooner or later the ocean will catch you by surprise and you'll find yourself upside down and out of your boat. This is natural and nothing to be ashamed of. Simply grab your boat at the bow or stern and tow it back to shore maintaining a grip with one hand on your paddle. Some surf kayaks have toggles instead of grabloops at each end, making it easier to keep control of your boat. Sometimes in heavy surf, a boat will roll over several times twisting a grabloop around in your hand.

After you feel comfortable running straight in ahead of a wave, try going out beyond where the waves are breaking, turn around, and catch a wave by paddling forward. Allow the boat to plane along the surface of the water in front of the wave. Using the paddle in a stern rudder position, angle your kayak so that it is cutting diagonally across a wave. You may notice a tendency for your craft to turn up and out of the wave. A firm stern rudder or bracing stroke can correct this if you wish to stay on the same wave and maintain your straight course toward shore.

If a wave is large, look along the crest of it in both directions and determine on which side the wave will start to break. Turn away from the breaking side and start planing diagonally away from the soup. On a good, long wave a competent surfer can move well over 100 yards sideways before heading appreciably toward shore.

Tricks to Try

Surf kayaks and surf skis are amazingly versatile craft. Here are a few stunts to add to your repertoire.

The 360 Degree Turn

Fortunately, a surf kayak has a flat bottom, making spinning and turning easy. As you plane down the front surface of a wave, a powerful stern rudder stroke in one direction should be enough to spin you around so that you're facing back out to sea. Complete the turn with a strong sweep stroke. Good surf kayakers can do as many as four 360's on the same wave.

Dropping and Climbing

Rather than being satisfied with running straight in to shore, try cutting back to the top of a wave, then dropping back down again. Your kayak will rise and fall on the face of the wave just ahead of the moving crest.

The turns can be made by a combination of stern rudder strokes and leaning the kayak into the wave to climb, and away from the wave to drop back down.

Cutting Back

This is a further refinement of dropping and climbing in which the boat heads down diagonally across the wave away from the soup, then turns and heads back toward the soup before turning back again to the original direction. Cutting back increases your use of the wave and lengthens your run. As before, the turns are made by strong stern rudder strokes and proper leaning of the kayak, coupled with an occasional sweep stroke if necessary.

Going Backward

Riding backward down the face of a wave can be quite a thrilling experience. Turn around so you are facing an oncoming wave. When the wave is a few yards in front of you, start paddling backward. Lean forward into the wave as soon as the angle on the face of the wave begins to steepen, and place your paddle blade near the bow to act as a rudder. This maneuver is not as easy as it sounds. The wave wants to spin your boat around into a forward position.

The Loop

Sooner or later as you surf down a steep wave, your bow will either bury itself in the sand (called pearling or pole vaulting) if the water is shallow, or simply plow deep into the reverse flowing water beneath the wave. In either case the wave itself won't stop for you, it will hurry on by, and in doing so it will literally push your kayak over forward in a loop. Contrary to your natural instinct to raise your head and arch your back, you should lean *forward*, duck your head and prepare to Eskimo roll. You'll be surprised that by the time you are ready to roll, the wave has gone by and the kayak will be rolled up in the deep water behind the wave.

Loops can be done both forward and backward. Some kayakers say that the backward loop is easier to learn because your back is presented to the water instead of your face, and your body is much nearer to the water during the loop.

The Half Loop and Flick

With the kayak in a vertical position about to be pushed over into a loop, reach down with the paddle blade into the water and make a quick sweep stroke while "flicking," snapping your hips in the opposite direction. The kayak will spin on its axis and come down right side up facing out to sea.

The Pirouette

This is the same maneuver as the half loop and flick except that the spin is strong enough for the kayak to turn 360 degrees or more on its axis.

Eskimo Roll Reverse Loop and Flick

Perfectly executed, this can be one of the most graceful and acrobatic tricks in surfing. As the kayak falls back down the face of a wave, the stern digs in. Just before the kayak becomes vertical, the kayaker assumes an Eskimo roll position and rolls into the wave. The bow continues in its arc beyond the vertical as the Eskimo roll is completed. Surprise! The kayak emerges right side up and is now heading forward on the same wave.

Pop Ups

Sometimes called *sky rocketing* or *pop outs*, these are possible on certain kinds of waves (you'll have to try the waves to see if they are right for them) to bury the bow but not quite do a loop. Your boat goes down deep and then acts as a ping-pong ball that has been immersed in a pail of water. The kayak will literally pop back up and sometimes actually clear the water.

The ultimate, of course, is an airborne 360 degree pirouette.

Summary

As you can see, surf kayaking adds a whole new, thrilling dimension to the sport of kayaking. With proper precautions taken, it is relatively safe. It can be exquisitely graceful as well as acrobatic. Since waves have so much variety to them, you can invent maneuvers that have not been tried before.

13. Touring

Exploring the waterways of the world can open an entirely new dimension for you. The spectrum is as broad as the imagination. Touring by kayak can simply mean traveling down the river that runs through your home town or exploring the shoreline of a nearby lake. It can also mean a major trip to a famous river in another part of the country, or even an international expedition to South America or to the Himalayas where rivers cascade from the highest peaks.

Going places, seeing unfamiliar sights, and learning new things in the great outdoors in relative safety and comfort with friendly companions can be one of life's greatest rewards. Land-based human beings are often intrigued by the smells and challenge of the sea. Urban people, surrounded by pavement, concrete, man-made noise, confusion, and visual pollution, can learn that there is natural incense in the air and a music to the wind. The world is out there for you to enjoy. A wilderness trip by kayak will renew you and refresh your senses and your appreciation of life. The kayak is an ideal vehicle to take you to some of the remote corners of the earth.

Taking the First Step

Whether you live in a city, in a small town, or in the country, the chances are good that you can find people who like to go kayaking. The American Whitewater Affiliation publishes a journal *American Whitewater* (Bart Jackson, editor, 7 Holland Lane, Cranbury, New Jersey 08512), which contains a list of clubs throughout the United States and even a few as far away as New Zealand, Chile, and Sweden. The American Canoe Association (P.O. Box 248, Lorton, Virginia 22079) and the annual Whitewater Program (Box 210 D, R.D. 2, Palmerton, Pennsylvania 18071) can be helpful to you. The Sierra Club on the West Coast, the Appalachian Mountain Club on the East Coast, and the Canadian Canoe Association may also be helpful.

You should check with the local Y.M.C.A., the Y.W.C.A., or the nearest college outing club. Often, wilderness outfitters, like Eddie Bauer's and Eastern Mountain Sports, have personnel who are knowledgeable about kayakers in your neighborhood.

If there is a club in your area, you should consider joining it. Here you can find access to kayaks, facilities for building boats, pool sessions, and instruction. Here, too, you're likely to find companions interested in the same kinds of adventure as you.

All the ingredients for a successful outing: boats, paddles, safety equipment, and a group of enthusiastic kayakers of all ages. (Ledyard Canoe Club)

Kinds of Trips

Touring by kayak and cruising the waterways can take any of four different forms. Each has unique demands. The easiest to plan and execute, of course, is the simple day trip. Your equipment, food, travel requirements, and expenses are minimal. It can be a simple lazy afternoon float down a nearby river, a visit to a surfing beach, or a picnic on an island in the middle of a lake.

The next step up in touring is the weekend excursion. This involves an overnight or two, more meals to consider, and perhaps considerable travel. These kinds of trips are enormously popular as a welcome break from life's daily routine. If done in moderation, you have helped yourself to the wilderness and returned to civilization refreshed and renewed.

The third kind of trip is often hatched in the minds of kayakers on dark winter evenings when the temperature hovers well below freezing: "Let's take a couple weeks off next summer and do the Middle Fork of the Salmon River in Idaho," or "Let's do a circumnavigation of Vancouver Island." Half the fun of these major trips is in the planning. These trips are likely to be taken on vacations. They require careful logistical planning and a considerable commitment on the part of the participants.

The most exciting prospect of all, however, is the major international expedition. It can be the high point of a person's life. To say that it requires a major dedication and commitment of time, money, and effort is an understatement, yet the rewards can be immeasurable.

Kayakers have traveled the entire navigable length of the Nile in Egypt, the Danube in Eastern Europe, as well as the Mississippi River. They have ventured into the mountain kingdoms of Nepal and Bhutan and Australia's outback, too.

There is still much, much more to explore. All the tallest mountains of the world have now been climbed, all the deserts have been crossed, and both polar caps have been inhabited, but most of the wild rivers of the world are still waiting. Rivers tumbling down the steep slopes of the 1,000-mile-long Andes mountain range in South America have barely been touched by kayak. For every mile of river that has seen a kayak in the huge Himalayan region of central Asia, there are hundreds and hundreds of miles still to explore. Truly, the wild rivers of the world are our last major frontier on this planet.

A Word About Commercial Trips

All of the above mentioned kinds of trips are also offered by enterprising commercial boating companies. For the most part these companies are registered with the U.S. Forest Service or with local authorities and are perfectly reliable. They are obliged to meet certain standards of safety and wilderness usage. Your comfort and safe return is important to their success. Outdoor outfitters and travel agencies can help you get in touch with commercial trips. Perhaps the best advertisement, though, is to talk with someone who has been on the trip you are thinking of taking.

You and Your Traveling Companions

The intriguing chemistry of interpersonal relationships can either make or break a cruising trip in kayaks. When possible, choose your companions carefully. Your group should be experienced enough to handle the normal hazards to be encountered on water. One paddler, weak in either boating skills or stamina, can spoil a trip for everyone. So can a hotshot boater who quickly becomes bored with slower-paced companions. There should not be too great a range in either skill level or physical conditioning of all members of the group.

Touring with friends. (Eric Evans)

You and your traveling companions should share the same basic goals. Is it agreed that this trip is to see how fast you can all paddle from point A on the river to point B? Or, are we agreed to stop and smell the flowers along the way? Tension can easily be created between those who want to push on down the river and those who wish to stay and play in a particularly attractive set of rapids. You should all be in agreement as to the purpose of the trip.

Unreconcilable differences in temperament among boating companions can cause unpleasantness. Naturally, some differences in political outlook and temperament are welcome. A healthy blend adds spice to an outing in kayaks.

One of the most helpful things you can do is to sit down in a quiet corner somewhere and write down a personal inventory of yourself. Try to make it a really objective assessment. First, consider your limitations as a boater, your skill level, and experience. Are they compatible with those of your companions and sufficient to meet the challenges of the trip planned? Do you have any physical handicaps, such as a bad back, that might act up part way through the trip? How far can you comfortably travel by kayak in a day? Is this trip realistic for you? Would you be a drag on the others? Is this excursion well below your level of skill and interest?

Second, what do you have to offer to the group? Fishing skill, water reading expertise, campsite experience, knowledge of the area to be covered, first aid, good humor, a good singing voice, or an inexhaustible supply of jokes?

Third, you should carefully examine your personal habits. Have you ever been accused of being a "me-firster"? Are you a chowhound? Do you talk too much or too little? Are you a heavy smoker, drinker, or a penny pincher? To what extent are you willing to share what you have with others when you don't have enough even for yourself? No person is perfect, of course, but when friends are thrown together on a kayak trip both the best and the worst traits blossom. It is important for the success of a trip to be ever mindful of your shortcomings and not burden your companions with them. It is also helpful if you ignore the shortcomings of others.

Fourth, leadership can take many forms, and touring by kayak can provide excellent opportunities for leadership. There is no single kind of leadership that is the best. Some people prefer consensus decision making: there is no real leader but people sit around, talk things out, and jointly agree upon what action to take. Others prefer the majority rule system where a vote is taken on decisions of importance. Still others feel more comfortable appointing a leader whom they can trust and bestow upon him all the decision-making responsibilities.

It would be smart before venturing out on a major kayak trip or an international expedition to do as the American Himalayan Kayak Descent did in the fall of 1981. In the words of one of the participants, "We met for a weekend at the Gauley River in West Virginia, disbursed our equipment, and discussed the philosophy of leadership. It was decided that our leader would have final decision-making power rather than leadership by majority rule. We also discussed chain of command, the goals of the expedition. We listed our priorities in rank order, and practiced rescue techniques."

As a result of such careful preparation, this expedition to a series of unknown wildwater rivers in the remote kingdom of Bhutan was an outstanding success in every way.

What Kind of Boat

The kind of craft you take touring or cruising may depend upon what you happen to own, but more importantly on what kind of trip is planned. Generally speaking for shorter day or weekend trips the common slalom or touring kayak is adequate. These craft are relatively stable (kayaks really aren't tippy—some kayakers are!), and, with their minimal draft and excellent maneuverability, are ideal for shallow water cruising, coastal touring, and the investigation of swamps. One can surf using a slalom type kayak, but it is better and safer to use a surf kayak designed specifically for that activity. The slalom kayak is also suitable for open water paddling on small lakes since its low profile prevents its being tossed about by the wind.

For more extended flatwater cruising your comfort is a concern. Larger volume, touring-style kayaks, while not so maneuverable, offer greater leg room. For the longer trips, you should consider a kayak's cargo capacity, because you'll need to take more gear along with you.

Cruising across really large bodies of water like the Great Lakes, the Chesapeake Bay, or the Gulf of Mexico can be done in almost any kind of kayak—then, a person can enter a footrace with heavy boots on, too, but shouldn't expect to do very well. Long, sleek, fast moving seagoing kayaks are available for ocean travel. Stable two-seater foldboats with built in air sponsons are also logical choices, as are those with sailing rigs. These craft ride the waves well, keep on course easily, and are comfortable. In summary, you should choose the type of kayak to fit the demands of the trip, just as a skier has the choice of cross-country, jumping, slalom, or downhill skis.

What to Wear

The two most important considerations for comfort and well-being on a kayak trip are to be warm and dry. With a little careful preparation you can tour all day long in a kayak in the pouring rain and still be totally comfortable. Actually, the very "defying the elements" can heighten the pleasure. If you go cruising and get wet, cold, and miserable, don't blame the weather. It is only your own shortsightedness and lack of preparation that cause the discomfort. Here's how to beat Mother Nature at her own game.

First of all, bring along a complete set of dry clothes. Leave them in the car so you can change into them at the end of the day. If you're camping out, bring them along but keep them in a waterproof bag tucked away under your deck. If you are kayaking for a couple of days or more and are not too far from civilization, make a detour to the nearest town and toss your wet clothes into the dryer at the local laundromat while you stop for gas and groceries.

Even if you usually wear a helmet while kayaking, it would be smart to bring along a wide-brimmed hat of some kind to keep the rain off while you're setting up the campsite. Always have a dry pair of sneakers and socks to sink your feet into at the end of a day. Sneakers are preferred over heavy boots, for you may wish to wear them while boating the next day. Heavy boots are not only clumsy inside a kayak, but are much more difficult to swim in.

Let's face it, in kayaking, your hands are going to get wet, but again, as previously explained, there are a variety of wind gloves or pogies that are excellent in protecting your hands from the cold wind and rain. Years ago paddles came supplied with rubber drip rings between the paddle blades and where the paddler gripped his paddle. These drip rings were designed to keep water from running down the paddle shaft as the paddle was raised on the return stroke. These have pretty well gone out of fashion, but the idea is still sound.

Fortunately, your spray cover and paddling jacket will do a fine job of keeping you warm and dry *while you're sitting in the kayak*. Once outside, a pair of rain pants together with your paddling jacket will come in handy and be appreciated.

There is nothing more yucky than squirming into a clammy, wet bathing suit in the morning. Take along an extra one. It doesn't take up much room, and a dry bathing suit in the morning is guaranteed to get you off to a good start.

For more rugged conditions a wool sweater under your paddling jacket can make a noticeable difference. In the most extreme weather or cold water conditions (see Chapter 3) wet suits are essential.

Since touring by kayak can be a wet sport, it is best to *overprepare* for cold and damp conditions rather than underprepare. It is easier to take a sweater off and stow it in your kayak, instead of shivering and wishing you had one to put on.

What to Take with You

The length and kind of trip you envision will dictate the quantity of gear you'll need to take with you. Many first-timers tend to cart along too many of the accoutrements of civilization. A good rule of thumb is: "If in doubt, leave it out." This is especially true when your kayak trip goes overnight well beyond the range of your automobile. Even the larger volume touring-style kayaks have only a limited amount of room for storage. Nevertheless, here are a few tips that might prove helpful.

Everything from matches to clothing should be encased in waterproof containers. No exceptions.

Five Little Bags

One bag should hold your toiletry articles. These could include soap, toothpaste, toothbrush, chapstick, sunburn cream, comb, insect repellent, a metal mirror, toilet paper, and (just in case) deodorant, shaving gear, or other personal items.

A second bag should contain a first aid kit with Band-Aids, a needle, thread, tweezers, aspirin, ace bandage, disinfectant, small scissors, and other items you might anticipate using on the trip.

A third bag should include a repair kit with the necessary fiberglass patching materials (see Chapter 3), duct tape, and bike tube repair material in case your flotation bags or air mattress leak. For the kayak itself, a spare collapsible paddle taped to the deck is worthy of consideration—especially when going deep into a wilderness area or to sea. A sponge placed beside your seat at the bottom of your kayak will serve double duty. It can be used as a bailer to get rid of any water collected in the bottom of your boat. Then, later at the campsite, the sponge can be used to wash up or even bathe with. Don't forget to include a safety rope with the kayak.

A fourth bag—always within easy reach—should contain your camera and extra film.

Finally, have you ever looked forward longingly to lunch only to find your sandwich watersoaked? A fifth plastic, waterproof bag should contain your noon repast. Your lunch in the wilderness can be an exquisite pleasure.

A discussion of appropriate kinds of tents, sleeping bags, cooking gear, axes, and saws goes well beyond the scope of this book. There are many good outdoors manuals that treat these topics in great detail. However, the kayaker's needs are like those of the mountaineer. All items must be as light as possible, and compact. Lest you overlook something though, make this a reminder not to forget: matches, a watch, pocket knife, can opener, and a flashlight. On a large lake or at sea—a compass, whistle, and flares.

Getting There

Classes of River Sections

Several things should be carefully considered before the actual arrival of the party at the launching site for the beginning of the trip. If you have chosen to travel a river, the section of it you intend to run will fall into one or more generally recognized classes of navigable difficulty:

Class I: Moving water with maybe a few riffles and small waves. Few or no obstructions. Most flatwater rivers are in this class.

Class II: Easy rapids with waves up to 3 feet high and wide, clear channels that are obvious without scouting. Some maneuvering is required, but nothing really tricky or difficult.

Class III: Rapids with high, irregular waves often capable of swamping in an open canoe or a kayak without a spray cover. Narrow passages that often require complex maneuvering. Rapids of this magnitude should be scouted from the shore first to determine the best route through.

Class IV: Long, difficult rapids with constricted passages that can require precise maneuvering in very turbulent waters. Scouting from shore is essential, and rescue may be difficult.

Class V: Extremely difficult, long, and very violent rapids with highly congested routes that must be scouted from shore before attempting. In the event of mishap, there could be a distinct hazard to life. All boaters attempting a Class V must be well-versed in all aspects of self-rescue and a rescue party should be available at the foot of the rapids.

Class VI: Difficulties of Class V carried to the extreme of navigability. To be run only by a team of experienced experts with all precautions taken.

Note: If the water temperature is below 50 degrees Fahrenheit or if the river is in a remote wilderness area, then it should be considered one class more difficult than normal.

Fortunately many of the major rivers in North America have been well described. Guidebooks are available classifying sections of rivers, from Class I to VI. Topographic maps of the U.S. Geological Survey are also helpful in locating dams and various access points, as well as noting elevation changes. Once you know what kind of water you can expect, you can plan your trip accordingly. This means you can change your mind on the stretch of the river chosen to be run to respond sensibly to the limitations of the group. Often a party will start their cruise just below major rapids and assure safety for all members of the party.

The river classification system is a handy yardstick, but one that should be used with caution. What might normally be Class III rapids in the spring or fall can quickly assume the proportions of a Class V after a hard rain, a heavy snow melt, or even an unexpected release of water from a dam upstream.

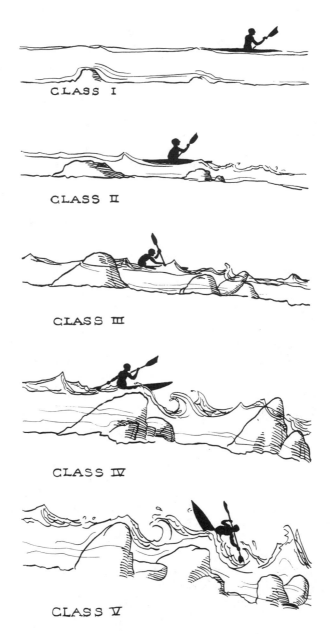

CLASS I

CLASS II

CLASS III

CLASS IV

CLASS V

Classification of rivers. Classes I-V comprise the range of navigable water. Class VI rivers —worse than Class V, if you can believe it—are avoided even by super-kayakers. (Walter Richardson)

Put-in and Take-out

The logistics of cruising a river are interesting and fun to work out. First to be selected is the put-in point. Look for calm water where it is easy to launch kayaks. There should be ample, safe parking space for automobiles. Most important, if the put-in point is on private land, be sure to ask permission of the landowner.

The take-out point chosen should be easily recognizable from the river. Preferably it will have a gentle, sloping bank and a place where automobiles can be parked. Again, if it is on private land, you must receive the landowner's permission.

Upon arrival at the put-in point, all kayaks and gear needed on the water should be unloaded. All but two people remain at the put-in point. These two then drive two vehicles to the take-out point and leave one vehicle there. Both drivers then return to the put-in point in the remaining car to join the "expedition."

Important

Make sure everybody in the party knows the whereabouts of the car keys for all vehicles stationed at either end of the river. It's embarrassing to arrive at the take-out point at the end of a very pleasant cruise only to discover that the car keys were left back at the start.

Warning

Always leave your vehicles locked, off the road, out of the way of traffic, and leave no valuable possessions in plain sight inside the car.

Upon arrival at the take-out point, two drivers (or more) use the vehicle left there to drive back to the start to pick up the remaining cars, and return them to the take-out point. Then, all boats and people can be loaded for the drive back home. Quite often the meanderings of a river make the water travel distance from start to finish much longer than it is by road. A 15-mile paddle might mean only a 6-mile drive.

If the party is small and only one car is used, a little more ingenuity is called for. It is possible, by pre-arrangement to hire someone at a nearby cabin, farmhouse, or ranch to drive you back at the end of the day. Or perhaps your spouse has other plans for the day and can drop you off at the river, then pick you up later on. Or, you can stash a moped or bicycle at the take-out point and use that to get back to your car.

Loading Up

Whether an overnight excursion is contemplated or a more extended river trip, it will be quite a challenge to store everything properly in a kayak. However, a few simple rules can help:

Rule 1: Take only what you really need.

Rule 2: Pack items in formless waterproof plastic bags. (Do not stuff a frame pack into a kayak. The formless, flexible plastic bag can be fitted in much more easily, and make much better use of the limited storage space.)

Rule 3: Beware of heavy articles. Take lightweight gear only. When a bag is unusually heavy, try to store it as close as possible to the center of the boat. (Perhaps tucked behind your hipbraces?) Avoid stuffing heavy objects at the extreme end of a kayak, since this will upset the trim of your boat, making steering more difficult.

Rule 4: It is OK to deflate your bow and stern flotation bags partially since they take up so much room. Stuff them as far as possible into the extreme ends of the boat. The rest of your gear—in waterproof bags—will help displace water in case of a capsize.

Rule 5: Examine your needs for the entire day. Items not needed until nightfall should be loaded first, toward the far ends of your craft. The repair kit, first aid kit, camera bag, and lunch should be packed close to the middle within easy reach. The kayaker obliged to unpack his entire kayak at lunchtime to get at something stashed at the far end of the boat is a poor planner.

Rule 6: Practice loading your kayak at home the day before you leave on the trip. This will give you ample time to redesign your gear if necessary. Such practice may sound time consuming, but it prevents awkwardness on the river bank—when the others are waiting for you.

The above rules pertain to those touring by kayak, independent of any support group. For some trips, however, it simply is not practical to take it all with you. In these cases predetermined campsites can be stocked ahead of time. But, make sure all cached gear is bear- and vandal-proof.

In cases where the river runs near a highway, a motorized escort can be arranged. This requires a person willing to carry the heavy camping gear and much of the food supply in a van or automobile. The driver sees you off in the morning, drives ahead to the evening campsite, and awaits you there. Most exotic, of course, is the periodic airdrop of supplies by a bush pilot who knows your route, timetable, and requirements.

Discipline on the Water

Under practically all conditions, the participants of a successful trip by kayak start together, stay together on the water, and arrive home safely together. Togetherness is important, not so much for sociability, but for the sake of safety, help, and rescue.

The "order of march" can be quite casual when there is no danger of rapids, fog, or other hazards, as long as *all kayaks stay within sight and shouting distance of each other at all times.* This rule holds for parties consisting of from a minimum of three to a maximum of six kayaks. Three is the smallest number for safe touring. Two kayaks is risky business— touring alone is foolhardy.

More than six kayaks can very quickly become a mob, if all try to stay close to each other in the water. When there are six or more boats in the same party, you should consider dividing into two independent groups. This does not suggest that each group can go its own way on its own timetable. Both groups should stay in reasonable proximity, but by dividing into two sections, they can prevent overcrowding on the river. Too many boats in the same place on the river can create a hazard for all concerned.

When a potential hazard appears, the most experienced boater, the one most familiar with the route, should lead. Other boats follow with plenty of space between to prevent crowding on the water. Last, comes the "sweep," one of the more skillful paddlers who trails the party, stopping to help anyone in difficulty.

Descending long rapids is often done in stages or sections. After carefully scouting from the river bank ahead of time, the party, in single file, heads through the top section and gathers at a quiet pool or eddy until all members have caught up. Should a less experienced boater inadvertently miss the stopping place, one of the more experienced kayakers should immediately peel off and head downsteam in pursuit. The others should follow as soon as possible.

Everyone in the touring party should have the ability to rescue paddlers and equipment. A brief discussion of rescue procedures before running a potentially hazardous stretch can help reduce confusion in an emergency.

There will be times when some members of the party may wish to run a set of rapids while others do not. This is perfectly acceptable. No boater should ever be peer-pressured into running a stretch of water he doesn't feel comfortable trying. These people can portage their boats around the rapids; and, more important, they can post themselves at the foot of the stretch on either side with a throw line as a safety precaution for the others as they come through.

Rescue Drills

In addition to the Eskimo roll, there are other rescue drills valuable to practice while touring. The Eskimo roll, of course, is the best, safest, and quickest means of self-rescue. Its importance can not be overemphasized.

The touring party should run through an Eskimo rescue drill before they go out on a trip. This procedure should be a reflex. Complete mastery of both the Eskimo roll and the Eskimo rescue is essential for all people contemplating coastal cruising or kayaking at sea or on large lakes.

In the Eskimo rescue, as described in Chapter 6, in a capsize, a second boater paddles quickly to the overturned boat and nudges its cockpit with his bow at a 90 degree angle. The capsized paddler can now grab the bow, and with a hip snap, pivot to an upright position again.

If it is not practical to approach the capsized kayak at a 90 degree angle, come alongside parallel. The rescuer places his paddle across both boats, holding it in place with one hand. (There should be not more than a couple of feet separating the boats.) With his other hand he can guide the overturned kayaker's hands to the paddle shaft, so the capsized boater can haul himself upright.

What happens if the capsized person comes out of his boat? Don't despair. In a river both boat and paddler can be towed to shore. In a large lake or at sea it is necessary to accomplish two things: First, with the help of a third boater, water can be emptied from the capsized kayak by quickly lifting one end as high as possible in an inverted position, so the water runs out. Then, with a kayak on each side and parallel to the empty boat, with paddles crossed over in front of the cockpit and grabbed by the two rescuers, the swimmer can lift himself up on the paddles and slip back into his boat. The kayaks on either side help to provide a stable platform made secure by each paddler holding on to each other's paddle as it rests on the deck of the empty kayak in the middle. It's clumsy and it takes effort, but it works.

Incidentally, for touring far from land or in the deep wilderness, it is advisable to bring along a quick release kayak tow assembly—just in case.

Rescue drills are fun to practice at home in a pool, or in warm, quiet water. For touring by kayak these rescue techniques are a necessary part of every boater's skills.

Setting Up Camp

Libraries and bookstores are full of excellent guidebooks explaining in great detail the procedures for camping out in the wilderness. The following points, however, should be remembered by those kayakers who wish to camp out in comfort and safety, and respect the wilderness:

- Know where you are going to set up camp before you start out. A pre-arranged place is almost always better than taking potluck.
- At the end of a day's trip, make sure your kayaks are pulled completely out of the water and tied down. A heavy rain upstream during the night can raise the river and float your boats away while you snooze.
- At the seashore always locate your campsite well above the high tide mark.
- If you can choose on which side of the river to camp, pick the one the morning sun strikes first.
- Plan your day on the water so you can erect your camp well before dark. The pleasures of a kayak trip can be greatly enhanced by making camp early.
- Avoid camping in poison ivy or in other poisonous plants.
- Avoid swampy ground near a river. Choose a higher location. It will be dryer and more bug free.
- Because of the danger of lightning, avoid camping under a tall tree.
- Be suspicious of all drinking water. Bring your own, use water purification tablets, or boil it for twenty minutes before you drink it.
- If the campsite is on private land, be sure to get the owner's permission.
- Keep all food securely battened down (or well out of reach above the ground) for the night. Your nocturnal forest friends love to scavenge through a campsite in the middle of the night.
- When striking camp, tidy up the area, carry your refuse and garbage out with you, and leave the site in *better* condition than you found it.

Kayaking for the Handicapped

By its very nature, the sport of kayaking is flexible enough to accommodate people with various handicaps. One of my earliest whitewater memories is of watching an incredibly skilled canoeist in whitewater out West. Only after the canoe finished its run below the rapids and the paddler stepped out on shore did I notice that the paddler had only one leg.

The Nantahala Outdoor Center in North Carolina has been a pioneer

162 The Kayaking Book

in devising instructional classes to aid boaters who are physically handicapped. Special fittings for arms and legs have been designed, and new
techniques are being taught.

Below-the-knee amputees can make normal use of the regular kneebraces important to successful boat control. The artificial limb below the
knee can work well against the footbrace. Above-the-knee amputees design their artificial limbs so that little control is lost between the upper
thigh and the kneebrace on the kayak. Thanks to modern science, artificial
hands and forearms are now designed so that people can hold a kayak
paddle adequately.

Those with impaired sight can learn to memorize the rapids and should
be accompanied by guides or boaters who remain close to them to give
voice signals as to which way to turn. The K-2 (two-person kayak) is
marvelously suited for the use by a boater and a friend with impaired
eyesight.

To those who have suffered hearing loss, kayaking through the rapids
may appear easy, at first glance. However, one reads water and plots a
course through the waves with more than just eyes alone. The various
sounds the river makes—the roar, gurgle, ripple, and swish—are all meaningful signals that, together with good eyesight, combine to help the kayaker make good judgments in the water.

Those whose hearing is impaired should act like a wise and cautious
boater approaching some rapids for the first time: He walks the river
bank studying the water currents and memorizing a logical course through.
On the first trip down, the smart boater—whether he has a hearing handi-
cap or not—will follow an experienced boater through.

It appears in kayaking that the biggest problem facing handicapped
people is not in cockpit or paddle shaft design, but simply becoming aware
of the possibilities open to them. Handicapped persons may, naturally, be
reluctant to try a new sport like kayaking, but they can be pioneers and
later help others to discover kayaking.

Listed below are a few organizations and sources that can provide more
information:

National Handicapped Sports-Recreation Association
Penn Mutual Building
4105 East Florida Avenue
Denver, Colorado 80221

New England Handicapped Sportsmen's Association
29 Woodcliff Road
Lexington, Massachusetts 02173

The Nantahala Outdoor Center
Star Route Box 68
Bryson City, North Carolina 28713

National Blind Organization for Leisure Development
533 East Main Street
Aspen, Colorado 81611

Norman Croucher, *Outdoor Pursuits for Disabled People*
Woodland-Faulkner Ltd., 8 Market Pasage
Cambridge, CB2 3PF England

PART IV. COMPETITION

14. Racing Kayaks

Several forms of kayak competition have evolved over the years, including racing on flatwater, in the surf, marathon racing, and two major divisions in whitewater: slalom and wildwater racing.

Surf, LD, and Specialty Racing

Competition in surf kayaking is still in its formative stages. In some cases a point system is used, surfers scored according to how they perform with their boats on the waves. This kind of performance is not unlike surfboard competition. In Australia, it's popular to race a kayak out through the incoming surf, around an anchored buoy, and back through the surf to the beach.

Marathon or LD (Long Distance) kayak racing is popular in England and continental Europe. In these races, mostly on flatwater, kayaks are timed over segments, some of which are many miles in length and require one or more portages. Longer races can include an overnight stop, the stop, of course, not being included in the racers' times.

Specialty races, combining skiing, bicycling, and kayaking, are popular in ski areas and other resorts toward the onset of spring. Actually, there is such a broad spectrum of possibilities for racing that almost anyone's needs and desires can be met. If yours are not, devise a competition of your own, invite a few friends, and hold your own race. Who knows? you may start a new trend.

Flatwater Racing

Flatwater racing, also known as sprint racing or paddle racing, has been part of the Olympic program for many years. Introduced in the 1932 Olympics at Long Beach, California, it became an official event at Hitler's 1936 Berlin Olympics.

Europe has been a stronghold for flatwater racing, its greatest competitors coming from Belgium, Bulgaria, Denmark, the two Germanies, Hungary, Rumania, Russia, and Sweden. Olympic kayak competition includes distances of 500 and 1,000 meters in five classes of kayaks:

K-1	One man in a kayak
K-2	Two men in a kayak
K-4	Four men in a kayak
K-1W	One woman in a kayak
K-2W	Two women in a kayak

and competition in single and double canoe. International regattas and world championships include relay races and a 10,000 meter event.

Kayaks designed for flatwater racing are highly stylized. They are built for one purpose—speed through the water. As a result, these beautiful craft are sleek and sharp. They slip through the water like needles; but for the uninitiated, they are somewhat unstable and definitely not meant to turn.

Flatwater racing requires that the competitor not only be in truly superb physical condition but also have an unusually well-honed and powerful forward stroke. Serious racers maintain year long training logs tracking their development and progress in both categories. Their forward strokes attain machine-like precision.

You might think at the outset that race strategy would not be particularly important in a 500, 1,000, or even a 10,000 meter race; simply point your boat straight ahead and go. You would, however, be quite wrong. Careful warm up before the race is essential. A lightning fast start is critical. Passing, jockeying for position, and the final sprint toward the finish line are all important factors that must be learned before you can hope to stand on the winner's platform.

Whitewater Racing

Racing kayaks in the rapids is by far the most popular form. Two distinct kinds have developed: slalom and wildwater. Since there are such large numbers of races of each kind held in Europe, North America, and elsewhere, each of these competitions is treated in some detail.

Slalom

The very first Olympic whitewater slalom was held in 1972 near Munich, with 38,000 people standing tensely by the edge of the course at the Eis Kanal. The race so fascinated the general public that in the following year the American Broadcasting Company filmed the kayak segment of the World Whitewater Championships from Muota, Switzerland, for a "Wide World of Sports" program shown on nationwide television. Truly, whitewater kayak racing had caught the fancy of the sporting world.

"Fishpole" gates mark the course in this beginners' slalom race. (Ledyard Canoe Club)

Very few racers will ever be fortunate enough to compete in the Olympics or World Championships with the eyes of world television upon them. But what may begin as a simple desire to sneak one's kayak between two rocks could develop into a taste for slalom or wildwater racing—and who knows where that may lead?

The Anatomy of Slalom

Whitewater slalom consists of paddling, in the fastest possible time, a stretch of challenging rapids whose demands have been increased tenfold by the introduction of additional, and artificial, obstacles. These obstacles are the gates—wooden poles dangling from a crossbar suspended over a stretch of highly turbulent water not more than 800 meters long.

There is no such thing as a standard championship slalom course like the 100-yard hurdles in track-and-field events. Rather, each slalom is laid out to create a unique series of challenges posed by the natural obstacles in the rapids in concert with the placing of the gates. Almost any number of gates will do, ranging from 12 or 15 in smaller local races to the 30 gates at most international competitions. The racer must go through each gate in the proper order (each is numbered), and in the proper direction (some must be negotiated upstream or backward).

Paddlers race separately against the clock, each trying for the least amount of time—and the fewest number of penalties for touching a gate or failing to follow the course correctly. The racer is given two runs on the course; the better run counts. The score is the total number of seconds taken to complete the course, plus the number of penalty points accrued, added in seconds.

If you touch a pole while negotiating a gate, 5 points (seconds) are added to your total time. Add another 5 points if you hit both poles negotiating a gate. If you get swept downstream, miss a gate entirely, and never get back to do it: 50 points added. If you manage to get close enough to touch a gate, but your body doesn't pass between the poles in the proper direction: 50 points added.

If you capsize as you go through a gate: 50 points added. If you get confused and pass through a gate in the wrong direction: 50 points.

There are other fine distinctions in the judging of gates, but these will do as starters. The thing to remember is to make your boat go through the gates properly *without touching*.

THE THREE KINDS OF GATES

For slalom you must think in terms of three major man-made obstacles: (1) the downstream gate; (2) the upstream gate; and (3) the reverse gate. In a full slalom course there may be as many as 30 gates. Most are downstream gates, but there are also several upstream and reverse gates in a well designed race course.

The Downstream or Forward Gate

This is the most common gate in whitewater slalom. In most situations the downstream gate should be taken at full speed, without interrupting your stroke, and at an angle that will line up your boat for getting quickly to the *next* gate.

COMMON MISTAKES:

Hitting a pole with the paddle as you stroke through the gate.
Not being lined up properly before you go through the gate.
Allowing your stern to touch a pole as you leave the gate.
Looking back as you go through the gate to see if you have cleared it. (It is too late for you to do anything at that point, and it will break your concentration on the next gate.)

Offset Downstream or Forward Gates

Two or more downstream (forward) gates in sequence set across the current from each other constitute *offset* gates. They can be quite difficult to reach, to say nothing of being negotiated swiftly and efficiently.

Offset gates can be done in three or four strokes. As you approach the first gate aim for the outside (left) pole, as in Diagram A. A boatlength in front of the pole, your first stroke should be a strong sweep on the left followed instantly by a Duffek stroke on the right. The Duffek should be planted just before your body passes between the poles. Those two

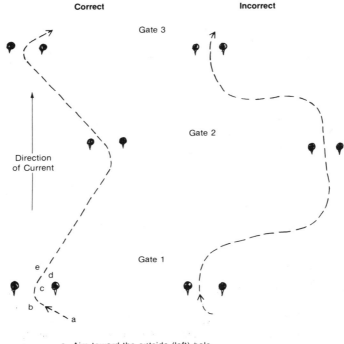

a. Aim toward the outside (left) pole
b. Sweep stroke on the left side
c. Duffek stroke as you enter the gate
d. Draw-pull stroke as you leave the gate
e. Sweep stroke on left side, boat flat, and leaning back.

Diagram A. Offset gate.

strokes pivot your boat. Now finish the Duffek with a sharp draw and a strong forward pull to slip through the gate unscathed.

If it appears that in pivoting your stern may touch the outside (left) pole, employ a forward sweep on the left wtih your boat flat on the water and you leaning back slightly in the cockpit. This will help get your stern to slip under the pole.

Remember, the quickest way to run offset gates is by turning *in* the gates.

COMMON MISTAKES:

Turning well before or after you have negotiated the gate. (This wastes time.)

Allowing your stern to touch the outside pole.

Touching the inside pole as you plant the Duffek stroke.

The Upstream Gate

This gate, often placed in eddies behind rocks can cost the racer a lot of time if his route is not carefully planned. The idea is to slip through the gate with the fewest strokes in the least possible time. This calls for unusually accurate depth perception as your boat closes in on the gate.

As you bear down hard on the approach, aim your boat upstream of the gate because the downstream current will carry you farther down beyond the gate than you need to go. If the pole near you is high off the water, you should sneak as much of your bow as possible under the pole (without touching it) as you Duffek into the gate. When conditions are right, an upstream gate can be negotiated in fewer than four seconds using only two strokes: the Duffek for the pivot, followed by a sweep stroke to clear the gate, as in Diagram B.

Upstream gates are often located near the shore where the water is shallow (on the shore side) and a rock or two stand out prominently on the river bank. If this is the case, don't hesitate to practice pushing off from the rock with your paddle—*if* this will speed up your gate negotiation. Be careful, of course, not to get the paddle caught on the rock or allow it to slip.

Diagram B. Upstream gate.

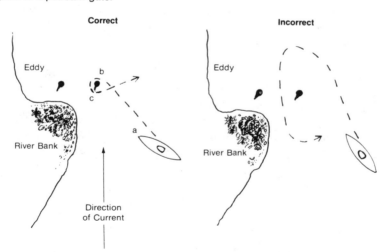

a. Aim boat toward a point upstream of the gate depending upon how strong the current is just outside the near pole.

b. Duffek stroke on left around the pole

c. Sweep stroke on the right to clear gate and get on to the next gate

Swinging too far below the gate into the eddy. (The current will tend to move you farther downstream than you expect.)

Misjudging the eddy current and thus making an outside (or inside) touch on a pole as you swing into and through the gate. (Study the current and the eddy carefully beforehand.)

Swinging out too far upstream after clearing the gate.

The Reverse Gate

This gate brings the most penalties in whitewater slalom, mostly because it is the gate that is practiced the least.

In approaching a reverse gate continue paddling forward toward it as long as possible. Paddling forward is always faster than paddling backward, so you obviously want to spend as little time as possible in backward paddling. Make your turn in front of the gate, taking advantage of the current by swinging your stern around into the faster moving water. Make the water work for you rather than trying to turn against the current.

Keep your eyes constantly on one pole (the easiest one for you to see as you turn). Turn your boat enough so you are *just a little more than broadside* as you slip between the poles in a slightly backward position. See Diagram C.

If the poles are high off the water, both your bow and stern will sneak under without danger of touching. If one pole is low to the water, you will have to turn your boat more before entering the gate to avoid touching the pole. Studying how other boaters negotiate a reverse gate and how the current affects their boats can be very helpful to you in deciding how to use the water in front of the gate to your benefit, as well as which poles, if any, can be sneaked under. As you pass through a reverse gate, keep your paddle in a vertical position and well down into the water. This will maintain positional control of your boat.

Proper exit from a reverse gate is as important as proper approach. Be sure to angle your boat so you are in position to go for the next gate in the sequence in the fastest possible time.

COMMON MISTAKES

Not looking at the gate soon enough as you approach it.

Not keeping your eye on the pole constantly as you turn in front of the gate.

Turning before the gate either too early or too late.

Floating through, rather than powering your way through, the gate.

Dropping below the gate too far (more than 1 inch) after the bow is clear.

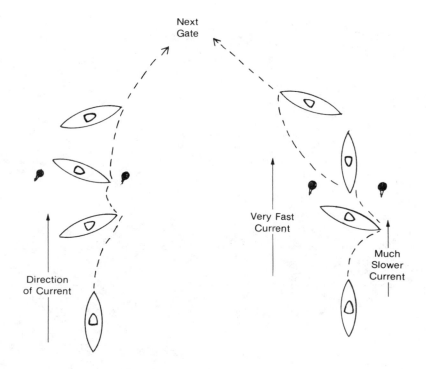

Next
Gate

Very Fast
Current

Direction
of Current

Much
Slower
Current

Above are depicted two ways to do a reverse gate depending upon current flow and the location of the next gate down the course.

Diagram C. Reverse gate.

"Pivotitis"—looking first over one shoulder, then over the other shoulder as you approach the gate. (If you are closing in properly on the nearer pole, you automatically know exactly how far away you are from the other one.)

Not twisting your body around enough so that *both* eyes can concentrate on the pole.

Not being a little more than broadside as you pass through the gate.

Putting the Slalom Together

MEMORIZING THE COURSE

From a close study of the course, preferably from both river banks, you must get the entire route firmly planted in your mind. Ideally it is best to arrive at the race site a day or two in advance to get settled, but short of that you should plan to get out early on the morning of the race to acquaint yourself with the water conditions and all details of the course.

A kayaker on the slalom course. (Evans Associates)

By this intensive study you should develop a clear-cut program of attack and get it firmly in mind. Take along a notebook and a pencil. Watch carefully to see how the good boaters do it if free practice is allowed on the course ahead of time. Those who have difficulty remembering a whole course might try clumping the gates in their minds. Think of several gates as a unit, and go over in your mind how you plan to tackle them.

The Decisions Involved

At each gate you must make three decisions:

1. At what angle should I approach so I get the fastest line on to the next gate?

2. Exactly where will I place my paddle the very moment I am clear of the gate?

3. If something goes wrong, can I duck into the nearest piece of friendly water and make a second attempt at the gate? (If the rules allow this, it is better to use an extra 15 seconds than to settle for a permanent 50-point penalty for missing the gate altogether.)

THE WARM-UP

Most people simply don't warm up enough before the race. A good warm-up prepares the body for the large load it will soon be asked to bear and—even more important—it helps to reduce nervous tension. If the race is held in the morning, you should get up at least several hours before your run to make sure that you are operating on all cylinders by race time.

Always remember that a full stomach prevents good breathing, so don't eat anything for at least a couple of hours before the race.

You should paddle hard for 10 minutes somewhere upstream of the start, out of the way. If this is impossible, jog and sprint along a nearby path or road, and do some limbering-up and stretching exercises. Your pulse rate should be up around 100, and you should have developed a pretty good sweat just before the countdown.

THE START

Shake your arms, shoulders, and wrists to loosen them. Relax your trunk muscles and take a few deep breaths to fill your lungs with oxygen. Make a final check of your spray cover. Listen carefully to the cadence of the countdown for other racers, so you can anticipate the split second when "Go" is called for your boat. (If the timing is by an electronic eye, you won't have to worry about that.)

At the start a standing boat must be brought into motion, and to overcome inertia and accelerate to top racing speed requires considerable strength. Also at the start, keep your boat pointed a few degrees inside of

Read from the Bottom of the Page Upward

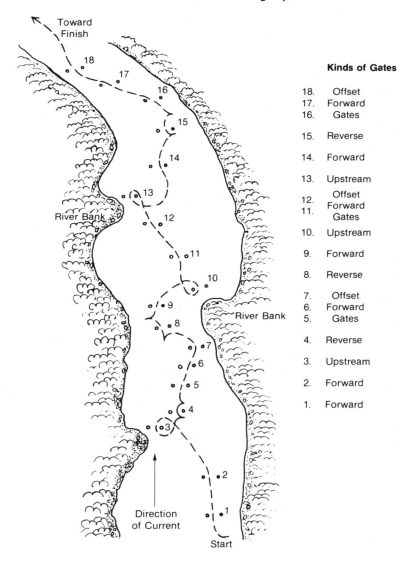

Toward
Finish

18

17

16

15

14

13

River Bank

12

11

10

9

8

7

6

5

4

3

2

1

River Bank

Direction
of Current

Start

Kinds of Gates

18.	Offset
17.	Forward
16.	Gates
15.	Reverse
14.	Forward
13.	Upstream
12.	Offset
11.	Forward Gates
10.	Upstream
9.	Forward
8.	Reverse
7.	Offset
6.	Forward
5.	Gates
4.	Reverse
3.	Upstream
2.	Forward
1.	Forward

Diagram D. Bird's-eye view of a slalom course (looking downstream).

the direction line you wish to follow so your first maximum power forward stroke can be employed without the immediate necessity of making a correcting stroke.

When the start is electronic, *if it is permissible*, back off a bit to try to get one or two strokes in so your boat will be well underway before the electric eye is triggered.

IT'S A RACE

You can waste much of the advantage gained from good gate technique if you loaf between gates. Keep in mind that an American National Slalom title was lost not too many years ago by 0.6 second! In world championship competition many a gold, silver, and bronze medal has been lost by less than half a second. Most gates are about 20 yards apart, so you have a chance to gain a little between gates if you hustle.

After the last gate is behind you, really pour it on and *sprint* not just to the finish line, but to a point at least one full boat-length beyond. This will guarantee that your boat crosses the real finish line in the fastest possible way.

Between Runs

After your run get into dry clothes as soon as possible. Get comfortable, but don't eat anything right away. Anything you ate, even pure sugar, wouldn't give you any energy until long after the end of the race, anyway.

You will probably wish to walk slowly up the course carefully studying how the other racers are negotiating the gates. Don't waste your time watching inexperienced boaters or engage in idle distracting conversation. Keep your mind clear for the second and final run. When the time comes for your run be sure to warm up as thoroughly as you did for your first run.

And good luck!

Wildwater Racing

Wildwater racing has become popular for a number of reasons: It is a simple, pure race. Your rewards are directly proportional to your skill, experience, and the quality of effort you put into the event.

What at first appears to be mainly physical labor is, in reality, very highly concentrated mental discipline. Each stroke is meaningful. You must constantly follow the shortest and fastest route down the river. The kayaks used are beautiful, highly specialized racing machines built primarily for speed. Training is less complicated than for slalom, and there

A Code for Whitewater Racers
(Slalom and Wildwater)

Whitewater racing is marvelously rewarding, thanks in part to its prevailing spirit of good fellowship and fair play. To make sure that this spirit is not eroded as the competitions grow, we propose the following code for racers.

Be realistic about your degree of competence. There are increasing numbers of boaters anxious to race who have not yet perfected the Eskimo roll, the most reliable way to get out of trouble. The answer to this problem rests largely in the hands of the race officials, who will determine that only competent kayakers may enter events that tax their skills. The kayaker has an obligation not to oversell his or her abilities.

Never enter a race without studying the course beforehand. Skill seldom compensates for bad judgment arising from ignorance of where obstacles lie. So get out to the river where the race will be run and study its haystacks, rollers, eddies, and chutes. Walk along its banks, spotting obstructions that lurk underwater.

Race with all the equipment necessary for safety. You owe it to yourself and everybody else to ensure that a mishap does not become a full-fledged emergency because you, and your boat, are not properly outfitted. This means lifejacket, helmet, and wet suit if it is indicated, for you; grabloops and flotation bags for your boat. To protect yourself against chill, use pogies or gloves and have warm clothing handy at the end of your run.

Bring your own equipment for every race. Borrowing equipment is poor form indeed, aside from being a nuisance. Bring an extra paddle, if possible. Have your name on each piece of your gear.

Follow the rules of any competition you enter. Race organizers have good reasons for the regulations they make. Therefore don't ask for special dispensation or consideration. Send your entry form in on time—completely filled out and with the correct entry fee attached. On race day, be patient with race organizers and be alert for chances to be helpful. Protest only for the most valid reasons.

Be gracious, win or lose. The true sportsman will congratulate the winner, and will never be a sore loser. (And a thank you note to the committee after the race will certainly be appreciated!)

In a wildwater race, "full speed ahead" is the basic strategy for all racers. (Klepper-Werke photo)

is very little need for extra equipment such as gates, wires, and a communications network. As a bonus, the scenery of the course can be spectacular.

Basically a wildwater race consists of a start somewhere upriver with a finish line anywhere from 2 to 15 miles or more downriver. No penalty points are involved and the winner is the racer with the shortest elapsed time between start and finish. While slalom rarely exceeds 4 minutes, a wildwater race will take anywhere from 9 to 30 minutes or more, depending upon the length of the course. The trick is to find the swiftest route through the rapids.

The Fastest Route

Familiarity with the course is not only helpful technically, but gives the racer a great psychological boost. Every rock in the river, every new view around the bend, should be a familiar, beckoning sight. Running the course many times at the same water level at which the race will be conducted, and experimenting with different routes, will add the knowledge necessary for winning.

Avoid eddies that will catch your bow and spin you around, and be wary of rollers and stoppers that slow your forward movement. Avoid "bottom drag"—an insidious braking action which measurably slows your boat when the water is too shallow.

Once the fastest route has been determined, go over each part of it in your mind just as carefully as you would the gates of a slalom. Develop a mental picture of it section by section.

The Start

In most wildwater races paddlers are started singly with 1-minute or 2-minute intervals between boaters. If this is the case, simply leap off that starting line as fast as possible and do everything in your power to close the gap between you and the boater who took off ahead of you.

In a multiple start (two or three boats at a time) when the field is particularly large, it is important to sprint out in front immediately and stay there. Let the rest of the pack jockey for position behind you.

Overtaking

If you catch up to a boater it is legal (except for flatwater racing) to ride his wake—assuming that he takes what you *know* to be the fastest route! Just being right on his tail may make him nervous, will make it easier for you to paddle, and can help you to pace yourself.

If you overtake another boater and are ready to pass him, he must give way to allow you room to pass. Simply yell "Track!" as in skiing, and he is obliged to move over.

Splits

Splits can be a handy way of keeping track of your speed in comparison with other boaters in a wildwater race. You need a confederate with a stopwatch, a bicycle or car, and a good working knowledge of the backroads and paths near the river.

Good Samaritans

Since much wildwater racing involves stretches of rapids often in a canyon or valley away from civilization, any racer who sees another boater in trouble and in need of help must stop, discontinue racing immediately and go to the kayaker's aid. Failure to do so can mean disqualification forever. Let's face it, human life is more important than a piece of blue ribbon, and besides, just put yourself in the other racer's wet suit for a moment. You'll be glad you helped. You can always race another day.

For example, your friend knows that the person you would like to beat is 2 minutes ahead of you in the starting order. The split-taker will be stationed at some mutually agreed upon place down from the start (bridges are always handy). He'll start his stopwatch as your adversary goes by. If you haven't gained on your opponent, then you should also pass by when the split-taker's stopwatch reaches the 2-minute mark. If you appear in 1 minute and 40 seconds, this means that you have gained 20 seconds on your opponent. The message will be shouted to you loud and clear by your friend on the bridge, and welcome news it is. And if you have fallen behind, the information thus relayed to you should give you renewed determination to step up the pace.

The Finish

As soon as the finish line comes into sight is the time for an all-out sprint. No need to conserve energy or to pace yourself any longer. Just keep constantly in mind that some races are won or lost by a fraction of a second. At the World Championships in 1973 the difference between a bronze and a silver medal in wildwater K-1 was only 0.8 second over a 17-minute course.

As in slalom, always paddle *through* the finish line, not simply *to* it. Then paddle around a bit to "warm down" until your pulse rate is reduced. Don't eat anything for at least half an hour after the race.

15. Organizing Whitewater Races

The popularity of whitewater competition is growing so fast that race organization requires efficiency and long-range planning. Running a race can be a source of enormous pride and satisfaction at seeing an event unfold smoothly, or it can turn into an endurance contest. By following a reasonably strict timetable spread over several months, it is possible not only to organize a race successfully but to enjoy it as well. The better the preliminary work behind the scenes before race day, the better the race turns out.

Six Months Before the Race

Where/When/Who

Choose the site, the time of the race, and the kind of race you want—slalom, wildwater, or possibly both. Obtain permission of the landowners on each side of the river where you propose to hold the events. Next, decide what kind of race it should be: experts only, beginners, or an all-comers race open to anyone. Determine what classes to offer. The ICF recognizes K-1, K-1W, C-1, C-2, and C-2M; you may want to add divisions for junior, senior, beginner, intermediate, and expert boaters. Decide the number of entries you can safely handle in terms of available manpower, camping, parking, and toilet facilities.

Publicity

After the basics have been decided, make sure the race gets listed in *Canoe* (the American Canoe Association magazine) and in the annual *Whitewater Racing Program* so people will learn about the race. Since most publications go to press months in advance of their cover date, be sure to check on the deadlines for getting your information to the editors.

At the same time, ask the American Canoe Association for sanction. Write for permission to hold the race, listing the date, location, kind of race, any limitations, and the name and address of the person who has been designated to provide information.

Finding a Sponsor

Races cost money to run. Quite often the local kayak or canoe club or a combination of clubs will bear the costs of organizing a race. Some businesses may be willing to underwrite at least part of the expenses of a race in return for a bit of advertising. As a race organizer, you can offer the business pre-race publicity, racing bibs and race programs bearing the sponsor's name, and results printed on the sponsor's stationery.

Finding sponsors also helps to bring the local community into the spirit of the event. It is nice to have the local townspeople take an active interest in a recreational event taking place in their community.

Three Months Before the Race

Paperwork

Entry forms for a well-run race should be mailed out a month to six weeks before the race date. Be sure to allow for the time it will take to prepare and print the forms and mail them out. Entry forms should include the following: time, place, date, starting time; description of the course, race categories, water conditions; liability release; entry fee and deadlines; and an address to which entries should be sent.

It is helpful, but not necessary, to mention whether there will be a shuttle service or food for sale and to give the addresses of conveniently located motels and campgrounds in the race area.

Manpower

Assign one person as the race registrar to keep track of all the entrants and whether or not they've paid the entry fee, so at any time he can report how many racers have entered and who is racing in what class. The registrar's duties last until race day is over and are linked closely with those of several other committees.

You should line up 50 percent more manpower than you think you'll need (most of your help will be volunteers, and therefore many well-meant promises might not be kept at the last minute). For a slalom race the following positions need to be filled: registrar, timers, scorers, recorders, gate judges, safety crew, gate-adjustment crews, protest committee, results coordinator, press officer, communications crew, and starters.

For wildwater, all these positions need to be filled except the gate judges and gate-adjustment crews needed for slalom races.

Numbering/Amenities/Water Level

The race registrar can also distribute and collect numbered racing bibs on race day. Bibs are available from ski areas and outing clubs, canoe companies, and some sports clothing outfitters. Paper bibs, which are beginning to replace the traditional cloth ones, will hold up well enough in whitewater to last a weekend, and make a nice souvenir of the race to take home.

Occasionally one will see a large white decal pasted on the deck of the boat with the racer's number written on the decal. This system works fine unless two racers want to use the same boat—in which case the first decal must be removed and a new decal applied in its place.

Check with groups that might want to set up food concessions. Inform local police about the race and alert them to any possible traffic problems.

If there is a dam upstream of the race site, investigate the possibility of having a water release timed for your race.

Equipment

Collect all the needed equipment several months in advance of a race including gates, wire, rope, string, communications materials, clipboards, scoreboards, typewriter, safety gear, and first aid equipment.

A Slalom Primer

The Course

A good slalom course should take advantage of the natural obstacles in the rapids yet should be laid out so that an expert racer can make a smooth and penalty free run. Whenever possible there should be as many turn-outs (or break-outs, as the British say) to the right as to the left, and the course should include several upstream gates and reverse gates. One North American K-1 champion gives this additional advice for designing a slalom course: "Rarely a reverse gate first, or last, or back-to-back."

A full-blown slalom of 30 gates will meet international specifications, but for most competitions 12 to 20 gates will do nicely. Don't be too ambitious: any more than that will overtax many paddlers' stamina, and problems of communications will begin to multiply for the race committee.

The Slalom Gate

A slalom gate consists of a wooden crosspiece with a pole dangling from each end. A small board hangs from the middle of the cross-piece to display the gate number. The gate hangs from a wire that has been stretched across the river high enough to let each dangling pole just clear the surface of the water.

The simplest form of gate has the poles permanently attached to the crosspiece, with the entire gate capable of being raised or lowered by adjusting the suspension wire over the stream. This rudimentary gate is not really satisfactory, however, because one pole should hang higher than the other if the rapids below are uneven. It is important in a race that *each pole*, regardless of its length, hang just clear of the water.

Gate Components

Crosspiece boards should be 6 or 7 feet long to allow for adequate spacing of the poles. According to ICF regulations, the width of the gate must be at least 1.2 meters (about 4 feet) and no more than 3.5 meters (just over 11 feet). At most slalom races, the gates are between 4 and 5 feet wide. Decide on the width of your gate and space 2 metal screw-eyes that distance apart, equidistant from the ends of the crosspiece. Also at the ends of the crosspiece, attach shower-curtain rings or metal loops through which a wire can be threaded when stringing gates across a river.

Two *poles* are needed for each gate. Paint one pole in alternating bands of white and green, the other in white and red. When you string the gate over the river, the green striped pole will be on the paddler's right as he goes through the gate, with the red and white pole on his left.

A *gate-number board* about 15 inches square hangs from the crosspiece between the poles to identify each gate. Paint both sides of the board yellow, with the gate number in black; add a diagonal red stripe on the backside of the board in the international sign for "no entry," so the racer knows which direction to approach it from. If the gate is a reverse or team gate, an additional "R" or "T" board must hang beside the number board.

Stringing a Gate

For the uninitiated, gate stringing seems quite a puzzle, but basically the setup is similar to that of a clothesline on pulleys, stretching between a porch and a garage. Just as you haul clothes toward you by pulling on the line, gate stringers move a gate from one side of the river to the other on a lead line.

The gate itself hangs from a wire; the gate's position is controlled by separate lines attached to the ends of the crosspiece. Another set of lines holds the poles to the crosspiece; these lines should be run from both poles to the same shore, so that individual poles can be adjusted easily from only one side of the river.

While a gate crew holds the lines that regulate the height of each pole, a crew on the other side of the river will pull this gate into position over the water. (Ledyard Canoe Club)

On Race Day

Safety

No matter what sort of waiver a racer may sign to release the organizing committee from liability for damage suffered during a race, the organizers are morally responsible to some degree for every boater's safety. There are increasing numbers of boaters eager to race before they've learned how to handle themselves in an emergency, much less come to the aid of anyone else.

Preventive Measures

The most important preventive measure is simple: *make sure each boater's ability is equal to the difficulty of the water.* A beginners' race should always be held in easy water. If you are holding a race in difficult water, pre-screen the entrants and allow only qualified boaters in the race.

Another precautionary measure is holding a boat inspection before the race, not so much to see that the boats are of legal length and width, as to make sure they have ample flotation and a grabloop in both bow and stern for controlling the boat and towing it to shore after a capsize.

I vividly recall the Mascoma River Slalom several years ago which took place under flood conditions. As the chief official, I allowed only the best qualified 13 out of 50 entrants to race in that dangerous water. Some people were angry that day, but I preferred that they be disappointed rather than injured.

Rescue

The best rescue of course is self-rescue, and for that, nothing quite compares with a reliable Eskimo roll.

The trouble comes with racers who have not perfected the roll. For them, a variety of arrangements for rescue from shore have been developed over the years.

A very effective measure is to ask at least *two boaters* to wait in their boats at the finish line while a third completes the course. This makes it easy to pick up paddles that come floating through, and to nudge a capsized boat toward shore.

Skin divers can be a great help—if they are familiar with the dynamics of rapidly moving water.

Throw-line rescue bags have now been perfected so that they can be very effective when thrown properly. (See Chapter 4.)

In preparing for a whitewater race, it is important to arrange for a standby emergency vehicle staffed by qualified emergency medical technicians to be *at the race course*. Large races draw spectators and other recreational boaters, some of whom might also need first aid assistance.

A rescuer on shore throws an innertube and line to a capsized boater. The kayaker has remembered to hang on to the boat and paddle. (Ledyard Canoe Club)

Communications

Effective communications are the key to a successful slalom. You need some means of knowing what's going on at the starting point, at a command post part way down the course, at the primary gate-checking stations, and at the finish line. At Olympic trials or major ICF races there is a gate checker with a portable telephone reporting to the command post the penalties at every gate as they happen. However, at less luxurious competitions, one telephone often will have to cover at least five gates, with the other gate judges signaling the penalties to the telephone operator.

Walkie-talkies also make an efficient communications system. Of course you'll make sure that the sets are powerful enough to cover the length of the course.

Scoring

Scores must be posted promptly. The Dartmouth instant-scoring system, devised by Sandy Campbell, a member of the 1972 Olympic team, is a good one for either telephones or walkie-talkies.

From the race starter, the recorder at the command post gets the name, class, and run-number of the racer about to depart. The recorder writes this information on an individual score sheet on a clipboard to which a stopwatch is attached. Over the walkie-talkie the recorder hears the starter give the racer the countdown, and starts his stopwatch as the racer begins. As the racer takes each gate, the gate judge reports any penalties over a walkie-talkie. The recorder follows the racer through the course, noting penalties as they are incurred, and clicks the stopwatch when the finish-line judge's report is heard that the boat has crossed the line. The

Gate judges with walkie-talkies stand near their assigned gate, ready to record and report penalties as they occur. (Ledyard Canoe Club)

recorder then hands over the stopwatch and score sheet to a scorer, who puts the results on the board for all to see.

In large, well established races and U.S. Team trials more sophisticated means are used, not only to provide quick race results, but also to insure greater accuracy.

Timing a Wildwater Race

In wildwater kayak racing, the most important single item, aside from safety, is *timing*. Make sure the timers are at the finish line when the first racer arrives. Synchronize the watches before the race begins so that the finish-line timers don't have to appear at the start at all.

Timers at the finish line need to have cool heads and keen eyes, because sometimes boats will cross the finish in a wild sprint and closely bunched, and it may be hard to see the race numbers.

A full finish-line crew should include one person who does nothing but read off the exact time, down to the nearest fraction of a second, as a given boat crosses the line. To verify the timekeeping, at least one assistant should be there with a backup stopwatch. In addition there should be two recorders ready to write down the racers' numbers and/or names and times as they cross the finish line. The cards can then be arranged according to time and class so the results can be posted immediately after the race. If the timing is electronic, there still should be a backup hand watch.

After the Race

Judge and Jury

In the event of a close call, in slalom, a gate judge must have written down what happened, in case the race jury asks him to testify to decide a protest. All protests should be submitted by a team captain in writing immediately after the posting of scores. The jury's decision is final.

The boater is probably the poorest judge of all as to whether he touched a pole or not: he simply is not able to see the entire length of his boat on both sides simultaneously.

Awards

Decide well ahead of time what kind of awards you will give and be sure they are on hand the day of the race. There is nothing like trophies to stimulate interest and enthusiasm among inexperienced racers. Utili-

An awards ceremony should be held immediately after a race. Here, an official presents medals to the top three competitors in the Colorado Cup races. (Ledyard Canoe Club)

tarian-minded race organizers sometimes offer paddles for awards, or mugs that can be used. I've seen pewter candlesticks given, and a nice leather briefcase was the prize for placing tenth in the K-1 class at Merano, Italy.

No matter what the awards are—mugs, cups, ribbons, or whatever—the important thing is for the awards ceremony to take place immediately following the race.

Dealing with the Press

When dealing with the press, remember that the Fourth Estate has the last word as well as the first word, and, at its discretion, no word at all. However, many sportswriters welcome the chance to report such a refreshingly different event as a kayak race.

Good press relations are important, and detailing a couple of people to act as a publicity committee can help. The committee should send out a *factual* news release to local and regional papers before the event. Committee members should be on hand at the race to escort reporters, if necessary, and to supply them with facts about the events and information about the competitors, plus any real human interest angles. A copy of the race results should be placed in each reporter's hands pronto.

In addition, send all race results to the American Canoe Association and to kayaking magazines.

16. Getting in Shape—
Physically and Mentally

Whitewater racing demands total body performance and mental concentration. It calls for stamina as well as strength, varying from a maximum output of effort of a couple of minutes in a slalom race to 30 minutes or more in a wildwater race. If your body is conditioned to putting out concentrated, sustained effort for the required period of time, you will be able to focus on the immediate obstacles of the race, how to deal with them, and on technique.

How Fit Are You?

If you wish to take up racing seriously, you should take an objective look at yourself. What kind of shape are you in *now*? First get medical clearance. Then find out how far you can jog or run in 12 minutes. According to Dr. Kenneth Cooper's book *Aerobics*, an average active person can do up to 1.75 miles in 12 minutes, while a gold-medal-category athlete can cover 2.25 miles or more.

After you have established your current physical fitness category, you can lay out a program for working up to your potential. You should have your doctor's permission to train. You should warm up thoroughly before each workout. Figure on a period of at least 6 months before expecting any substantial improvement, and try to work out at least 5 days each week.

Building Stamina

Any or all of the following exercises will increase your stamina. If you can't do them for the prescribed length of time, simply do them for as long as you can, and gradually work up. If these exercises are too easy for you, you're only cheating yourself unless you set your sights higher.

Interval Training

When water is available, get into your boat and try 50 rapid maximum effort forward strokes followed by a 10-second rest. Repeat this exercise six times or more. On land, run six 200-yard sprints, keeping track of your time. Try to lower your time with each sprint.

Tempo Training

Paddle at full racing speed for 20 percent of the length of time it takes to cover a race. If you are training for slalom, try paddling all-out for 1 minute; for wildwater, paddle all-out for 2½ to 3 minutes, once for each quarter of the race. Repeat about five times. If you don't have access to water, run six consecutive ½-mile stretches in not more than 3 minutes each, taking a 1-minute rest between each ½ mile.

Distance Training

Ideally, this involves prolonged paddling for 30 minutes to an hour at racing speed against a stopwatch. Try to increase the distance you cover from week to week. If you can't get to water, jog or run for at least an hour nonstop.

Building Strength

Strength is the power your body has available to accomplish a particular task. Stamina and strength go hand in hand as essential ingredients for good physical fitness. Do these exercises every day or at least every other day. The important thing is to establish a definite routine and keep at it until it becomes a regular part of your life.

Chin-ups

How many you can do will depend on your body weight and frame, but if you are not physically out of proportion, you should aim for two groups of 25 each in a period of a couple of minutes. Chin-ups develop the muscles of the forearm and the biceps.

Push-ups

Push-ups work wonders to develop the triceps as well as the forearm. Aim for three groups of 40 push-ups in a couple of minutes.

Sit-ups

Do three groups of 20 sit-ups (knees bent) in a couple of minutes. Hold your hands behind your head and your body rigid at a 45-degree angle for 20 seconds afterward, until those abdominal muscles really begin to shout for relief.

Circuit Exercises

A six-station circuit exercise that requires only a barbell and weights, a 1-inch diameter wooden dowel, and about 5 feet of rope is recommended. Complete the "cricuit" three times in a row, allowing about 5 minutes for rest between each station.

1. With a 10-pound weight held behind your head, do 20 *sit-ups*.

2. Lying on your back with weights equal to two-thirds of your body weight attached to the barbell, *bench-press* the barbell 10 times.

3. Standing, with a quarter of your body weight attached to the barbell and with your arms at your sides, palms out, raise the barbell to your chin, then lower it back to waist level; do this *curl* 10 times.

4. Standing, with a quarter of your body weight on the barbell and with your hands at your sides, palms in, raise the barbell to your chin with elbows high, then lower it; do this *upright row* 10 times.

5. Sit with your forearms resting on top of your thighs, wrists extending just beyond kneecaps and palms facing out: *wrist-curl* the barbell up as high as you can until your forearms leave your thighs, 50 times.

6. Stand with your arms fully extended in front of you, grabbing the dowel with both hands. Roll the dowel up, turning it so that a rope attached to the dowel will gradually lift a 10-pound weight tied to the other end of the rope; do this *roll* 10 times.

Race Training

Although there are many different kinds of kayak races, luckily training will cover all of them. There is much overlap in technique from one kind of racing to another. The following exercises will help you train for almost any kind of race.

Pool Training

There are municipal or private indoor pools in most communities. The local kayak club can usually organize pool sessions by arrangement with public or private owners.

Pool training offers several advantages. The space limits make coaching easier, and there is guaranteed lighting for the use of visual aids. The trick is to devise basic training techniques that call for very little water space but at the same time simulate outdoor conditions.

The Roll

Above all, that pool water is warm! Those trying to conquer the Eskimo roll on their weak sides will find this a great help. You can make a game of it. Anyone can learn to roll using a paddle—eventually—but how about with a pair of ping-pong paddles, or better yet, using hands only?

Stunt men will be interested in seeing how many rolls they can do in 60 seconds. A competent roller in reasonably good physical condition should be able to complete up to 20 rolls in a minute. (The first time you try it, though, you'll believe that it is the longest minute of your life.)

The English Gate

The English Gate—developed in England, where it's called the "Wiggle Test"—is a complicated, back-and-forth, in-and-out maneuver to add flavor to flatwater, in which a paddler goes all around and through a single gate without touching a pole. It is particularly effective training for slalom and helps develop the quick, precise movements you need for wildwater racing. It can be practiced in a pool indoors, or outdoors in a river.

First, pass through the gate in a forward direction three times. Next, back your kayak down the outside of a pole, roll, then go forward through the gate and repeat the process on the other side. In the third phase, move again down the outside of a pole, pivot, and then go backward through the gate. Once through, pivot again and go backward through the gate. For the final phase, move forward past the outside of a pole, roll, then go

Pool training. (Evans Associates)

Strenuous training exercises include the English Gate, a sequence of maneuvers around a single gate, performed at full speed. (Ledyard Canoe Club)

backward through the gate and repeat the process on the other side. (See Diagram A.)

The English Gate should be done flat-out at full speed. The occasional weekend racer really ought to complete an English Gate in 80 or 90 seconds, a U.S. Team prospect in 60 to 70 seconds.

Diagram A. The English Gate.

Phase I

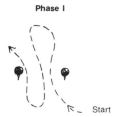

Forward through three times

Phase III

Reverse down outside, then reverse through twice

Phase II

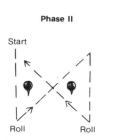

Reverse down outside, roll, forward through on both sides

Phase IV

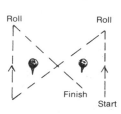

Forward down outside, roll, reverse through, on both sides

The Rack

A rack consists of two wooden 2 × 4's connected by wooden crosspieces like a ladder, with a molded kayak seat set in the middle. Attach the rack firmly to the side of the pool so that it projects directly out into the water, and support it from below so that it won't move. Place a full-length mirror in front of the kayak seat so that a boater can see his own strokes.

Using a stopwatch, take a stroke a second, and paddle in the rack for 5 minutes without once breaking rhythm. This exercise begins to simulate the physical strain that a boater experiences during a 20- or 25-gate slalom. You can vary the 5-minute time limit for interval and tempo training.

Don't try the rack with a full-bladed paddle: it has too much water resistance. Take an old paddle and shave the blades to about 3 inches wide.

Pool Games

The Chase

A three-man chase lasting for 5 minutes straight adds zest to any practice. At top speed, the paddler in Boat No. 1 leads the other boats on an unpredictable route for 5 minutes, through and around 4 or 5 gates that have been strung across the pool; he can also include an occasional Eskimo roll. The object of the chase is for the lead boat to gain enough on his followers to approach and touch Boat No. 3 from the rear. All gates must be negotiated without touching the poles.

Sprints

A fast start is important in track racing and equally so in kayak racing. Line three or four boats up at one end of the pool and start them off at a given signal to sprint almost the entire length of the pool. The sprinting should be backwards as well as forwards, and even sideways using sculling and draw strokes.

Sequences

One of the most popular ways to train for slalom is to design a course through several gates. The leader makes a demonstration run while the other boaters watch and try to memorize the course. Then, by starting a couple of boats only 10 seconds or so apart, it is possible to maintain two racers on the course at a time—always under the relentless hand of the stopwatch.

Backward paddling, especially through a gate, is an art often neglected. Entire sequences can be designed in which all the gates are negotiated in reverse, one after another. To add a little spice throw in an Eskimo roll or two as well.

Exergenie Contest

An exergenie provides extra drag against which the boater must paddle. It is a small metal tube through which you thread a rope, twisting the rope inside: the amount of twist determines the degree of resistance. Exergenies are for sale in sport shops.

Thread a nylon rope as long as the pool through the exergenie and fasten one end of the rope to the stern grabloop of a kayak. At a signal, the boater springs forward, drawing the entire length of rope through the exergenie to the far end of the pool. When a boater has pulled the rope the length of the pool under a stopwatch several times, he is usually quite ready to suggest switching places with the timers. This exercise is best done with a fairly narrow-bladed paddle.

Kayak Polo

Kayak polo, a favorite sport in England, can be played in an indoor pool (2 boats per side) or outside in flatwater (3 or 4 boats per side) in either K-1's or C-1's. A good fast game builds stamina, increases paddling skills and maneuverability and is a worthwhile change from formal training.

Players use their paddles as mallets and try to hit a volley ball or water polo ball into the opponent's goal (a loose net inside a rectangular frame about 3 feet above the water). Every boat should have a rubber tip on its bow, and players should wear helmets. Players cannot use hands or elbows to touch the ball, an opponent, or a boat. Some polo games are played with bat boats—kayaks with rounded ends to prevent injury.

Outdoor Training

If you are fortunate enough to live near water with a moving current or rapids, you can have a lot of fun working out various practice routines to develop basic moves and skills during the warm weather months. Most of the exercises and games recommended for pool training are just as effective outdoors, especially sequences, English Gates, sprints, the chase and, of course, kayak polo. Unless vandalism is a problem, or the sensitivities of fishermen are involved, you may be able to set up permanent gates on a river.

You don't need to have real rapids and lots of whitewater in your backyard in order to train outdoors. Check the topographic maps, visit the nearest dam. There is more whitewater around than you may think. You don't need much. The Czechoslovakian national whitewater team, for example, conducts much of its practice in moving current under a bridge in the heart of the city of Prague.

Mental Preparation

Lots of attention has been paid to getting in shape physically for a kayak race, and attention has also been paid to proper technique, but we are still at the threshold of knowledge about mental preparation. Physical gains are easily measurable and obviously noticeable. However, scientific data on sports psyche are still quite limited. How does one measure concentration, nervousness, anxiety, or fear of failure?

Fear of Failure

Until significant breakthroughs are made in this fascinating field of inquiry, we are limited to personal observation, coupled with the practice of strict mental discipline. Those who have entered competition are well aware that many races have been lost, not because of poor physical conditioning (a national championship was won not too many years ago by a person who had been bedridden with a 102 degree fever) or poor technique, but as a result of fear of failure. More often, racers complain about the judges, the condition of the race course, the water level, the weather, the food they ate or didn't eat, the wind, the lack of sleep the night before, or the long drive to the race site. All of these items are common excuses for a deeper, underlying symptom—fear of failure.

Fear of failure, especially in our success-oriented society, is a common malady that afflicts us all in one degree or another. The thing to do is simply to recognize it for what it is, then treat its symptoms. Fear of failure manifests itself as tension. The entire body becomes tight. Movements and maneuvers that were easy in practice now feel awkward under race conditions. Fear of failure makes you think about where you're going to place in the race rather than how to get the job done. It is far better to take the approach that you are going out there on the river and do the very best you can. If someone is lucky enough to do better, then that person deserves to win.

A second method of dealing with tension caused by fear of failure is to get plenty of racing experience. The more you sit in that starting gate the more you will feel accustomed to it. Experience is a wonderful banisher of worries.

Concentration

Another major mental facet of kayak racing is concentration, control of the flow of thoughts that pass through your head while on the race course. Avoid thoughts which destroy your concentration on the task at hand, such as

> "I've simply got to win this one."
> "Why do I feel so tired so early in the race?"
> "Who is that person standing on the shore?"
> "Someone shouted at me and I should answer back."
> "What if I goof gate 13?"
> "My foot is going to sleep."

Thoughts which improve concentration center on the immediate task at hand: get off to a fast start, remember to exit left immediately after gate 1, shave the upcoming rock close to the right, sneak the green pole on gate 2, head directly for gate 3, plant the Duffek immediately on front of gate 4, on to other gates and the finish.

Rarely does everything go according to plan in a race. Surely, something unexpected will pop up to throw your concentration off. If such an eventuality occurs:

- Don't fuss over the problem. Utter no cry of despair or curse; don't slam your paddle down in frustration. All this does is to draw attention to the mistake and allows the valuable seconds to tick away.
- If an error has been made, there is nothing you can do about it now. Put it out of your mind instantly and start concentrating on the next item coming up on the course. Don't dwell—even for a fraction of a second—on the mistake. You have no way of knowing how well or how poorly others may be doing.

At a national slalom championship held in the Northwest, one racer got a 50 point penalty near the start of the course by hitting gate 2. Instead of losing heart—because there was no way he could win the national title with a 50 point penalty—he *increased* his concentration for the rest of the course and turned in such a remarkable score that he won the silver medal.

Concentration is an acquired habit. Practice it, master it, and you might reap enormous rewards later in life where it really counts.

Just remember, nervousness, anxiety, and tension are all natural feelings that spring from fear of failure. Recognize them for what they are. Get as much experience as you can, and keep winning (or at least trying to win) in its proper perspective. A loss is not the end of the world, and a victory is only for today.

PART V. USEFUL INFORMATION

Glossary

A.C.A. The American Canoe Association.

A.M.C. Appalachian Mountain Club.

Aft. Toward the stern or rear of a kayak.

Amidships. Midway between the bow and stern.

Astern. Behind the kayak.

A.W.A. The American Whitewater Affiliation.

Back ferry. See ferry.

Ballast. Weight concentrated at the bottom of a kayak that increases its stability by lowering the center of gravity of the boat.

Bat boat. A shortened version of "bath boat," a snub-nosed kayak popular in the British Isles for training in indoor pools.

Beam. The transverse measurement at the kayak's widest part.

Bilge. In a cross section of a kayak hull, the point of greatest curvature between the bottom and the side.

Blind drop. Rapids, the end of which cannot be seen from the top.

Boil. A (water) current welling up into a convex mound. Often found in big eddies.

Broaching. Running a kayak up sideways against an obstacle in the river, or to veer broadside to the wind or waves in a lake or in the ocean.

Buoyancy. The characteristic that provides good flotation for a lifejacket or for a kayak.

Cartwheel. A training exercise in which a kayak peels out of an eddy, spins around and re-enters immediately. It can be done both forwards and backwards.

Center of gravity. The single point of resolution of all weight in a kayak.

C.F.S. Cubic feet per second, the volume of flow in a river.

Channel. A navigable route through rapids or a designated stretch of water in a harbor or estuary.

Chine. The line of intersection between the side and bottom of a flatbottom or V-bottom kayak.

Chute. A gap or drop in rapids, steeper than the surrounding water.

Coaming. The raised lip around the cockpit of a kayak.

Cockpit. The open hole in the deck of a kayak to accommodate the boater.

Crest. The highest point of a wave.

Deck. The covering for the hull of a kayak to prevent water from entering.

Draft. The vertical distance from the bottom of a kayak to its waterline.

Draw stroke. A basic kayak stroke in which the paddler plants his paddle out and away from the kayak and pulls the boat toward the paddle.

Duct tape. Common plumber's gray or silver tape used in the repair of boats. Sometimes called gray tape.

Duffek stroke. A high bracing stroke, named after the Czechoslovakian kayaker Milovan Duffek.

Ebb. The falling away of a tide.

Eddy. An area of relatively motionless water in a river often found directly downstream of an exposed obstacle or downstream from an outcropping from a river bank.

Eddy line. The line of demarcation between the main current and an eddy. It is sometimes marked by turbulence and small whirlpools. In heavy water this is sometimes called an eddy fence or an eddy wall.

Eddy turn. A maneuver used by a kayak to enter an eddy.

Ender. A situation in which a kayak stands momentarily on end in a vertically upright position while surfing or playing in a roller or sousehole. Enders are also called pop ups, endos, end-overs, nose-stands or tail-stands.

Endo. See ender.

End-over. See ender.

English Gate. A timed training exercise around a single gate. It also involves four Eskimo rolls. It helps to develop quick, precise movements and boat control. In England it is called the wiggle test.

Eskimo roll. A self-rescue maneuver in which the kayaker rights his capsized kayak, bringing it and himself back into an upright position.

Extended paddle roll. An Eskimo roll in which the paddle is slid forward in the kayaker's hands to obtain greater leverage.

Faltboat. See foldboat.

Feather. To recover the paddle upon completion of a stroke by leading with one edge to reduce wind or water resistance.

Feathered blades. The blades on a kayak paddle that are set approximately at right angles to one another.

Ferry. A movement laterally across a river or an ocean swell. The kayak is paddled diagonally against the current. When facing upstream it is called an upstream ferry. When facing downstream and paddling in reverse it is called a back ferry or setting. Sometimes the maneuver is called ferry gliding.

Flat water. Lake, river, or ocean water where no rapids or strong current exist.

Foldboat. A collapsible kayak, consisting of a frame covered by a waterproof material. The kayak can be dismantled and packed into two bags. Sometimes called a Faltboot (German).

Footbraces. Part of a kayak's internal bracing system designed to support a kayaker's feet.

Freeboard. The vertical distance from the waterline to the lowest part of the kayak's gunwale. The freeboard plus the draft should equal the kayak's depth.

F.R.P. Fiberglass reinforced plastic. Woven fiberglass cloth held rigid in a matrix of resin.

Gate. Two wooden poles, separated by a cross piece, suspended over rapids. The poles are color-coded and the cross piece is numbered to inform the slalom racer in what manner he should pass his kayak between the poles.

Grabloop. A coil of rope at each end of a kayak. Used for lifting, carrying, and tying down a kayak.

Gradient. The average rate of descent of a section of a river, usually specified in feet per mile.

Gunwale. The uppermost portion of the hull of a kayak, all the way around.

Hanging strokes. Basic maneuvers employing a paddle in which the kayaker leans out away from the boat and relies on the paddle blade in the water for stability.

Haystacks. A succession of standing waves often found toward the end of rapids.

Heavy water. Big rapids, a very large volume of water passing down a river characterized by fast current and large standing waves.

High brace. A hanging stroke in which a kayaker leans out away from the boat with the upper paddle blade high and away from him while the lower blade digs into the water.

Hipbraces. Interior supports for the hips in the cockpit so the body will fit snugly.

Hip snap. A movement of hips, lower torso, and knees to adjust the position of a kayak. An important part of the Eskimo roll.

Hole. A depression in river water where a portion of the current is recirculating or falling back on itself. Also called: sousehole, roller, stopper, keeper, and reversal.

Hypothermia. Loss of body heat enough so that the body's core temperature begins to drop. Can lead to death if not treated promptly.

I.C.F. The International Canoe Federation.

Kayak. It is believed this word evolved from the Eskimo expression for a hunter's boat. It describes a small streamlined craft paddled by one or two people using double-bladed paddles.

Keel. A projecting strip along the bottom of a kayak located on the outside of the hull to improve tracking and prevent sideslipping.

Keeper. See hole.

Kneebraces. Interior support for the knees just forward of the cockpit.

Lateral resistance. The resistance of the part of a kayak below the waterline to being pushed sideways by the wind.

Lay up. An expression used to describe the soaking in resin of two or more layers of fiberglass cloth over a mold. When done by hand it is called a hand lay up.

Ledge. The edge of a rock stratum in the river bed which acts as a natural low dam or as a series of such dams.

Lee. (Leeward) the sheltered or downwind side.

Left bank. The left side of a river looking downstream.

Lining. Allowing a kayak to drift down the edge of rapids while the kayaker walks along the shore holding the kayak under control with a rope. Or, pulling a kayak up rapids from shore with a rope.

Low brace. A bracing stroke in which the paddler pushes down on the water usually with the back side of a paddle blade holding his arms and wrists in a low position.

Mold. A specially prepared shaped form from which a kayak can be constructed.

Nonpower face. The face of a paddle blade that is not being used to push water.

Nose-stand. See ender.

Paddle Jacket. A waterproof parka or anorak type of outer clothing designed to protect the kayaker from splashing waves.

Painter. A line attached to the bow or stern of a kayak.

Pawlata roll. An Eskimo roll performed with the paddle extended beyond the normal grip to increase leverage. Named after the Austrian Hans Pawlata, the first modern European to master the Eskimo roll.

Pillar. A reinforcing structure on the interior of a kayak that reinforces the top deck. Often made of foam.

Pirouette. A maneuver in which a kayak, while doing an ender, turns before assuming a horizontal position again.

Pitch. A steep section of a rapids. Sometimes also referred to as a drop.

Pogie. Waterproof and windproof mitts that attach directly around the paddle shaft to protect the kayaker's hands. Also called wind gloves and smittens.

Pool. A section of the river where the current is slower and the riverbed deeper than normal.

Pop up. See ender.

Port. The left side of a kayak, facing forward.

Portage. The act of transporting a kayak between two stretches of water, or carrying it overland around a rapid.

Power face. The concave side of a paddle blade. Sometimes called the business side of the paddle.

Put-in point. The location on a river at the start of a kayak trip.

Reversal. See hole.

Reverse sweep. The same as a normal sweep except that it starts at the rear of the kayak and arcs widely out toward the front.

Riffle. A stretch of shallow water producing small waves and a little turbulence.

Right and left control. Right control indicates that the kayaker's right hand remains fixed during the normal forward stroke. In left control the kayaker's left grip remains fixed.

Right bank. Looking downstream, the right side of a river.

River left. A directional term indicating the left side of the river, looking downstream.

River right. A directional term indicating the right side of a river, looking downstream.

Rock garden. A stretch of rapids in a river heavily obstructed by rocks and boulders.

Rocker. The amount of upward curvature in the hull of a kayak from the center toward the bow and stern.

Roller. See hole.

Screw roll. An Eskimo roll performed with the paddle shaft gripped in the normal paddling position.

Sculling. A series of figure eight strokes on one side of a kayak which provides stability for the kayaker while at the same time tends to pull the kayak toward that side.

Setting. See ferry.

Shaft. The handle of a kayak paddle between the blades. Sometimes called the loom.

Sheer. The upward curve of the sides of a kayak's hull from amidships to the ends.

Shuttle. A transportation arrangement in which vehicles are parked at both the start and finish of a kayak run on a river.

Slalom. A race through the rapids usually not over 800 meters in length, the object of which is to pass through a numbered series of gates in order from start to finish in the shortest time.

Soup. The name given to that part of a wave that breaks and forms white foam (whitecaps) in front of it.

Sousehole. See hole.

Splash cover. See spray cover.

Spray cover. A neoprene or cloth material that fits over the cockpit rim and snugly around the kayaker, making the cockpit waterproof. Sometimes called a spray deck, a spray skirt, or a splash cover.

Spray deck. See spray cover.

Spray skirt. See spray cover.

Standing wave. A permanent wave in a river which is formed when water flows over a submerged obstacle.

Starboard. The right side of a kayak when facing forward.

Stopper. See hole.

Strainer. A river obstacle, such as partially submerged trees or bushes. If current flows through a strainer, it is possible for an unwary boater to become trapped.

Surfing. A kayaker balances his boat on a standing wave in a river. Also riding ocean waves on to a beach at the seashore.

Swamp. To fill the inside of a kayak with water.

Sweep boat. The last kayak down a stretch of river. It is the sweep's responsibility to make sure no kayakers are left behind.

Sweep stroke. A widely arcing stroke that creates a turning motion to the opposite side. There are both forward and back sweep strokes.

Tail-stand. See ender.

Take-out point. The location on the river where the kayaker finishes his run and leaves the water.

Throat. The section of the paddle shaft just above the blade.

Thwart. A transverse brace, from gunwale to gunwale.

Tip. The extreme end of a paddle blade.

Tongue. The final stretch of smooth water at the top of a rapid at the point of a V.

Trim. The angle to the plane of the water surface at which the kayak rides. A kayak can ride down at the stern, down at the bow, or be trimmed evenly.

Trough. A hollow depression between two waves.

Upstream ferry. See ferry.

V. The angle formed by flat water as the river approaches the top of rapids. The pointed part of the V extends down into the rapids a short way.

Volume. A measure of the total enclosed space within the shell of a kayak. Volume can also refer to the amount of water in a river.

Wake. The wave(s) a kayak makes as it travels through water.

Weathercocking. The turning in a beam gale of a kayak into the wind unless proper correction is made.

Whitewater. Rapids filled with a lot of aerated water.

Wildwater. A stretch of untamed rapids. Also a type of kayak race.

Windage. The wind acting on the exposed area of a kayak above the waterline.

Windward. The direction from which the wind is blowing.

Wind-water couple. A balance in the kayak between windage and lateral resistance so that the kayak will not turn into the wind.

Weir. A low level dam on a river.

Wet exit. The maneuver by which a kayaker extricates himself from a kayak while underwater, instead of performing an Eskimo roll.

Wet suit. A close fitting garment of neoprene rubber which helps hold body heat.

Wind gloves. See Pogies.

Wrap around. A situation where a kayak has broached against an obstacle and is bent around it by the force of the current.

A Selected Bibliography

Below is a representative, alphabetic sampling of books and manuals for readers who wish to delve further into the sport of kayaking.

Adney, Edwin Tappan, and Howard I. Chapelle, *The Bark Canoes and Skin Boats of North America* (Washington, DC 20560: Smithsonian Institution, Bulletin 230, 1964). A beautifully illustrated and diagrammed history of the development of hand paddled water craft in the arctic regions.

American Red Cross, *Canoeing* (Garden City, NY 11530: Doubleday & Company, 1977). Although primarily devoted to the canoe, this well known manual also has valuable information on first aid, camping, competition, and kayaks. Unusually well illustrated. A new, condensed version (1981) is now available.

Burmeister, Walter F., *Appalachian Water*, Vols. I, II (Washington, DC: published privately by the Canoe Cruisers Association of Washington, D.C. 22101, 1962). The material for these volumes was collected in the late 1950's. Nevertheless they stand as classic source books of rivers in the eastern part of the United States.

Crantz, David, *The History of Greenland* (John Gambold, ed.), 2 vols. (London: Moravian Bretheren Society, 1767). David Crantz, a European missionary, described ten different methods the Eskimos in Greenland used to Eskimo roll.

Denis, Keith, *Canoe Trails through Quetico* (Toronto: Quetico Foundation, University of Toronto Press). An informative guide to the Canadian part of the Quetico-Superior river country.

Endicott, William T., *To Win the Worlds* (Baltimore 21202: Reese Press). For those athletes wishing to excel in international slalom competition. This is an enormously helpful and detailed account for the serious and talented paddler. It is equally essential for coaches and trainers. It is *the* definitive book on slalom for both kayaks and canoes.

Endicott, William T., *The River Masters* (available from 6537 Broad Street, Bethesda, MD, 20016). A detailed and well documented history of the World Championships in Whitewater Racing from their inception in 1949 through 1978.

Evans, Eric, and John Burton, *Whitewater Racing* (New York 10020: Van Nostrand Reinhold). This is a comprehensive, basic guide to whitewater slalom and wildwater racing in kayaks and canoes. Written with much personal insight and touched with humor, it is an excellent primer for those seriously interested in making a commitment to competition.

Granek, Istvan, *Paddling Kayaks and Canoes* (available from the National Paddling Committee of the American Canoe Association, Box 194, Kenilworth, NJ 07033). With the assistance of the United States Olympic Committee, this excellent text on flatwater kayak and canoe racing has been translated into English from Hungarian. It is an excellent source book for training and techniques. Although published (in English) in 1969, it still contains much relevant and helpful information for the serious flatwater racer.

Hutchinson, Derek C., *Sea Canoeing* (London: Adams and Charles Black, 1976). An authoritative work devoted exclusively to handling kayaks in the ocean. This is a comprehensive guide for beginners, and also contains a great deal of information for more advanced sea paddlers. It also offers a chapter on kayak surfing and the Arctic origins of the kayak.

Jenkinson, Michael, *Wild Rivers of North America* (New York: E. P. Dutton & Co. Inc., 1973). Nine classic rivers are described in detail, with notes on over 100 more.

Peekna, Andres, *Guide to Whitewater in the Wisconsin Area* (Madison, WI 53706: Hoofers Outing Club, University of Wisconsin). A very thorough and useful river guide to the waterways of Wisconsin.

Steidle, Robert, and Walter Pause, *Alpenflüsse-Kajakflüsse* (Munich: BLV Verlag, 1969). In German. It describes 50 well-known whitewater runs in the Alps. Well illustrated.

Tutko, Thomas, and Umberti Tosi, *Sports Psyching* (New York: Hawthorne Books). This book discusses mental factors involved in sports. It offers specific exercises to help a person control tension and reduce fears.

Walbridge, Charles, *Boatbuilder's Manual* (Penllyn, PA 19422: Wildwater Designs, Inc.). Anyone contemplating the construction of a kayak should have this book at his side. Indispensable.

Kayak Films

A MARGIN FOR ERROR 16 mm, color, sound, 22 minutes, Stock # 321529. Boating safety is stressed in an exciting narrative form focusing on proper preparations and procedures. Order from your local Red Cross chapter.

FAST & CLEAN 16 mm, color, 36 minutes, optical sound. 1980. This film follows the best U.S. racers on their year-long quest for gold at the 1979 World Championships. Available from Nichols Productions 6016 Hawthorne St. Cheverly, MD 20785.

PADDLING TO THE OLYMPICS A.C.A. Paddling Committee 17 minutes 16 mm color, sound. 1978. A promotional film for flatwater Olympic kayaking including equipment, technique, and training. A.C.A. Film Library Special Services Building, University Park, PA 16802 Catalogue number 22050.

PADDLES UP Wolf Ruck Productions, 19 minutes, 16 mm, color, sound. 1977. Olympic C-1, K-1, K-2, and K-4 kayaks are depicted as well as war canoes. A.C.A. Film Library, Special Services Building, University Park, PA 16802. Catalogue number 22053.

THE UNCALCULATED RISK American Red Cross. 15 minutes, 16 mm, color, sound. 1978. A strong statement in regard to river safety. Catalogue Number 22051. A.C.A. Film Library Special Services Building, University Park, PA 16802.

WHITEWATER PRIMER American Red Cross 23 minutes 16 mm, color, sound. 1978. Catalogue number 32390. Instructional film on how to handle whitewater safely. A.C.A. Film Library Special Services Building, University Park, PA 16802.

WHITEWATER SELF-DEFENSE: THE ESKIMO ROLL Nichols Productions. 14 minutes, super 8, color, magnetic sound. 1977. Catalogue number MS8C-0061. A.C.A. Film Library Special Services Building, University Park, PA 16802.

WILDWATER Jon Fauer. 16 mm color, sound 20 minutes. 1971. The story of the U.S. Team at the 1971 World Championships in Merano, Italy. Available from Jon Fauer, 500 E. 83rd St. N.Y., NY 10028.

Manufacturers and Distributors

California Rivers
P.O. Box 468
Geyersville Avenue
Geyersville, CA 95441

Seda Products
P.O. Box 997
Chula Vista, CA 92010

Wet Dreams Products Company
P.O. Box 2229
Van Nuys, CA 91404

Colorado Kayak Supply
P.O. Box 291 r
Buena Vista, CO 81211

W.A. Clark Associates
Sugarloaf Star Route
Boulder, CO 80302

ExtraSport
3050 Biscayne Boulevard
Miami, FL 33137

Kayakamaran
Box 1692
Gainsville, GA 30503

Northwest River Supplies
P.O. Box 9186
Moscow, ID 83843

Voyageurs Ltd.
P.O. Box 409
Gardner, KS 66030

Phoenix Kayaks
Rte 421
Tyner, KY 40481

Baldwin Boat Company
R.F.D. 2 Box 141
Orrington, ME 04474

L.L. Bean, Inc.
Freeport, ME 04033

Old Town Canoe Company
Old Town, ME 04468

Poseidon Kayak Imports
Route 129
Walpole, ME 04573

Bart Hauthaway
640 Boston Post Road
Weston, MA 02193

Eastern Mountain Sports
1041 Commonwealth Avenue
Boston, MA 02215

Iliad Paddles
199 Weymouth Street
Rockland, MD 02370

Iliad, Inc.
168 Circuit Street
Norwell, MA 02061

Omega Corporation Lifejackets
266 Border Street
East Boston, MA 02128

Carlisle Paddles Inc.
Box 488
Grayling, MI 49738

Country Ways, Inc.
15235 Minnetonka Boulevard
Minnetonka, MN 55343

Mitchell Paddles
Canaan, NH 03741

Apple Line Company
Washout Road
Scotia, NY 12302

Cascade Outfitters
Rte 1, Box 524
Monroe, OR 97456

Danny Broadhurst Surf Kayaks
409 A Wading River Manor Road
Manorville, NY 11949

Hans Klepper Corporation
35 Union Square West
New York, NY 10003

Sea Eagle
Dept. CB-1, St. James
New York, NY 11780

Waveskis, Inc.
86 Lafayette Drive
Mastic Beach, NY 11951

West Side Boat Shop
P.O. Box 151, Station B
Buffalo, NY 14267

Sports Equipment Company
Box TW
Mantua, OH 44255

West Hills Outfitters Ltd.
8425 SW 88th Avenue
Tigard, OR 97223

Dauber Canoe and Kayak Company
P.O. Box 59W
Washington Crossing, PA 18977

Elizabeth Metzler Kayaks
220 Hillview Drive
Springfield, PA 19064

Nippenose
330 Government Place
Williamsport, PA 17761

John R. Sweet
118 So. Buckhout Street
State College, PA 16801

Wildwater Designs
230 Penllyn Park
Penllyn, PA 19422

Windfall
330 Government Place
Williamsport, PA 17701

Folbot Corporation
Stark Industrial Park
Charleston, SC 29405

Perception Boats
P.O. Box 686, Dept. CM
Liberty, SC 29657

Whitewater Boats
P.O. Box 483
Cedar City, UT 84720

Hurka Products
RD 3 Box 47
Shelburne, VT 05482

Easy Rider Fiberglass Boat Company
10013 51st Avenue S.W.
Seattle, WA 98146

Eddyline Northwest Ltd.
8423 Mukilteo Speedway
Everett, WA 98204

Mariner Kayaks
1005 E. Spruce
Seattle, WA 98122

Natural Designs
4849 West Marginal Way SW
Seattle, WA 98106

Pacific Water Sports
Dept. G
16205 Pacific Highway South
Seattle, WA 98188

Life Link International
P.O. Box 345
Wilson, WY 83014

Grey Owl Paddle Company
101 Sheldon Drive
Ontario Canada N1R 6T6

A.C. Canoe Products Ltd.
P.O. Box 62
Chester England

Avoncraft
Burrowfield Industrial Estate
Welwyn Garden City Herts AL74SR
  England

Baron Canoes Ltd.
Hatch Moor
Ind. Estate Great Torrington
North Devon England

BMS Plastics (Midlands) Ltd.
Tollerton Aerodrome
Tollerton, Nottingham England

Canoesport U.K.
97 High St. Hampton Wick
Kingston-upon-Thames
Surrey England

Capel Canoes Ltd.
Five Oak Green
Nr. Tonbridge Kent England

Dolphin Wetsuits
2/4 Ashwell St. St. Albans
Herts England

Gaybo
Bell Lane Bellbrook Industrial Estate
Uckfield East Sussex TN22 1QL
  England

Granta Boats (CN) Ramsey
Huntingdon England

Harishok Ltd.
Unit 3 Clarendon Trading Estate
Hyde Cheshire England

Howarth Sports
18 Brookdale Belmont
Bolton England

Insports
31–39 High Bridge
Newcastle on Tyne NE1 1ES England

Lendal Products Ltd.
18/20 Boyd St.
Prestwick KA9 1LG Ayrshire
England

Ottersports Ltd.
Ash Street
Northampton England

P & H Fibreglass Ltd.
Old Stanley Colliery Station Road
West Hallam Ilkestom Derby DE7 6JA
  England

Palm Canoes and Kayaks
Unit 15 Marsh Lane Easton-in-Gordano
Nr. Bristol BS20 0NW England

Seasports
119 Seamer Rd.
Scarborough
YO12 4EY England

Shepperton Design Studios
76 The Green
Twickenham England

Trylon
Wollaston Northants
NN9 7QS England

Valley Canoe Products Ltd.
Private Road Colwick Estate
Nottingham England

Wye Kayaks
31 East Street
Hereford England

CYMRU Canoes
St. Hilary's Rd.
Llanrhos Llandudno
Cwynedd LL30 1 PU Wales

Whitewater Slalom Racing Rules

Effective 1 January 1980 and
Amended 1 January 1981

AUTHORITY: The National Slalom & Wildwater Committee, as constituted under Article VIII(1) of the A C A Constitution, and as empowered under Chapter V(8) of the Bylaws, hereby promulgates the following rules to govern slalom competition.

ARTICLE 1 OBJECT

The object of slalom competition is to negotiate a rapid-river course, defined by gates, without fault, in the shortest possible time.

ARTICLE 2 COMPETITIONS

A. Championship Competitions
  1. Championship competitions are here defined to be A C A Divisional, Regional, or National Championships, or trials races for any United States Team. These must be run in accordance with these A C A rules.
  2. International competitions, where other nations are invited to participate, must be run in accordance with the I C F rules.
B. Non-Championship Competitions
  1. Non-championship or local races should be run in general compliance with these rules, though some reasonable adaptations to suit local conditions may be made after discussion with the Divisional Slalom & Wildwater Chairman.
  2. A non-championship race may be conducted in conjunction with a championship event provided the additional entries can be accommodated without jeopardizing the championship event.

ARTICLE 3 ELIGIBILITY OF COMPETITORS

A. Only amateur canoeists who are members in good standing of the A C A may compete in championship competitions, except as provided in Article 3.C. In addition, for National Championships or team trials, the competitor must be a citizen of the U S A, or a bona fide resident of the U S A for two years, and must be registered with the National Slalom & Wildwater Committee (NSWC) of the A C A. For divisional championships, the competitor must be a member of that A C A division.
B. In all races the competitor must be a bona fide member of the club or federation under which he registers, or he must race unattached. He must also comply with the A C A Amateur Rules in Chapter XIII of the Bylaws of the A C A, which also appear as Article 38 of these rules.
C. A Race Organizer may, if desired, permit the entry of visiting foreign competitors, provided they are members of their National Federation, though such competitors are not eligible for any championship awards.

ARTICLE 4 COMPETITION CALENDAR

By December 1st of each year, each Divisional Slalom & Wildwater Chairman shall send in duplicate to the National Slalom & Wildwater Chairman the dates of the competitions proposed to be held in his division in the coming year. Proposed championships should be noted, and for each race it should be indicated which ranking levels (ABCD) of paddlers will be permitted to enter. By February 1st the competition calendar shall be published in one or more widely circulated publications.

ARTICLE 5 BOATS

A. Slalom is carried out in the following boat types:
  1. Single kayak (K-1): minimum length 4.00 m, minimum width 60 cm.

2. Single canoe (C-1): minimum length 4.00 m, minimum width 70 cm.

3. Double canoe (C-2): minimum length 4.58 m, minimum width 80 cm.

B. All boats must be used without rudder. All kayaks must be propelled by a double-bladed paddle. All canoes must be propelled by single-bladed paddles. Any boat which does not conform to these requirements shall not be accepted. It is not permissible to make the boats meet the required dimensions by the addition of taped-on extensions or by similar means. Soft foam ends are specifically permitted for safety reasons. The boat should be designed to, and remain within, the required dimensions. To be permissible, corrective measures must be of a permanent nature except where applied to repair damage occurring during an event, and must in no case constitute a potential safety hazard. No other dimensional or shape requirements apply.

C. During championship competitions and during training it is forbidden to indulge in commercial publicity. Boats, accessories, and clothing shall carry the same trademarks as the corresponding articles on sale to the public. Any boat or accessory not complying with these requirements shall not be accepted.

ARTICLE 6 CATEGORIES

A. Individual Classifications

1. The international categories are K-1 (men), K-1W (women), C-1 (men), C-2 (men), and C-2M (mixed). These shall be offered at all competitions.

2. Additional U S.A categories are C-1W (women) and C-2W (women). These shall be offered at all races where the demand for them is sufficient, at least three starting boats being required to form a class.

3. Optional or special categories may be formed at the discretion of the Organizers, at non-championship races where the demand for them is sufficient. These may include, but are not limited to, classes for open canoes, junior-size boats, and special designations such as C-2 Father/Son, etc.

B. Team Events

When team events are offered, teams of three boats may be formed in any of the categories listed in Article 6.A. Combining categories to form teams is at the discretion of the Organizers.

C. Age-Group Categories

1. Any or all of the categories in Article 6.A may be subdivided according to age groups if the demand for such subdivision is sufficient. The definitions of these categories are as follows:

a. A Junior is one who has not reached his or her 17th birthday as of 1 January of the current year.

b. A Master is one who has reached his or her 40th birthday as of 1 January of the current year.

c. The Senior Open is the remaining age group, 17 through 39, but is open to any contestant regardless of age.

2. Competitors in a Junior or Master category are eligible for awards only in that category, and may not win an award or be given a place ranking in the Senior Open category.

D. Ranking Categories

Any or all of the categories in Article 6.A.1 and 6.A.2 may be subdivided according to the A C A National Paddler Rankings at the discretion of the Organizers. All four ranking groups may be used separately, or only a partial subdivision into AB and CD groups may be used if desired. When age-group categories (Article 6.C) are offered, only the Senior Open may be subdivided by ranking.

E. Limitation on Entries

A competitor may take part in two individual categories and, if offered, two team categories. This limit may be waived by the Organizers if they wish to accept the additional entries, and can accommodate them without jeopardizing the smooth operation of the race.

F. Combination of Categories

In the event there are not three boats registered and starting in a given class, the competitors in this class may be included in a comparable class of higher difficulty rating. For example, C-2M may be merged with C-2, Junior K-1 with K-1, C-1W with C-1, etc. However, a competitor may not be permitted to compete twice in the same class as a result of such a merger. For example, if C-2W is merged with C-2M, a competitor entered in both of these events would have to drop one of them, or could choose to have her C-2W entry merged with C-2 rather than C-2M. A competitor may withdraw and receive a refund of entry fee if he does not wish to compete in such a combined class.

ARTICLE 7   OFFICIALS

A. According to its nature and importance, a slalom shall be supervised by the following Officials:

1. Race Chairman*	6. Starter*	11. Section Judges*
2. Registrar	7. Assistant Starter	12. Chief of Scoring
3. Course Supervisor*	8. Finish Judge*	13. Boat Scrutineer*
4. Communications Officer	9. Timekeepers	14. Safety Officer
5. Chief Judge*	10. Gate Judges	

B. Those Officials indicated by * should be A C A certified Slalom Experts. It is imperative that the Chief Judge and the Section Judges be so certified. Additionally, for National Championships and team trials, gate judges should be certified Slalom Experts insofar as possible.

C. Jury

1. The Race Chairman of every slalom shall appoint a Jury of 3, 5, or 7 members. The Chief Judge shall be the chairman of the Jury, and at National Championship competitions shall be appointed by the NSWC. All members of the Jury shall be A C A certified Slalom Experts, and shall come from different clubs or Federations among those participating in the slalom.

2. The Jury controls the correct running of the slalom, receives any protests concerning the non-observance of these rules, and ultimately decides in the event of disagreement on the interpretation of these rules. The decisions of the Jury shall be guided by these rules insofar as possible, but it must also decide on all matters arising during the race which are not covered herein. The Jury can disqualify a competitor for all or part of the race.

3. A member of the Jury must not vote in a decision involving a member of his own club or Federation, or (if he is a competitor) a decision involving his own category of competition.

ARTICLE 8   DUTIES OF OFFICIALS

A. The *Race Chairman* directs the preparation and execution of the race in accordance with these rules. He appoints the Jury and other officials as needed to assure the smooth execution of the race.

B. The *Registrar* is responsible for the processing of all race entries, verification of entry qualifications (if any), and preparation of the starting order. He is responsible for the post-race distribution of results and the filing of other reports.

C. The *Course Supervisor* is responsible for the course design and the correct hanging of the gates. He must be prepared to have necessary adjustments and repairs effected as needed.

D. The *Communications Officer* is responsible for the setup and maintenance of lines of communication between start and finish, and between the judges and the scoring office.

E. The *Chief Judge* is responsible for the correct running of the race in accordance with these rules. He interprets these rules, and has the right to disqualify or grant a rerun. He is the chairman of the Jury. He shall ensure that all gate judging stations are properly manned, or he may appoint an assistant to carry out this function. If correctable changes in the course occur, he will stop the competition until the original conditions are reestablished.

F. The *Starter* ensures that competitors start in the correct order.
  1. He can refuse to start a competitor if the latter:
    a. fails to respect the safety rules;
    b. fails to present himself on time for his run after being called;
    c. appears without his correct number bib; or
    d. fails to follow the Starter's orders.
  2. If a false start occurs, the Starter determines if a second start is to be given, and notifies the Chief Judge.

G. The *Assistant Starter* is responsible for checking in boats at the start, calling competitors, enforcing the safety rules (see Article 16), and checking that the boats have been marked by the Scrutineer. He must prevent any competitor from starting if the required safety measures have not been followed.

H. The *Finish Judge*, in conjunction with the Starter, ensures that times are properly taken. He must rule on disqualification for capsize at the finish line, and may disqualify for violation of the safety rules.

I. The *Timekeepers* shall assist the Finish Judge in taking times. All stopwatch times must be *independently* read by two timekeepers.

J. The *Gate Judges* shall judge the negotiation of gates in accordance with Articles 22 and 27. Each judging station shall be manned by at least two Gate Judges for individual runs, and by at least three Gate Judges for team runs. No station may be manned solely by members of the same club unless it is the club which is organizing the race, and the judges involved are non-competitors. A single judging station may judge several gates, provided all may be clearly seen. Gate Judges shall take special care to note any disagreement on scoring on their score sheets. Gate Judges must whistle a competitor off the course in the event of overtaking, in accordance with Article 28. Judges must notify the Course Supervisor of necessary adjustments to the gates.

K. The *Section Judges* shall oversee all the duties of the Gate Judges in the section of the course allotted. A section consists of one or more judging stations.

L. The *Chief of Scoring* is responsible for the calculation, tabulation, and posting of the results. He shall indicate the time of posting for each category as it is completed.

M. The *Boat Scrutineer* ensures that the dimensions and safety equipment of all boats conform to the regulations and marks them accordingly.

N. The *Safety Officer*, assisted by his team and according to the circumstances, shall do his utmost for the rescue of competitors who have capsized and shall make a reasonable effort to recover their equipment. He shall have overall responsibility for safety measures. The nature of the safety measures employed shall be commensurate with the difficulty of the course and the skill of the competitors.

O. An official can, if need be, take on two or more functions. Officials are forbidden to give competitors on the course technical advice by calling or in any other way.

ARTICLE 9 INVITATIONS

The invitation and entry form for a slalom should be distributed at least four weeks prior to the entry deadline. The invitation should include the following information:

A. Time and place of the competition.

B. Description of the course, including water conditions and degree of difficulty.

C. Categories to be run. All those listed in Article 6.A.1-2 must be offered.

D. Sequence and approximate starting times of the heats.

E. Any specific championships to be contested.

F. Safety measures.

G. Address to which entries should be sent and amount of entry fee to be paid.

H. Last date for entries to be postmarked.

I. Whether late entries will be accepted, and if so amount of extra fee.

J. Time and place of the draw.

K. Limitations on entries, if any.

L. Nature of awards to be given.

M. Required work assignments for competitors, if any.

N. Regulations on training runs.

O. Camping, meals, other accommodations for competitors and officials.

P. Any other information as deemed necessary by the Organizers.

ARTICLE 10 ENTRIES

A. Entries for a slalom shall be on the official form provided with the invitation or a suitable facsimile, and shall be in accordance with these rules and any additional rules as given on the invitation. An entry shall always include the name and address of the competitor, his A C A number and/or NSWC registration number, the club he represents (if any), the categories he wishes to enter, the names of his partner(s) and team member(s) as applicable, and his ranking division for each category. The entry form, including the safety waiver, must be signed and must be accompanied by the applicable entry fee. A competitor under the age of majority in the state where the race is held (usually 18, but 21 in some states) must also have a parent or guardian sign the form.

B. Whenever possible, acknowledgment of entry, with acceptance or rejection (with reasons for the latter), shall be sent by mail to all competitors. Withdrawal of an entry for good cause prior to race day, or cancellation of the race by the Organizers, should result in at least a partial refund, an amount being held by the Organizers to cover handling costs. Alteration of entries after the deadline may be accepted only at the discretion of the Race Chairman.

ARTICLE 11 THE DRAW

The starting order within each category shall normally be determined by a draw of all competitors registered by the entry deadline. In order to make the race run more smoothly when a wide range of ability levels are entered, the competitors may be divided into two or three groups and a draw done for each group. Late entries, if allowed, shall be placed at the beginning of each class. After the draw a start list shall be printed and made available to the competitors prior to the start of the race. Changes in the starting order after the draw may be made only for a demonstrable good reason.

ARTICLE 12 WORK ASSIGNMENTS

All competitors may be expected to perform some task necessary to the running of the race. Failure to perform the assigned task, unless excused by the Race Chairman, will result in disqualification. The assignment list should be printed and attached to the start list. In making assignments, the Organizers should make every effort to ensure that late entrants do not escape an assignment by virtue of being late.

ARTICLE 13 RACE SANCTIONING

Application for race sanctioning shall be made to a Divisional Slalom & Wildwater Chairman, or to the National Slalom & Wildwater Chairman.

ARTICLE 14 PRACTICE

A. During the official training, and circumstances permitting, each competitor shall be allowed one training run over the course with the gates in position for each individual category in which he is entered. The Organizers are responsible that the training is done in a correct manner. They must ensure that during the runs:
  1. An official is put in charge and his instructions are carried out.
  2. Starting numbers are used.
  3. Safety measures are carried out, and if no rescue service is available, the competitors are so advised and they are required to lend each other assistance as necessary.
  4. All runs are non-stop, with each gate being done only once. Repeated passage of a gate is allowed only when it is one of a sequence of gates that constitutes a single technical maneuver, so recognized by the Course Supervisor.
B. Open or unlimited training may be permitted at the discretion of the Organizers. All the above rules should be adhered to, including required non-stop runs, in order that the training be carried out smoothly and safely.
C. Non-observance of any of these requirements can lead to disqualification. If a paddle breaks during training, outside assistance is permitted. In the event of a capsize, or rendering aid to another who has capsized, the training run can be resumed from the point of capsize or the point of departure from the course to give aid.
D. Particularly for important races, the Organizers are advised to have all personnel at their stations and all systems activated for testing during practice.

ARTICLE 15 INSTRUCTIONS TO COMPETITORS

A. At a meeting held prior to the start of the race, all competitors shall be given any pertinent information regarding the running of the race, such as: start and finish lines, starting times, intervals, and order, starter's commands (countdown or electronic signal), safety regulations, procedures for protests, boat transport, and any other matters of importance. It is particularly important to cover any late changes in the course, hazardous spots, or gates to be omitted by some classes. Competitors may ask questions about the course or the operation of the race. Additional meetings may be held as deemed necessary by the Race Chairman. Information presented at these meetings shall also be posted on a bulletin board for the benefit of competitors who missed the meeting.
B. Particularly for important races, the Organizers are advised to deal with competitors through Team Leaders, thus allowing the competitors to concentrate on race preparation by freeing them from meetings.

ARTICLE 16 SAFETY MEASURES

A. All boats must be made unsinkable. In doubtful cases, boats will undergo flotation testing, which will require the boat filled with water to float nearly level on the surface of the water.
B. All boats must be equipped with endloops, for which the point(s) of attachment must be no more than 30 cm from the end of the boat. The loops must be large enough to allow the easy insertion of the entire hand, and the cord from which

they are made must have a minimum diameter of 6 mm. Flat webbing with a minimum cross section of 2 by 10 mm may be used. Aside from their points of permanent attachment, the endloops must be free and unfettered. They may not be held in place by tape, rubber bands, Velcro, or any other means.

C. Each competitor shall wear a safety helmet and a lifejacket with a minimum buoyancy of 6 kg. Competitors failing to observe such decision shall be refused the right to start. Organizers are advised to make spot checks of the buoyancy of life jackets at either the start or finish. A solid iron weight of 6 kg is to be used. A child under 90 pounds may wear a lifejacket with buoyancy rate approved by the U S C G for his or her weight in lieu of the above buoyancy requirement.

D. Competitors must at all times be in a position to free themselves immediately from their boats.

E. In all cases competitors participate at their own risk. Neither the A C A nor the Organizers can be held responsible for accidents or material damage which may occur during a competition.

F. Three boats must remain at the end of the course at all times for safety. The number may be reduced to two at the discretion of the Organizers. This function will always be required of competitors unless specifically relieved and other measures have been provided by the Organizers. The Organizers should make every effort to provide other safety measures, particularly for the first boats in each class and following breaks (as per Article 16.G).

G. According to the difficulty of the course and the experience of the competitors, safety boats and/or other safety measures shall be provided along the course.

H. Non-observance of any of these requirements can lead to disqualification. Every official is required to observe that the safety measures are adhered to. The Starter and the Assistant Starter must prevent boats or competitors from starting if they fail to meet the requirements of this Article. Any time lost at the start as a result of safety violations goes against the competitor.

ARTICLE 17   MINIMUM PARTICIPATION

For an individual or team contest to take place, at least three boats or three teams must take part. It is, however, not necessary for all three boats or teams to complete the course for the contest to remain valid. Less than three may race informally if the Organizers approve, or categories may be combined (see Article 6.F).

ARTICLE 18   STARTING NUMBERS

Starting numbers shall be provided by the Organizers. They shall be fixed to the body of the competitor in such a manner that they can be seen clearly. In C-2 only the bow paddler wears the number. Each competitor is responsible for his starting number. The number should be unique for each boat and must not be reused by another competitor, or by the same competitor in another class at the same race. The numerals must be at least 15 cm high, and have a line width of at least 1.5 cm.

ARTICLE 19   THE COURSE

A. The course shall have a maximum length of 800 meters measured from the start through all the gates to the finish line. As far as possible it should include natural and artificial hazards such as current, eddies, rapids, rocks, bridge piers, wiers, etc. It shall contain at least 25 (non-championship courses may reduce this number) and not more than 30 gates, of which at least four are reverse gates and only one a Team gate. No gate shall be closer than 25 meters to the finish line. The finish line must be clearly marked on both sides, and downstream of the final gate.

B. The Organizers are advised to design the course in such a manner that smooth and continuous runs may be expected from the better paddlers in all categories at the level of skill for which the competition is intended. Excessive crisscrossing should be avoided, and the gates must not be so close together as to impair negotiation or judging. Reasonable balance between left and right-handed moves must be provided. The course must be navigable throughout, without excessive hazard to life, limb, or equipment. Particularly difficult gates may be omitted for some categories at the discretion of the Organizers or upon a vote of the Jury. The final approach and negotiation of a gate must not be unduly hindered, such as by an isolated submerged rock or other obstruction. The Team gate should be positioned in such a manner that on approaching it, contact with subsequent gates may be avoided as far as possible. The final course layout must be approved by the Jury prior to the start of competition.

ARTICLE 20 MARKING AND HANGING OF THE GATES

A. All gates shall be numbered in the order of their negotiation and painted in the international shipping colors, according to the direction of negotiation, i.e.:
  1. Green—always to the right of the competitor (starboard).
  2. Red—always to the left of the competitor (port).
B. The width of the gates is 1.2 m minimum, and 3.5 m maximum, measured between the poles. The poles must be round, at least 2 m long and 3.5 to 5 cm in diameter. Poles shall be painted throughout their entire length with five white and five red or green rings, the ring nearest to the water always being white. The bottom ends of the poles must be a minimum of 10 cm above the water surface, and the pole must not be put in motion by the water. The gate number boards and the indicating boards for reverse and team gates ("R" & "T") must measure 30 cm by 30 cm. The numbers and the letters R and T must be painted on both sides of the board, black on a yellow background, and must be at least 20 cm high and have a line width of at least 2 cm. The side facing the direction from which the gate must not be entered must, in addition, be painted with a red diagonal line.
  1. Forward Gate: A forward gate is defined by two poles, one red-and-white and one green-and-white, and a number board.
  2. Reverse Gate: A reverse gate is arranged like a forward gate with the addition of a letter "R".
  3. Team Gate: For team contests a single forward gate is marked with a letter "T".
C. The gate supports should not be placed so high as to permit excessive motion due to the wind. If such placement is unavoidable, a second crossbar and/or additional strings should be used to stabilize the gate.
D. The course must be the same for both heats as nearly as practicable. Gates and gate poles should not be changed after competition has begun unless to restore the course to its original condition. Such changes may only be made by the Course Supervisor or with explicit permission and direction from the Course Supervisor or the Chief Judge.

ARTICLE 21 NEGOTIATION OF GATES

A. All gates must be negotiated in numerical order. Forward gates shall be negotiated in accordance with the colors, bow first. Reverse gates shall be negotiated in accordance with the colors, stern first.
B. Negotiation of a gate begins when the gate is *engaged*, which means either of the following:
  1. A pole is touched by boat, paddler, or paddle; or
  2. The head or torso of the competitor (in C-2 either competitor) has broken the line between the poles (gate line).

C. Negotiation of a gate is *completed* when either of the following applies:
1. The head and entire torso of the paddler (in C-2 both paddlers) and part of the boat has crossed the gate line in the correct direction *and* the boat has continued through, either onwards or sidewards, and left the gate line (a hand, arm, or paddle remaining within the gate after the boat and torso have cleared is not considered when judging completion); or
2. A 50-second penalty is incurred by any of the means described in Article 22.A.4-9.
D. Negotiation of a gate is *correct* when it occurs as described in Article 21.C.1, provided that no 50-second penalty is incurred by any of the means described in Article 22.A.4-9. Negotiation of a gate is *faultless* when, in addition to being correct, neither pole has been touched by the boat, paddler, or paddle.
E. Negotiation of the Team Gate must be completed by all three boats of a team within 15 seconds. The time will start from the moment the first team member engages the Team Gate, and will end when the third team member has completed negotiation of the gate.

ARTICLE 22 JUDGING
A. Penalties are not cumulative at a single gate. If more than one infraction occurs, only the one highest penalty is assessed.
1. No penalty—Faultless negotiation.
2. 5 second penalty—Correct negotiation, but touching one pole.
3. 10 second penalty—Correct negotiation, but touching both poles.
4. 50 second penalty—Gate engaged but not negotiated. Lack of negotiation is judged to have occurred only when the competitor clearly abandons the attempt and continues down the course.
5. 50 second penalty—Intentional pushing aside of a pole in an attempt to lessen a penalty. This penalty is assessed only if the intentional pushing materially affects the negotiation of the gate.
6. 50 second penalty—Eskimo rolling while the body (in C-2 either body or between the bodies) is within the gate. A roll is judged to have occurred if the entire torso (trunk of the body, not including arms and head) of the competitor (in C-2 either competitor) is momentarily under water.
7. 50 second penalty—Negotiation of a gate contrary to the color indications or the R sign according to Article 21.A. A contrary negotiation is judged to have occurred if at any instant, during the passage of the head and torso of the competitor (in C-2 both competitors) between the poles, the boat is situated contrary to the colors or the R sign.
8. 50 second penalty—Gate omitted. A gate is judged to have been omitted only when the competitor clearly abandons the attempt and continues down the course.
9. 50 second penalty—Repeated attempt at a gate after the body of the competitor (in C-2 either competitor) has broken the gate line. This means that once a competitor has broken the gate line he must continue onward until clear of the gate without dropping back or moving sidewards such that his body leaves the gate. In the case of an upstream gate in current, if dropping back is so minor as to have occurred between normal paddling strokes, it is not to be judged a repeated attempt. In C-2 neither body may drop back so as to leave the gate line, nor may the boat leave the gate sideways after one body has crossed and then return.
10. 50 second penalty—Failure to negotiate the Team Gate in accordance with

Article 21.E. This penalty is assessed to the team as a whole, in addition to any individual penalties incurred on the Team Gate.

B. Interpretations

1. Once negotiation of a gate is completed (Article 21.C), that gate is immediately dead and no further penalties can be incurred.
2. The *gate line* is an imaginary line drawn between the tips of the two poles at any instant, whether they are hanging straight down or have been brought into motion by wind or contact. An imaginary extension of a pole may be needed to define the gate line in some cases involving large motions.
3. Passing underneath a pole without touching (undercutting) is not penalized.
4. In all doubtful or borderline cases, the competitor is given the benefit of the doubt and the lower penalty. For *example:*
   a. If a Judge is in doubt as to whether movement of a pole was caused by contact or by a water splash, no penalty for a pole touch may be given.
   b. With regard to forward or reverse negotiation, when the boat is so nearly broadside that correct or incorrect direction cannot be determined, benefit of the doubt is given.
5. Repeated attempts at a gate are not penalized provided the body of the competitor (in C-2 either body) has not broken the gate line.
6. Repeated touching of the same pole is only penalized once.
7. In addition to the interpretations listed here, there shall be a series of numbered diagrams which shall depict various judging situations. These shall be considered an integral part of these rules.

C. Placement of Judges

Judging stations, or individual Gate Judges, must be located so that all situations can be clearly observed. Particular attention must be given to having a Judge exactly on the gate line where problems of boat orientation are likely to be severe, or where a post-negotiation touch may occur as at some upstream gates. It is advised that Judges have two distinct viewpoints for each gate when possible.

ARTICLE 23 CAPSIZE

The Eskimo roll is not regarded as a capsize. In team races the members of a team may help each other to roll up. If a competitor leaves his boat he is disqualified for that heat. He *must* immediately leave the course in the most expeditious manner. If a member of a team leaves his boat in a team contest, the whole team is disqualified for that heat and must leave the course in the most expeditious manner. Failure to leave the course after capsize will result in disqualification for both heats.

ARTICLE 24 HEATS

A slalom is run in two heats, the better of which counts as the final result. For the team contest this may be reduced to one heat. Where a competition is held on uncontrolled water, both heats in a category must be on the same day.

ARTICLE 25 TIMING

A. The time of a run is taken from the moment of the Starter's signal, with the boat held at a fixed starting point, to the moment the finish line is cut by the competitor's body (in C-2 the first body). If electronic timing is used, the clock may be started by the paddler or his boat. In team events, the finish time is taken when the finish line is cut by the competitor's body in the third boat. Crossing the finish line upside down disqualifies for that heat. The boat is regarded as upside down when the whole of the competitor's torso (trunk of the body, not including arms and head) is under water. A competitor's run is complete when he crosses the finish line. He may not cross the finish line more than once.

B. If the timing is done by stopwatches, only those with 60 or (preferably) 100-second-sweep second hands shall be used. Those with 30-second-sweep hands *must not* be used. In any case, all watches used should be of the same type to avoid confusion among timers.

C. The Organizers should be aware that the accuracy of most stopwatch timing cannot exceed ½ second, and should report the results accordingly. If 60-second watches are used, the times must be recorded in minutes and seconds, then converted to seconds on paper. Precise timing and rounding methods must be specified prior to the start of the race.

D. All stopwatch times must be *independently* read by two Timekeepers. The Organizers are advised to provide backup timing, which should be *read and recorded independently* of the main timing. This is mandatory for National Championships and team trials.

ARTICLE 26 CALCULATION OF RESULTS

A. For the calculation of the results, the following formula applies:

$$\text{Time in seconds} + \text{Penalties} = \text{Score}$$

Example of an individual result:

Time elapsed	2 minutes, 20.8 seconds	= 140.8 seconds
Penalties	5 + 10 + 50 + 50	= 115.0 seconds
Total score		= 255.8 points

B. For a team event, the individual penalties for each of the three boats and the Team Gate penalty (if any) are all added to the total elapsed time in seconds to arrive at the team score.

ARTICLE 27 SCOREKEEPING AND SIGNALING BY GATE JUDGES

A. Gate Judges shall mark the penalties incurred by each boat on penalty sheets provided for this purpose. Unusual or questionable circumstances, or disagreements on scoring, should also be noted. Care should be taken to number these sheets sequentially, and to clearly indicate first and second heats, and reruns, if any. Gate Judges' penalty sheets shall be picked up periodically throughout the race and delivered to Scoring. All penalty sheets shall be delivered to Scoring at the end of the day's events. If telephones are available, penalties shall be reported to Scoring as frequently as practicable, but such reporting must not interfere with the direct recording of penalties by the Judges.

B. If Gate Judges are provided with marked disks to communicate with the Chief Judge, Section Judges, and the public, they shall be marked as follows: a double-sided red disk marked with a white "0", and three double-sided yellow disks marked with black figures 5, 10, and 50. Results are signaled as follows:

1. Negotiation with penalty: The appropriate yellow disk held steady.
2. Disqualification: The red disk waved from side to side.

At National Championships and team trials the penalty disks must be provided and used.

C. Judges are forbidden to communicate with the competitors on the course in regard to their faults or their technique in any manner whatsoever. Competitors are forbidden to interfere with the Judges at any time.

ARTICLE 28 CLEARING THE COURSE

A. Whistling over

The signal to clear the course is repeated short whistle blasts, given by the nearest Gate Judge. Upon hearing such a signal, a competitor must immediately pull in to shore and await further instructions from the Judge. Reasons for whistling a competitor over include overtaking, as well as difficulties with the timing of his run, or a gate out of position further down the course. In the latter cases a rerun will always be granted.

B. Overtaking

1. When overtaking occurs, the normal procedure is to whistle over the overtaken boat, and permit the overtaking boat free passage. The Judge must ensure that the interrupted run is not resumed so soon as to cause immediate re-overtaking. Any time lost goes against the overtaken boat, and he will be granted no rerun unless highly extenuating circumstances prevail.

2. On rare occasion the overtaking boat may be whistled over and held, allowing the overtaken boat to continue. This could occur if the overtaken boat is running the course correctly, while the overtaking boat is doing so by running largely out of control and missing gates (the "Mad Bomber"). Any time lost goes against the boat whistled over, and there will normally be no rerun.

C. Interference

1. If a competitor has been interfered with by another boat, he may be granted a rerun with the authority of the Chief Judge. To merit a rerun, interference must be substantial and unavoidable, presenting a material impediment to the course.
   a. Contact usually, but not always, is interference.
   b. Lack of contact usually, but not always, is not interference.
   c. Intentional contact where it could have been avoided, or other unsportsman-like conduct in attempting to create interference to obtain a rerun will not be tolerated, and could result in disqualification.

2. Normally a rerun will be granted only to the overtaking boat. Only under highly extenuating circumstances would a rerun be granted to the overtaken boat (for example, see Article 28.B.2) or to both boats. Extra care must be taken to ensure that no overtaking occurs during a rerun.

ARTICLE 29 STARTING INTERVAL

In principle, only one competitor is on the course at a time. If entries are numerous and the time is limited, the Race Chairman can decide on a shorter starting interval. This can be a fixed time interval, or it can be based upon progress of the preceding boat to some point down the course. The latter is recommended if the competitors are of varied abilities and are not seeded (see Article 11). If the starting interval is not fixed, a competitor should be able to request extra time before or after his run if the preceding boat is markedly slower.

ARTICLE 30 DEAD HEAT

In the event of two or more competitors obtaining the same result, their order shall be decided by the better of the two non-counting runs. If this again produces a dead heat, both competitors or teams shall be given the same placing.

ARTICLE 31 LOSS OR BREAKAGE OF PADDLE

If a competitor loses or breaks a paddle, only a spare carried on the boat may be used. In team events, the spare paddle of another member of the team may be used.

ARTICLE 32 PROTESTS

A. Any action by a race Official, or lack of action where action is called for, is protestable unless specifically prohibited.

B. All protests must be lodged with the Chief Judge in writing, together with a fee set by the Organizers but not exceeding $5.00. This fee is refunded if the protest is upheld by the Chief Judge or by the Jury. If it is not upheld, the Organizers retain the fee.

C. A protest concerning the right of a competitor to participate must be handed to the Race Chairman not later than one hour before the start of the competition. Protests against the right of a competitor to participate may be lodged with the

National Slalom & Wildwater Committee within 30 days of the competition if they are based on facts which became known later than one hour before the start of the competition.

D. Protests against decisions made during the competition must be lodged with the Chief Judge in writing not later than 30 minutes after the official results of the particular category have been posted. If this time limit conflicts with the competitor's work assignment, then the time shall be extended to 30 minutes after his relief from duty. An informal protest, without fee, may be filed by verbally requesting the Chief Judge to check the correctness of a posted score. If dissatisfied, the protester may still file a written protest provided the score in question is his own. No one may protest the score, time, or penalties of another competitor.

E. The Chief Judge shall evaluate the legitimacy of a protest. He shall obtain testimony from the race officials and inform himself as to any other matters relevant to the decision. His decision shall be transmitted in writing.

F. If dissatisfied with the decision of the Chief Judge the protester may file an appeal to the Jury within 15 minutes of having received notice of the Chief Judge's decision. An appeal to the Jury must be in writing. The original $5.00 fee is refunded if the protest is upheld. If it is not, the Organizers retain the fee.

G. The Jury shall, after interviewing the Officials, competitor(s), and witnesses involved, rule on all protests in accordance with these rules and the following guidelines insofar as possible.

1. Timing
   a. If backup timing is provided by the Organizers, and both times are in substantial agreement, no protest is allowed.
   b. If there is no backup timing, or if the main and backup times disagree, a protest will be considered.
   c. If faced with compelling evidence of a specific error in a time, the Jury may adjust the time accordingly. A frequent cause of such error would be a one-minute error in reading a watch.
   d. If faced with compelling evidence of an irretrievable error in a time, or if the official time is lost, the Jury may grant a rerun.

2. Judging
   a. No rerun may be granted when the protest involves a gate penalty.
   b. None of the following limitations are intended to prevent the protesting of an alleged misinterpretation of the rules.
   c. If two Gate Judges, or a Gate Judge and Section Judge, operating independently and from different vantage points, agree, no protest is allowed. If they disagree and the disagreement cannot be otherwise resolved, the lesser penalty must be assessed (see Article 22.B.4), so there will be no protest allowed. If one Judge assesses a penalty but the other is uncertain or did not see it clearly, a protest will be considered.
   d. If only one Judge saw the disputed infraction, or if two Judges were operating together from the same vantage point, a protest will be considered.
   e. To be considered, a judging protest must be accompanied by the signatures of two witnesses. The Jury must consider both the vantage points and credibility of the witnesses. To dispute the agreed call of two Judges, as in (d) above, the vantage point(s) of the witnesses must be clearly superior to that of the Judges. If it upholds the protest, the Jury will direct the Chief of Scoring to reduce the disputed penalty.

3. Interference

If a competitor is interfered with by another boat or by an act of an Official, he may be granted a rerun in accordance with Article 28.C.

ARTICLE 33 APPEAL

A. A competitor has the right of appeal to the National Slalom & Wildwater Committee against a decision of the Jury. Such an appeal must be lodged through his Divisional Slalom & Wildwater Chairman within ten days of the event. A fee of $5.00 plus $5.00 for costs must be paid, which is in addition to any protest fee paid to the Organizers. The NSWC shall hold a hearing only after fair notice is given to decide the matter. If the appeal is denied, only that portion of the cost fee not expended in conducting a mail vote of the Committee is refunded. Appeal to higher authority shall be directed first to the National Judicial Committee, and finally to the A C A Congress. If the appeal is upheld, the entire $10.00 is refunded, as is the original protest fee, and the Organizers must bear the cost of the mail vote up to a maximum of $5.00.

B. If the appeal involves a matter of scoring, the NSWC must rule on whether, and in what manner, the score is to be changed. The appeal fee is handed to the Chief Judge at the race as notification and assurance that an appeal is to be filed. He must forward it promptly, along with his report on the matter, to the competitor's Divisional Slalom & Wildwater Chairman. The written appeal is sent by the competitor as prescribed above. If results lists are printed before the outcome of an appeal is known, the fact of the appeal must be noted on the list and the outcome must be published when it is known.

C. If a protest involving the course or any aspect of the race organization is denied by the Jury, the protester's only recourse at that time is to withdraw from the race and demand a refund of entry fees. If such demand is not agreed to, it may be appealed to the NSWC.

D. If the appeal involves a denied rerun, the Chief Judge, upon notification of the intent to appeal and receipt of the appeal fee, must grant the rerun. It will be timed and scored as usual, but its effect is conditional upon the outcome of the appeal.

ARTICLE 34 DISQUALIFICATION

A competitor may be disqualified from a single heat, from both heats in a category, or from an entire race, depending on the nature and severity of an infraction.

A. Which course of action to choose is at the discretion of the Chief Judge in the following cases: Any competitor attempting to win a competition by irregular means, who breaks the present rules, fails to follow an Official's order, fails to observe the safety rules (Article 16), or starts in a boat which does not conform to the requirements (Article 5) shall be disqualified.

B. Failure to perform a work assignment unless excused (Article 12) or failure to remain for safety unless relieved (Article 16.F) will entail disqualification for the entire race.

C. Deliberate misrepresentations on an entry form or in statements to Officials will result in disqualification from the category involved or from the entire race, depending on their nature.

D. Non-observance of the rules for practice (Article 14) or failure to leave the course after a capsize (Article 23) will result in disqualification from the category involved.

E. The following will result in disqualification only for the run in which it occurred:

1. Capsize on the course (Article 23).

2. Being upside down crossing the finish line (Article 25).
3. Being unready to start in the published sequence, or appearing without his correct starting number, if negligence on the part of the competitor can be established.
4. Acceptance of outside assistance during a run. In the sense of this Article, the following is taken to mean outside assistance:
   a. Any help by a second party given to a competitor or boat, such as:
      i) to hold out, slide, or throw a competitor's lost paddle or a replacement paddle;
      ii) to guide, slide, or set in motion a boat;
      iii) however, nothing in this Article shall prevent team members from helping each other.
   b. Communication with the competitor by means of an electric loudspeaker or radio.

ARTICLE 35   PRIZES

A. Prizes will generally be awarded for the first three places in each category. Medals, if used, should be of gold, silver, and bronze, denoting first, second, and third place. Ribbons, if used, should be of blue, red, and white respectively. Other types of trophies or prizes may be given provided they conform with Article 38.B.8. Additional places may be given awards if the depth of the class merits it. In the C-2 classes, both members of the crew shall receive the appropriate award.
B. For championship events, care must be exercised to assure that awards are presented only to those who are eligible for them in accordance with Article 3.

ARTICLE 36   RESULTS AND REPORTS

A. The results list shall include the full name of each competitor, his A C A number and/or NSWC number if given, his club if any, and his times, penalties, and scores for *both* runs, and shall be listed in order of finish place within each category. The outcome of any formal protests shall also be given.
B. Two copies of all race results must be sent to the Divisional Slalom & Wildwater Chairman of the Organizer's A C A division, and to the NSWC Race Records Officer for use in the rankings and for permanent file. It is recommended that they also be submitted to appropriate regional and national publications.
C. Organizers should be aware of the importance of all results in computing rankings, and should strive for completeness and accuracy. Full names, including Jr., III, etc., where applicable, are essential, and A C A numbers are an excellent cross check on identity.

ARTICLE 37   AMENDMENTS

A. These rules may be amended at any time by a ⅔ vote of the National Slalom & Wildwater Committee. At least 30 days before such a vote is taken, all proposed amendments must be submitted in writing to all Divisional Slalom & Wildwater Chairmen and to the NSWC Rules Committee, and must be published in the NSWC Newsletter or a national publication of the A C A. Amendments shall take effect on 1 January of the year following adoption by the NSWC. Article 38 on Amateurism may be amended only by vote of the A C A Congress, as provided in Article XIV of the A C A Constitution.
B. The NSWC may issue interpretations and supplementary rulings on questions as they arise. Such rulings shall take effect immediately upon publication, and shall be noted within the body of the rules.
C. Fundamental changes in the negotiation and judging rules by the I C F will automatically become effective on 1 January of the year following adoption by the

I C F. Less substantive changes in I C F rules must be voted on as above for incorporation in these rules.

ARTICLE 38 *AMATEUR RULES OF THE AMERICAN CANOE ASSOCIATION*
(Chapter XIII, A C A Bylaws)

A. An amateur canoeist is one who devotes himself to sport for pleasure and for moral and physical well-being without deriving therefrom, directly or indirectly, any material gain. He is not permitted:

1. to engage as a professional in any sport or to have contracted to do so while participating in an amateur competition;

2. to have allowed his person, name, picture, or sports performance to be used for advertising, except when the American Canoe Association or his or her National Activity Committee enters into a contract for sponsorship or equipment. All payments must be made to the American Canoe Association or to the National Activity Committee concerned and not to the individual;

3. to carry advertising material on his person, clothing, or equipment in any amateur competition, other than trademarks on technical equipment or clothing. Standards for trademarks may be established as required;

4. to have acted as a professional coach or trainer in any sport;

5. to have competed for or to have received any financial rewards or material benefit in connection with his or her sports participation except as permitted specifically in this Bylaw.

B. The following specific rules define more closely the provisions given above, and further apply to American canoeing competition.

1. An amateur canoeist may not receive pay for training or coaching competitive canoeing.

2. A professional athlete may be invited to participate in amateur competition without jeopardizing the amateur status of others.

3. A professional athlete may not be awarded a Divisional or National amateur title.

4. A professional athlete may not participate in any international competition under the jurisdiction of the I C F or on a national team or in any team trials which lead to participation in an event under the jurisdiction of the I C F.

5. Anyone who is declared a professional canoeist may not become an amateur again. Anyone who is declared a professional in any branch of canoeing (paddling, sailing, slalom, whitewater open canoe, marathon, or canoe poling) automatically becomes a professional in all branches.

6. An amateur canoeist may not compete in canoeing activities as a representative of a corporation or business in which he is employed, unless he has a minimum of two years of service, and the canoeing (or closely allied activity) is purely amateur in nature.

7. No canoeist shall lose amateur status by reason of the fact that his livelihood in total or in part is derived from the designing or construction of canoes, or any parts of canoes, or accessories of canoes, or sails, or from advertising or other profession connected with canoes, providing there is no capitalization of his fame. He may also write or publish articles on canoeing or engage in other artistic endeavors relating to the sport for money provided there is no capitalization of his fame.

8. An amateur canoeist may not compete for a medal or a prize on which it is not possible to engrave or place an inscription commemorating the event. The value of individual prizes shall not exceed $50.00.

9. An amateur canoeist may not bet or risk money on canoeing events.

10. An amateur canoeist may not enter or compete under any name that is not his own.

C. An amateur canoeist may:

1. be a physical education or sports teacher who gives elementary instruction. (Teaching canoeing and its allied skills for pay is not in itself a professional act.)

2. accept, during the period of preparation and actual competition, which shall be limited by the rules of each National Activity Committee:

   a. assistance administered through his or her National or Divisional Activity Committee for: food and lodging; cost of transportation; pocket money to cover incidental expenses; insurance to cover accidents, illness, personal property, and disability; personal sports equipment and clothing; cost of medical treatment, physiotherapy, and authorized coaches;

   b. compensation, authorized by his or her National Activity Committee in case of necessity, to cover financial loss resulting from his or her absence from work or basic occupation, on account of preparation for, or participation in Olympic Games and International sports competitions. In no circumstances shall payment made under this provision exceed the sum that the competitor would have earned in the same period. The compensation may be paid with the approval of the National Activity Committee at its discretion.

   c. prizes won in competition within the limits of the rules established by the respective National Canoe Federation (pertains to competitions other than within the United States).

   d. academic and technical scholarships.

D. Enforcement of this Bylaw shall be the responsibility of the National Activity Committee concerned. Appeals from the actions of the National Activity Committee shall be to the National Judicial Committee as provided in Article IX, Section 1 of the Constitution of the A C A.

WILDWATER SLALOM RACING RULES

Effective 1 January 1980 and
Amended 1 January 1981

AUTHORITY: The National Slalom & Wildwater Committee, as constituted under Article VIII(1) of the A C A Constitution, and as empowered under Chapter V(8) of the Bylaws, hereby promulgates the following rules to govern wildwater and downriver competition.

PREFACE: These rules make frequent reference to the A C A Slalom Rules, and should be attached thereto. Where a wildwater rule is identical to, or substantially the same as, a slalom rule, the slalom rule is referenced and not reproduced here. It is assumed that the user of these rules can ignore some minor slalom-specific wording which, in the interest of brevity, has not been edited out. Where a wildwater rule is substantially different from the corresponding slalom rule, the complete wildwater rule is presented here.

The following ARTICLES are the same as those in the A C A Slalom Rules, except as noted:

Article 2   Competitions
Article 3   Eligibility of Competitors

ARTICLE 1   OBJECT

A. The object of Wildwater racing is to demonstrate a competitor's mastery of his boat in whitewater of class III difficulty or greater, while running a prescribed downstream course in the shortest possible time.

B. The object of Downriver racing is identical, but is carried out on streams of less than class III difficulty.

ARTICLE 5   BOATS

A. Wildwater racing is carried out in the following boat types:
  1. Single kayak (K-1): maximum length 4.50 m, minimum width 60 cm.
  2. Single canoe (C-1): maximum length 4.30 m, minimum width 70 cm.
  3. Double canoe (C-2): maximum length 5.00 m, minimum width 80 cm.
  4. All boats may have only a single hull, with a single bow and a single stern.

B, C. Refer to Slalom Rules.

ARTICLE 6   CATEGORIES

E. Limitation on entries.

  A competitor may take part in one individual category and, if offered, one team category. This limit may be waived by the Organizers if they wish to split the race into sections in order to permit the additional entries, and if they can do this without jeopardizing the smooth operation of the race.

A, B, C, D, F. Refer to Slalom Rules.

ARTICLE 7   OFFICIALS

Refer to Slalom Rules, except delete sections 7.A.4 and 7.A.10.

ARTICLE 8   DUTIES OF OFFICIALS

C. The *Course Supervisor* is responsible for the layout of the course and the determination of its navigability. He is responsible for the erection of any gates if they are to be used to mark dangerous sections, or chutes over dams, or any other structures that are needed for the race.

E. The *Chief Judge* is responsible for the correct running of the race in accordance with these rules. He interprets these rules, and has the right to disqualify. He is the Chairman of the Jury. If correctable changes in the course occur, he will stop the competition until the original conditions are reestablished.

K. The *Section Judges* shall observe the race from various vantage points to help ensure that the competition occurs in a sportsmanlike manner.

A, B, F, G, H, I, L, M, N, O. Refer to Slalom Rules. D & J of Slalom Rules are deleted.

ARTICLE 14   PRACTICE

A. Training runs must be provided at least a day before the competition and under the same technical conditions that will prevail during the competition. The water level during the official training must, except for circumstances beyond control, be the same as during the competition. If no rescue service is available the competitors must be so advised. In any case, they are required to lend each other assistance as necessary.
B. Particularly for important races, the Organizers are advised to have all personnel at their stations and all systems activated for testing during practice. In this case, training shall be run in race order, and starting numbers shall be used.

ARTICLE 16   SAFETY MEASURES

I. Since wildwater competition is as much a contest against the elements as against other competitors, it is required that any competitor finding another in real danger must immediately render him rescue assistance at pain of disqualification for life.

A–H. Refer to Slalom Rules.

ARTICLE 19   THE COURSE

A. The course must be at least three kilometers in length, and part of it must be of at least class III difficulty to qualify as a Wildwater race. Courses of lesser difficulty shall be termed Downriver races.
B. The course must be navigable throughout; i.e. there must always be a route where a boat may pass without touching the bottom. Dangerous passages may be marked with gates to indicate the correct channel. Portages are not allowed.
C. The course must be approved by the Jury prior to the start of the competition. If the course is not approved, the competition may be moved to a replacement course.
D. It is permissible to have a shortened course for the women's classes if the Organizer's so desire.

ARTICLE 20   THE START

A. Starts take place in categories, with the fastest categories started first:
   K-1, C-2, K-1W, C-2M, C-1, C-2W, C-1W.
B. In individual categories the boats are separated by at least a 30-second interval. In team categories the teams are separated by at least one minute. The start interval must remain the same for the entire competition.

ARTICLE 21   TIMING

B. All watches used for timing should be of the same type to avoid confusion among timers. The Organizers should be aware of the degree of accuracy of the timing methods they are using, and should report the results accordingly. Precise timing and rounding methods must be specified prior to the start of the race.

A, C. Refer to Slalom Rules, Article 25.A and 25.D.

ARTICLE 22   OVERTAKING

Any competitor overtaken by another competitor shall allow the overtaking boat free passage if the overtaking competitor shouts, "FREI" or "TRACK!"

ARTICLE 23   CAPSIZE

A. If a competitor capsizes during his run and is able to perform a self rescue of himself and his equipment, he may continue the race. If he accepts or receives any outside assistance (see Article 27.C), he is disqualified and must quit the race.
B. If a competitor capsizes in a team race, he may be assisted by his teammates.
C. Crossing the finish line upside down disqualifies (see Article 21.A).

ARTICLE 27 DISQUALIFICATION

A competitor may be disqualified from the competition for:

A. Attempting to win a competition by irregular means, breaking the present rules, or failing to follow an Official's order.
B. Being unready to start in the published sequence, or appearing without his correct starting number, if negligence on the part of the competitor can be established.
C. Accepting outside assistance during a run. In the sense of this Article the following is taken to mean outside assistance:
   1. Any help by a second party given to a competitor or boat, such as:
      a. to hold out, slide, or throw a competitor's lost paddle or a replacement paddle;
      b. to hold, guide, slide, or set in motion a boat;
      c. however, nothing in this Article shall prevent team members from helping each other.
   2. Communication with the competitor by means of an electric loudspeaker or radio.
D. Making deliberate misrepresentations on an entry form or in statements to Officials.
E. Starting in a boat which does not conform to the requirements, Article 5.
F. Failure to perform a work assignment unless excused, Article 12.
G. Non-observance of the rules for practice, Article 14.
H. Failure to observe the safety rules, Article 16.
I. Being upside down crossing the finish line, Article 23.C.
J. Failure to assist another competitor in real danger may result in disqualification for life, Article 16.I.

ARTICLE 29 RESULTS AND REPORTS

A. The results list shall include the full name of each competitor, his A C A number and/or NSWC number if given, his club if any, and his time for the race, and shall be listed in order of finish place within each category. The outcome of any formal protests shall also be given.
B, C. Refer to Slalom Rules, Article 36.B and 36.C.

Because of anticipated rule changes, we suggest you contact

The American Canoe Association, Inc.
7217 Lockport Place
P.O. Box 248
Lorton, VA 22079

for current information about whitewater and wildwater slalom rules.

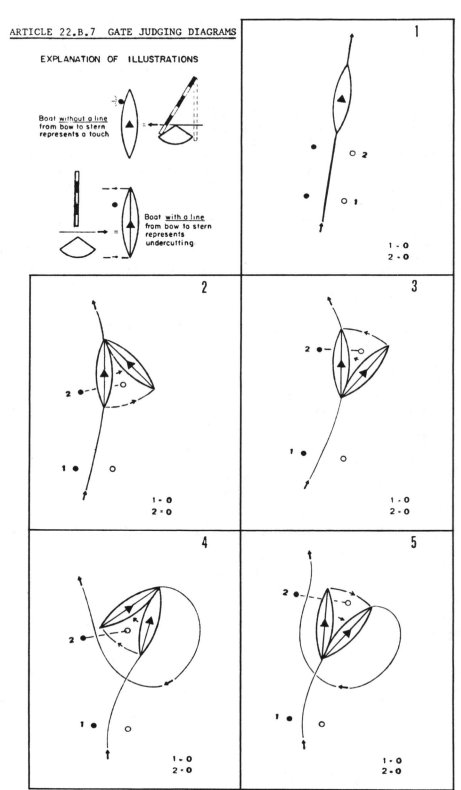

ARTICLE 22.B.7   GATE JUDGING DIAGRAMS

EXPLANATION OF ILLUSTRATIONS

Boat without a line from bow to stern represents a touch

Boat with a line from bow to stern represents undercutting.

1
1 - 0
2 - 0

2
1 - 0
2 - 0

3
1 - 0
2 - 0

4
1 - 0
2 - 0

5
1 - 0
2 - 0

230

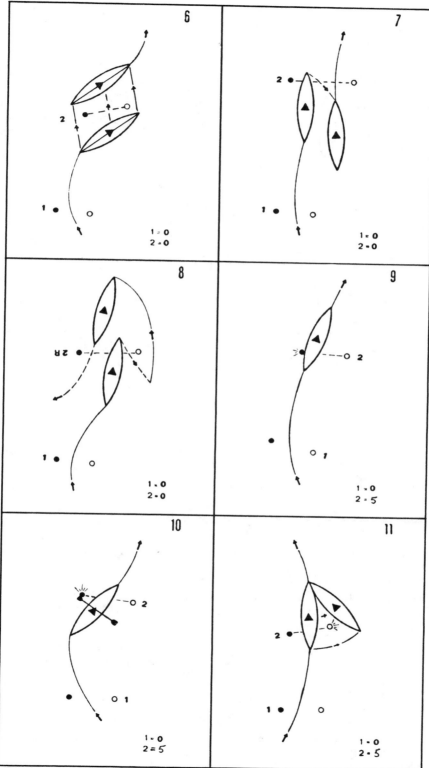

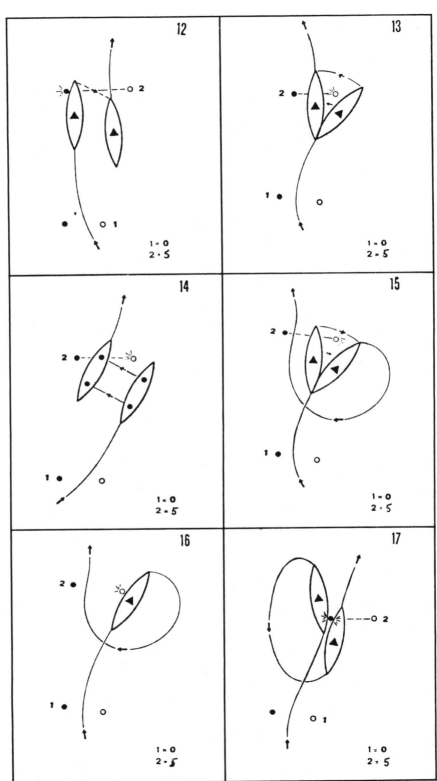

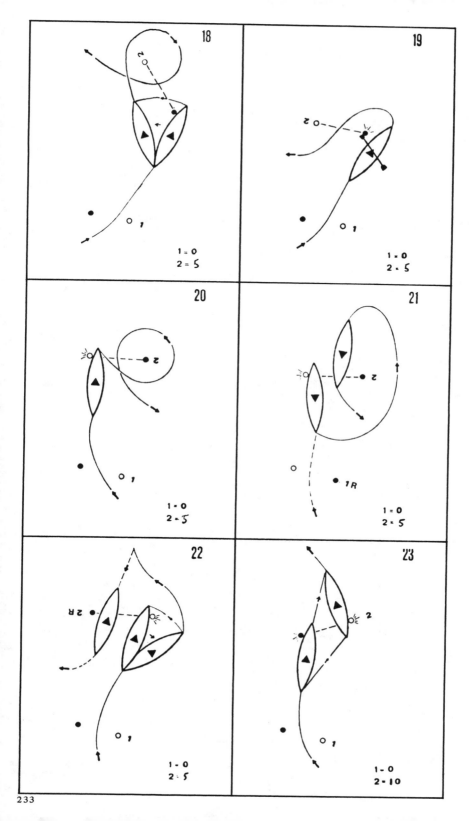

233

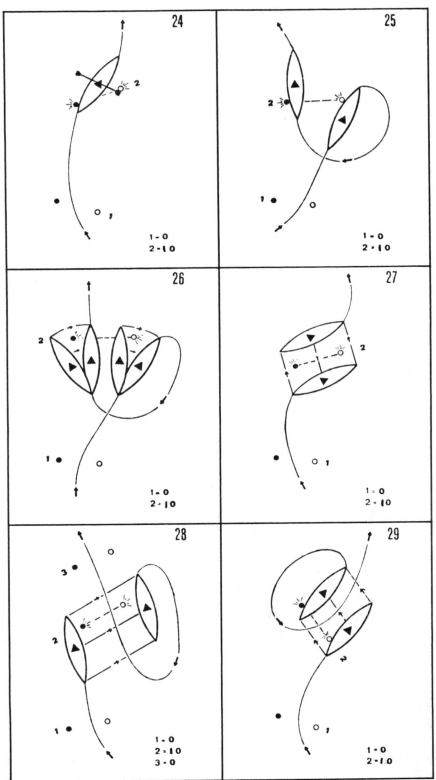

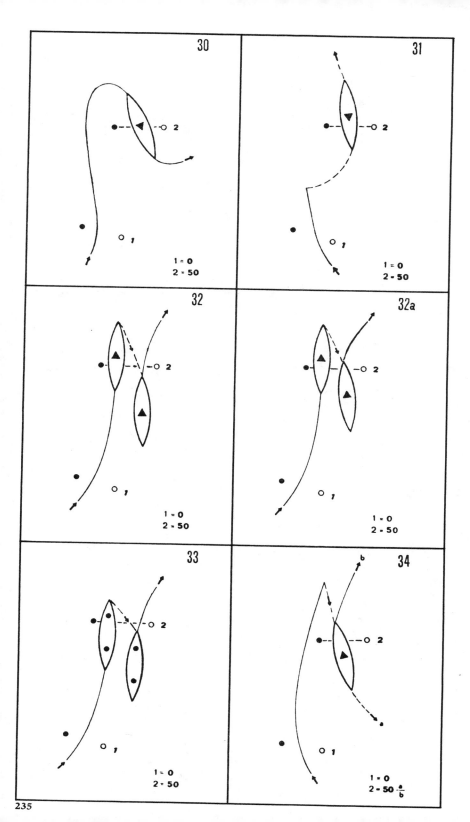

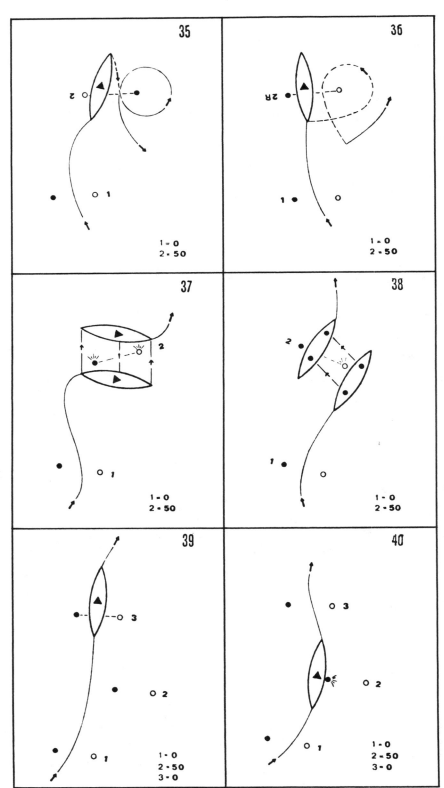

35

1 = 0
2 = 50

36

1 = 0
2 = 50

37

1 = 0
2 = 50

38

1 = 0
2 = 50

39

1 = 0
2 = 50
3 = 0

40

1 = 0
2 = 50
3 = 0

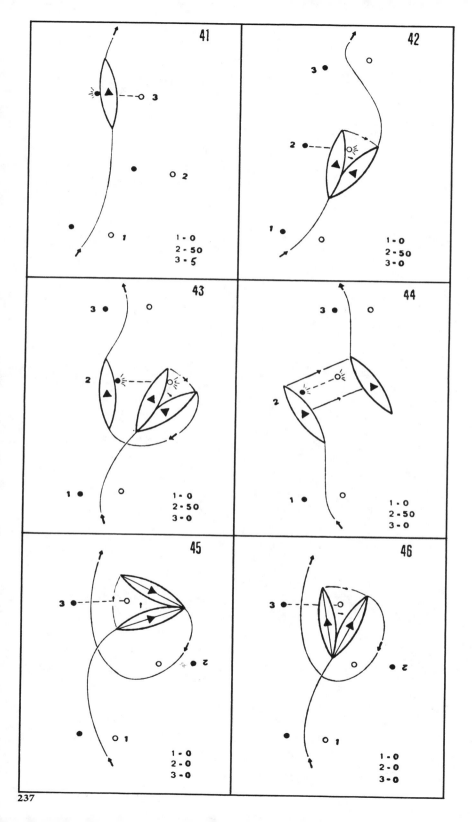

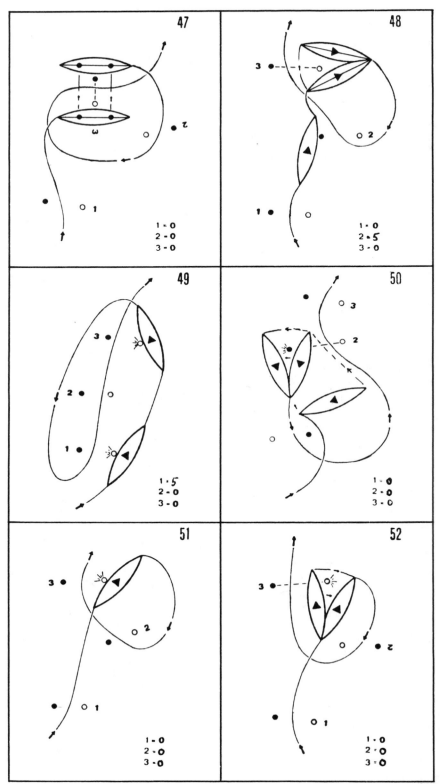

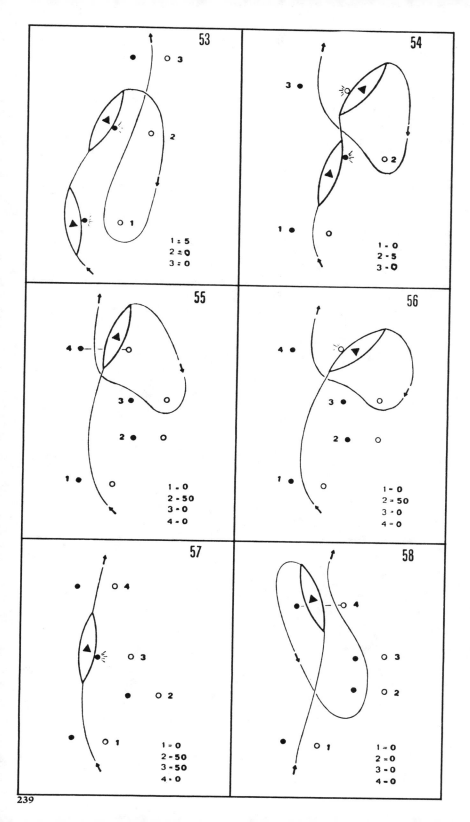

53

1 = 5
2 = 0
3 = 0

54

1 - 0
2 - 5
3 - 0

55

1 - 0
2 - 50
3 - 0
4 - 0

56

1 - 0
2 = 50
3 = 0
4 = 0

57

1 = 0
2 = 50
3 = 50
4 - 0

58

1 = 0
2 = 0
3 - 0
4 - 0

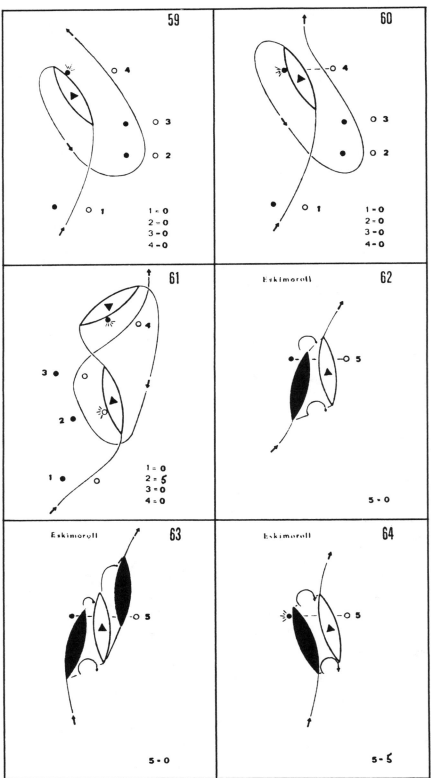

59

1 = 0
2 = 0
3 = 0
4 = 0

60

1 = 0
2 = 0
3 = 0
4 = 0

61

1 = 0
2 = 5
3 = 0
4 = 0

62

Eskimoroll

5 = 0

63

Eskimoroll

5 = 0

64

Eskimoroll

5 = 5

240

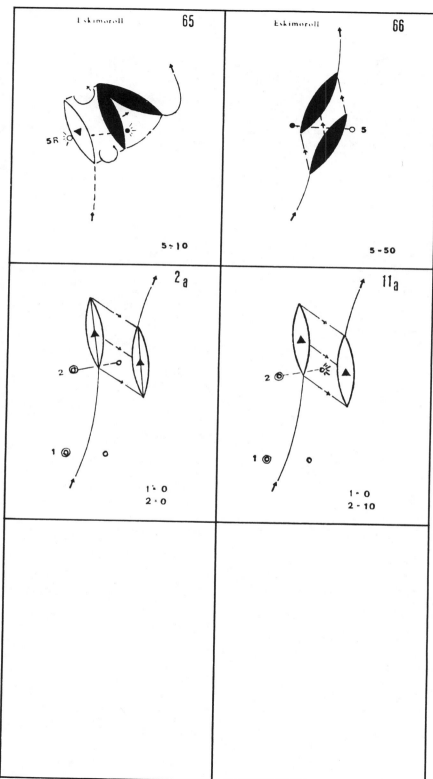

65   Eskimoroll

5R

5 ÷ 10

66   Eskimoroll

5

5 - 50

2a

2

1

1 ÷ 0
2 ÷ 0

11a

2

1

1 - 0
2 - 10

Kayak Schools and Clinics

(See also Organizations and Clubs.)
   The following organizations offer instruction in kayaking. They may range from one day or weekend clinics to courses lasting several weeks in length.

P = Private Location   C = City Recreation   I = Institutional

ALABAMA

Canoe Trails (P)
Broad & Dauphin St.
Mobile, AL 36608
205-344-6433

Cahaba Canoe & Kayaks Too (P)
2468 Cuchura Rd.
Birmingham, AL 35244
205-967-9241

ALASKA

Canoe Alaska (P)
1738 Hilton
Fairbanks, AK 99701
907-456-2999

Valdez Medical Clinic (P)
Box 789
Valdez, AK 99686
907-835-4811

ARIZONA

Grand Canyon Youth Expeditions (P)
R.R. #4, Box 744
Flagstaff, AZ 86001
602-774-8176

ARKANSAS

Ozark Canoe School (P)
Rt. #2, Box 387
Springdale, AR 72764
501-756-9514

Ozark Outdoor Supply (P)
5514 Kavanaugh
Little Rock, AR 72207
501-664-4832

Take A Hike (P)
2611 Kavanaugh
Little Rock, AR 72205
501-664-2423

Moore Outdoors (P)
1001 N. Arkansas
Russellville, AR
501-968-6324

CALIFORNIA

American Touring Assoc. (P)
1307 Harrison St.
Oakland, CA 94612
415-465-9355

California Rivers (P)
P.O. Box 468
Geyserville, CA 95441
707-857-3872

National Outdoor College
P.O. Box 962
Fair Oaks, CA 95628

EPIC Adventures (P)
550 South 1st St.
San Jose, CA 95113
408-294-5676

Otter Bar Lodge
Forks of the Salmon, CA 96031

Robbins Mountain Shop (P)
7257 N. Abbey Rd.
Pinedale, CA 93650
209-431-7152

Sierra Kayak School (P)
P.O. Box 682
Lotus, CA 95651
916-626-3461

Ultrasports Kayak School (P)
P.O. Box 581
Lotus, CA 95651

Western Mountaineering (P)
550 South 1st St.
San Jose, CA 95113
408-298-6300

World Of Whitewater (P)
P.O. Box 708
Big Bar, CA 96010
916-623-6588

Adventure Sports (P)
303 Potreo #15
Santa Cruz, CA 95060
408-423-3648

CANADA

Canadian Outward Bound School (P)
P.O. Box 370
Keremos, B.C. 40X INO
604-499-5582

Madawaska Kanu Camp (P)
2 Tuna Court Don Mills
Toronto, Ont. Canada M3A 3L1

Similkameen Wilderness Centre (P)
Box 97
Cultus Lake B.C. VOX 1H0
858-6775

COLORADO

Aspen Kayak School (P)
P.O. Box 1520
Aspen, CO 81612
303-925-4433

Boulder Kayak School (P)
525 So. 40th St.
Boulder, CO 80303
303-494-2061

Outdoor Leadership Training (P)
P.O. Box 20281
Denver, CO 80220
303-333-7831

Rocky Mountain Kayak Supply (P)
611 East Durant Box 1520
Aspen, CO 81612
303-925-4433

Roger Paris Kayak School (P)
0171 Ute Trail
Carbondale, CO 81623
303-963-2433

CONNECTICUT

Main Stream Outfitters (P)
590 Old Albany Rd.
Canton, CT 06019
203-693-6353

DELAWARE

Wilmington Canoe Trips, Inc. (P)
Wilmington Trail Club
P.O. Box 1184
Wilmington, DE 19899
302-751-5370

IDAHO

Leonard Expeditions (P)
P.O. Box 98
Stanley, ID 83278
208-774-3656

Boise City Recreation (C)
Fort Boise Community Center
Boise, ID 83702

INDIANA

Fluid Fun Canoes (P)
200 East Jackson Blvd.
Elkhart, IN 46514
219-848-4279

St. Joe Valley Canoe & Kayak Club (P)
200 East Jackson Blvd.
Elkhart, Ind. 46514
317-295-6915

Water Meister Sports (P)
P.O. Box 5026
Ft. Wayne, IN 46895

IOWA

Mid America River Voyageurs (P)
Box 125
Spencer, IA 51301
712-262-5630

KANSAS

Trail Phernalia (P)
6404 East Central
Wichita, KS 67218
316-684-8129

LOUISIANA

Canoe & Trail Shop (P)
624 Moss St.
New Orleans, LA 70119
504-488-8528

Delta Wilderness Outfitters (P)
1817 Veterans Blvd.
Metairie, LA 70005
504-835-1932

Outdoors Adventures (P)
410 N. 6th St.
West Monroe, LA 71201
318-387-0128

MAINE

Eastern River Expeditions (P)
P.O. Box 1173
Greenville, ME 04441
207-695-2411

Unicorn Rafting Expeditions (P)
Box 1135
Greenville, ME 04441
207-695-2535

MARYLAND

The Potomac Kayak School (P)
P.O. Box 30061
Bethesda, MD 20014
301-530-8733

MASSACHUSETTS

Hampshire College Kayak Program (I)
% Robert Crown Center
Amherst, MA 01002

Magnolia Boat Co. (P)
11 Lexington Ave.
Magnolia, MA 01930
617-525-3756

MINNESOTA

The Cascaders Kayak & Canoe Club (P)
710 W 98th St.
Bloomington, MN 53420
612-884-4315

MISSOURI

Mountain People, Inc. (P)
836 North Glenstone
Springfield, MO 65802
417-869-0775

Wilderness Access (P)
4110 Baltimore
Kansas City, MO 64111
816-531-6185

San Souci River Sports (P)
Rt. #5, Box 121
Joplin, MO 64801
417-623-0253

MONTANA

The Trailhead (P)
501 South Higgins
Missoula, MT 59801
406-543-6996

Outdoor Rescources Center (I)
University of Montana
Missoula, MT 59801
406-243-5072

NEW HAMPSHIRE

Ledyard Canoe Club (I)
Dartmouth College
Hanover, NH 03755
603-646-2753

Saco Bound (P)
Box 113
Center Conway, NH 03813
603-447-2177

NEW JERSEY

Boats & Paddles (P)
11 Hillview Dr.
Madison, NJ 07940
201-377-5569

NEW YORK

The Original Waveskis (P)
86 Lafayette Dr.
Mastic Beach, NY 11951
516-281-6650

West Side Boat Shop (P)
254 Rano St.
Buffalo, NY 14222
716-883-8548

NORTH CAROLINA

Nantahala Outdoor Center (P)
Star Rt. Box 68
Bryson City, NC 28713
704-488-2175

New River Outfitters (P)
P.O. Box 433
Jefferson, NC 28640
919-246-7711

University of North Carolina at
   Charlotte (I)
Cone University Center UNCC Station
Charlotte, NC 28223
704-597-2521

OHIO

Base Camp, Inc. (P)
1600 W. Mill Ave.
Peninsula, OH 44264
216-657-2110

Blackhand Gorge Canoe Livery (P)
1101 Staddens Bridge Rd.
Newark, OH 43055
614-763-4000

River Horizons, Inc. (P)
Box 395
Neapolis, OH 43547
419-875-5292

OREGON

Aquarian Enterprises (P)
1088 S.E. Oak St.
Milwaukie, OR 97222

Rivers West (P)
2909 Hilyard
Eugene, OR 97405
503-686-0798

Sundance Expeditions (P)
14894 Galice Rd.
Merlin, OR 97532
503-479-8508

Portland Community College (I)
4336 N.E. 20th Place
Portland, OR 97211
503-246-6985
or 503-284-6412

PENNSYLVANIA

Bottoms Up Canoe Club (I)
RD #2, Box 266
Pittsfield, PA 16340
814-563-7138

Coats Canoes (P)
1 Walnut Valley Rd.
Chadds Ford, PA 19317
215-388-7613

Love's Canoe Rentals (P)
Hilltop Drive Box 17
Ridgeway, PA 15853
717-776-6285

Pocono Whitewater Center (P)
Box 44 Rt. 903
Jim Thorpe, PA 18229
717-325-3656

River Path Outfitters (P)
R.D. #1, Box 15B
Confluence, PA 15424
814-395-3136

Riversport School of Paddling (P)
P.O. Box 100
Ohiopyle, PA 15470

Whitewater Challengers (P)
Star Route 6A1, Box C
White Haven, PA 18661

Wildwater Outfitters (P)
46 South Pershing Ave.
York, PA 17401
717-846-3132

SOUTH CAROLINA

Alpine Outfitters (P)
P.O. Box 18143
Hillcrest Shopping Center
Spartanburg, SC 29318
803-583-8688

Wildwater Ltd. (P)
General Delivery
Long Creek, SC 29658
803-647-5336

TENNESSEE

C&C Canoe Crunchers (P)
Box 42 Rt. #1
Winchester, TN 37398
615-967-3008

Cumberland Transit (P)
2807 West End Ave.
Nashville, TN
615-327-4093

Nolichucky Expeditions (P)
P.O. Box 484
Erwin, TN 37650
615-743-3221

TEXAS

Far Flung Adventures (P)
P.O. Box 31
Terlinga, TX 79852
915-371-2489

Whitewater Experience (P & I)
3835 Farnham
Houston, TX 77098
713-721-7299

Goynes Canoe Livery (P)
Rt. #1, Box 55R
Martindale, TX 78655
512-357-6125

UTAH

Slickrock Kayaks
P.O. Box 1400
Moab, UT 84532

Moki Mac River Expeditions (P)
6829 Bella Vista Dr.
Salt Lake City, UT 84121
801-564-3361

Timberline Sporting Goods (P)
3155 Highland Dr.
Salt Lake City, UT 84106
801-466-2101

Whitewater Sports (P & I)
3495 W. 8245 S
West Jordan, UT 84084
801-255-2295

VIRGINIA

Appomattox River Company (P)
P.O. Box 68, 610 N. Main St.
Farmville, VA 23901
804-392-6645

James River Experience (P)
11010 Midlothian Tpk.
Richmond, VA 23235
804-794-3493

New River Canoe Livery (P)
P.O. Box 188
Ripplemead, VA 24150
804-626-7189

Wilderness Challenge School (P)
P.O. Box 809
Norfolk, VA 23501

Wind & Water Sports (P)
7720 Lisle Ave.
Falls Church, VA 22043
703-821-1053

WASHINGTON

NWOC (P)
P.O. Box 3116
Seattle, WA 98103
206-523-1982

Whitewater Sports, Inc. (P)
817 No. 1 St.
Tacoma, WA
206-627-8068

WEST VIRGINIA

Appalachian Wildwater (P)
P.O. Box 126
Albright, WV 26519
800-624-8060

Class VI River Runners (P)
P.O. Box 264
Fayetteville, WV 25862

Class VI River Runners (P)
P.O. Box 78
Lansing, WV 25862
304-574-0704

Cooper Canoes (P)
401 Dunbar Ave.
Dunbar, WV 25064
304-965-3552

North American River Runners (P)
P.O. Box 81
Hico, WV 25854
304-658-5276

Trans Montane Outfitters (P)
P.O. Box 325
Davis, WV 26260
304-259-5117

WISCONSIN

Steeds Wolf River Lodge (P)
White Lake, WI 54491
715-882-2182

Wheel & Sprocket (P)
10575 N. Forrest Home Ave.
Hales Corner, WI 53130
414-425-7930

Whitewater Specialty (P)
White Lake, WI 54491
715-882-2182

Hike Out Ltd. (P)
#3 Menard Plaza
Wausau, WI 54401
715-842-0805

WYOMING

Snake River Kayak School (P)
P.O. Box 1533
Jackson, WY 83001
307-733-3595

Teton Mountaineering (P)
P.O. Box 153
Jackson, WY 83001
307-733-3595

Periodicals

American Whitewater
% Bart Jackson
7 Holland Lane
Cranbury, NJ 08512
(Published bimonthly)

Canoe
2410 No. Clinton
Fort Wayne, IN 46805
(Published six times per year)

Canoeing
Ocean Publications Ltd.
34 Buckingham Palace Road
London SW1W ORE England
(Published monthly)

International Canoeing
The International Canoe Federation
    Bulletin
% Hans Egon Vesper, Am Muhlenberg
19/V D-4100 Duisburg 1
Federal Republic of Germany

River Runner Magazine
Powell Butte, OR 97753
(Published quarterly)

River Safety Task Force Newsletter
230 Penllyn Pike
Penllyn, PA 19422
(Published twice a year)

The American Canoeist
P.O. Box 248
Lorton, VA 22079
(Bimonthly Newsletter of the American
    Canoe Association)

Whitewater Program
Box 210, RD #2
Palmerton, PA 18071
(Published annually)

Organizations and Clubs

(See also Kayak Schools and Clinics)

ALABAMA

North Alabama River Runners
8120 Hickory Hill Lane
Huntsville, AL 35802

ALASKA

Alaska Kayak Club
5413 Emmanuel Ave.
Anchorage, AK 99504

Alaska Rivers Company
P.O. Box 827
Cooper Landing, AK 99572

Alaska Whitewater Association
Bill Kenyon
Glenn Allen, AK 99588

Knik Kanoers and Kayakers
3014 Columbia
Anchorage, AK 99504

Valdez Alpine Club
P.O. Box 1872
Valdez, AK 99686

ARIZONA

Dry Wash Canoe and Kayak Club
Chemistry Department
Arizona State University
Tempe, AZ 85281

Northern Arizona Paddlers Club
P.O. Box 1224
Flagstaff, AZ 86002

ARKANSAS

The Bow and Stern
1408 Rockwood Trail
Fayetteville, AR 72701

Arkansas Canoe Club
1408 Rockwood Terrace
Fayetteville, AR 72701

CALIFORNIA

Alpine West
1021 R Street
Sacramento, CA 95805

American Guides Association
P.O. Box B
Woodland, CA 95695

American Youth Hostels
Santa Clara Valley Club
5493 Blossom Wood Avenue
San Jose, CA 95124

Antioch Whitewater Club
40 North Lake Drive
Antioch, CA 94509

Bear Boaters
6925 Wilton Drive
Oakland, CA 94611

Cakara
675 Overhill Drive
Redding, CA 96001

Chasm Outing Club
Box 5622
Orange, CA 92667

Echo Wilderness
2424 Russell St.
Berkeley, CA 94705

Feather River Kayak Club
1773 Broadway Street
Marysville, CA 95901

Haystackers Whitewater Canoe Club
P.O. Box 675
Kernville, CA 93238

Idlewild Yacht Club
800 Market Street
San Francisco, CA 94102

Lera Canoe Club
200 Almond Ave.
Los Altos, CA 94022

Lerc Voyageurs Canoe and Kayak Club
12814 Arminta Street
North Hollywood, CA 91605

Lorien Canoe Club
P.O. Box 1238
Vista, CA 92083

Marin Canoe Club
P.O. Box 3023
San Rafael, CA 94902

Mother Lode Whitewater Experience
Pacific High School
581 Continental Drive
San Jose, CA 95111

Outdoor Adventures
688 Sutter St.
San Francisco, CA 94102

Outdoors Unlimited
Millberry Union Recreation Dept.
500 Parnassus
San Francisco, CA 94143

Powell Boating Club
University Calif. Berkeley
5499 Claremont Avenue
Oakland, CA 94618

RAFT Kayak School
Box 682
Lotus, CA 95657

Sierra Club Loma Prieta Paddlers
185 Loucks Ave.
Los Altos, CA 94022

Sierra Club River Touring Bay Chapter
62 Hancock Street
San Francisco, CA 94102

Sierra Club T.S.
1760 Walnut Street
Berkeley, CA 94709

Southern California Canoe Association
3906 Mento Avenue
Los Angeles, CA 90037

The Confluence
Box 76
Vallecito, CA 95251

Tomales Bay Kayak Club
Box 468
Point Reyes Station, CA 94956

Truckee River Kayaks
Box 1592
Tahoe City, CA 95730

Valley Canoe Club
10363 Calvin Avenue
Los Angeles, CA 90025

Voyageur Canoe & Kayak Club
12814 Arminta Street
No. Hollywood, CA 91605

Western Mountaineering
550 South First Street
San Jose, CA 95108

Westlake Canoe Club
3437 Gloria
Newbury Park, CA 91320

Whitewater Voyages
River Exploration Ltd.
1225 Liberty Street
El Cerrito, CA 94530

YMCA of San Joaquin County
640 North Center Street
Stockton, CA 95202

COLORADO

Aspen Kayak School
P.O. Box 1520
Aspen, CO 81611

Colorado Kayak Club
University of Colorado
Boulder, CO 80309

Colorado Rivers
P.O. Box 1386
Durango, CO 81301

Colorado State Whitewater Club
Activities Center Box 411
Colorado State University
Fort Collins, CO 80533

Colorado White Water Association
4260 East Evans Avenue
Denver, CO 80222

Fibark, Inc.
Box 762
Salida, CO 81201

National Organization for River Sports
314 North 20th Street
Colorado Springs, CO 80904

Otero Junior College Recreation Club
La Junta, CO 81050

Whitewater Expeditions
P.O. Box 9541
Colorado Springs, CO 80932

CONNECTICUT

AMC Connecticut Chapter
20 Dyer Avenue
Collinsville, CT 06022

Amston Lake Canoe Club
Deepwood Drive
Amston, CT 06231

Columbia Canoe Club
Lake Road
Columbia, CT 06237

Good Earth Inc.
539 Broad Street
Meriden, CT 06450

Great World
250 Farms Village Road
West Simsbury, CT 06092

OGRCC Family Paddlers
20 Arcadia Road
Old Greenwich, CT 06870

University of Connecticut Outing Club
Box 110
Holcom Hall
University of Connecticut
Storrs, CT 06268

Waterford Canoe Club
Box 111
Waterford, CT 06385

Water Works
Box 111
Cornwall Bridge, CT 06754

DELAWARE

Buck Ridge Ski Club
R.D. #1, Box 426 E
Arthur Drive Wellington Hills
Hockessin, DE 19707

Wilmington Trail Club
324 Spaulding Road
Wilmington, DE 19803

DISTRICT OF COLUMBIA

Potomac Boat Club
3530 Water Street, NW
Washington, DC 20007

Washington Canoe Club
3700 K Street, NW
Washington, DC 20007

FLORIDA

Citrus County Kayak Club
Route L, Box 475
Floral City, FL 32636

Everglades Canoe Club
239 Northeast 20th Street
Delray Beach, FL 33440

Florida Sport Paddling Club
133 Hickory Lane
Seffner, FL 33584

Polivalues Inc.
101 Maplewood Avenue
Clearwater, FL 33515

Seminole Canoe and Yacht Club
5653 Windermere Drive
Jacksonville, FL 32211

GEORGIA

Camp Merrie-wood
3245 Nancy Creek Road, NW
Atlanta, GA 30327

Coweta County Canoe Club
P.O. Box 1218
Newman, GA 30264

Dean's Club
6277 Roswell Road, NE
Atlanta, GA 30328

Explorer Post 49
1506 Brawley Circle
Atlanta, GA 30313

Georgia Canoeing Association
Box 7023
Atlanta, GA 30309

HAWAII

Kayak Club
407 D Keariani Street
Kailea, HI 69734

International Hawaiian Canoe
  Association
1638 A Kona
Honolulu, HI 96814

IDAHO

American Indian Center Canoe Club
115 North Walnut
Boise, ID 83702

Idaho Alpine Club
1953 Melody
Idaho Falls, ID 83401

Idaho State Outdoor Club
Box 9024, I.S.U.
Pocatello, ID 83209

Northwest River Supplies
430 West 3rd Street
P.O. Box 9186
Moscow, ID 83843

Sawtooth Wildwater Club
1255 Elm Street
Mountain Home, ID 83647

ILLINOIS

American Youth Hostels
3712 North Clark Street
Chicago, IL 60613

Belleville Whitewater Club
No. 3 Oakwood
Belleville, IL 62223

Caterpillar Canoe Club
344 West Arnold Road
Sandwich, IL 60548

Chicago Whitewater Association
5460 South Ridgewood Court
Chicago, IL 60629

G.L.O.P. Kayak Club
1510 Lombard Avenue
Berwin, IL 60402

Illinois Paddling Council
2316 Prospect Avenue
Evanston, IL 60201

Le Brigade Illinois
451 South St. Mary's Road
Libertyville, IL 60018

Lincoln Park Boat Club
2737 North Hampden Court
Chicago, IL 60614

Mackinaw Canoe Club
120 Circle Drive
East Peoria, IL 61611

Northern Prairie Outfitters
206 N.W. Highway
Fox River Grove, IL 60021

Prairie Club Canoeists
517 Miller Road
Barrington, IL 60010

Prairie State Canoeists
5055 North Kildare Avenue
Chicago, IL 60630

Sauk Valley Canoe Club
R.R. #2
Morrison, IL 61270

Sierra Club Canoeists
625 West Barry
Chicago, IL 60657

Southern Illinois Canoe & Kayak Club
R.R. #1 Box 263
Makunda, IL 62958

St. Charles Canoe Club
1074 Cherry Lane
Lombard, IL 60148

Tippecanoers
1270 West Green Street
Decatur, IL 62521

University of Chicago Whitewater Club
933 East 56th Street
Chicago, IL 60637

Chicago Whitewater Association
5460 South Ridgewood Court
Chicago, IL 60629

Wildcountry Wilderness Outfitters
516 North Main Street
Bloomington, IL 61701

INDIANA

Bloomington Canoe and Kayak Club
2221 Maxwell
Bloomington, IN 47401

Connersville Canoe Club
R.R. #3
Connersville, IN 47331

Elkhart YMCA Canoe Club
229 West Franklin Street
Elkhart, IN 46514

Hoosier Canoe Club
824 Aumen East Drive
Carmel, IN 46032

Kekionga Voyageurs
1517 Werling Road
New Haven, IN 46774

Maumee Whitewater Club
9962 Diebolo Rd.
Fort Wayne, IN 46825

Paddle Pushers Canoe Club
2506 Rainbow Drive
Lafayette, IN 47904

Prairie Club Canoeists
364 Rose Ellen Drive
Crown Point, IN 46307

Purdue Canoe Club
% Recreational Gym
Purdue University
West Lafayette, IN 47906

St. Joe Valley Canoe & Kayak Club
112 North Second Street
Elkhart, IN 46514

Sugar Creek Paddlers
R.R. #8
Crawfordsville, IN 47933

Tukunu Club
952 Riverside Drive
South Bend, IN 46616

Whitewater Valley Canoe Club
1032 Cliff Street
Brookville, IN 47012

Wild American Paddlers
R.R. #7 Box 66D
Greenfield, IN 46140

IOWA

Mid-America River Voyageurs
Box 125
Spencer, IA 51301

KANSAS

Johnson County Canoe Club
7832 Rosewood Lane
Prairie Village, KA 66208

KENTUCKY

Blue Grass Pack & Paddle Club
216 Inverness Drive
Lexington, KY 40503

Bluegrass Wildwater Association
Box 4231
Lexington, KY 40504

Four Rivers Canoe Club
523 Alben Barkley Drive
Paducah, KY 42001

Kentucky Canoe Association
2006 Marilee Drive
Louisville, KY 40272

Louisville Paddle Club
Route #1
Smithfield, KY 40068

Sage School of Outdoors
209 East High Street
Lexington, KY 40507

Viking Canoe Club
5117 West Pages Lane
Pleasure Ridge Park, KY 40258

LOUISIANA

Bayou Haystackers
624 Moss Street
New Orleans, LA 70119

MAINE

ANorAK (The Association of North-
   Atlantic Kayakers)
% James Chute
R.R. #3 Box 20B
Freeport, ME 04032

Bates Outing Club
Box 580
Bates College
Lewiston, ME 04240

Mattawamkeag Wilderness Park
P.O. Box 104
Mattawamkeag, ME 04459

Penobscot Paddle and Chowder
   Association
Box 121
Stillwater, ME 04489

Saco Bound Canoe & Kayak Club
Fryeburg, ME 04037

Sunrise County Canoe Expeditions
Cathance Lake
Grove, ME 04638

MARYLAND

Appalachian River Runners Federation
Box 107
McHenry, MD 21541

Baltimore Kayak Club
1099 Tollgate Rd.
Bel Air, MD 21014

Mason Dixon Canoe Cruisers
222 Pleasant Terrace
Hagerstown, MD 21740

Monacy Canoe Club
Box 1083
Frederick, MD 21701

Potomac River Paddlers
Sea Scouts #489
18505 Kingshill Rd.
Germantown, MD 20767

St. Mary's College of Maryland
Outing Club
St. Mary's City, MD 20686

Terrapin Trail Club
University of Maryland
Box 18 Student Union Building
College Park, MD 20742

MASSACHUSETTS

AMC Berkshire Chapter
Knollwood Drive
East Longmeadow, MA 01028

AMC Boston Chapter
5 Joy Street
Boston, MA 02108

Cochituate Canoe Club
99 Dudley Road
Cochituate, MA 01760

Decorum Paddlers Ltd.
% R.C.C.
Hampshire College
Amherst, MA 01002

Experiment With Travel Inc.
Box 2452
281 Franklin Street
Springfield, MA 01101

Foxboro Camp Canoe Club
32 Taunton Street
Bellingham, MA 02019

Hampshire College Kayak Program
Robert Crown Center
Hampshire College
Amherst, MA 01002

Kayak & Canoe Club of Boston
Bolton Road
Harvard, MA 01451

Lake Chaogg Canoe Club
P.O. Box 512
Webster, MA 01570

MIT Whitewater Club
R 6432 M.I.T.
Cambridge, MA 02139

Northeast Sports & Recreation
  Association
2 Fairmont Terrace
Wakefield, MA 01880

Northeast Voyageurs
West Street
Kingston, MA 02360

Waumpanoag Paddlers
13 Borden Street
North Scituate, MA 02060

Westfield River Canoe Club
90 West Silver Street
Westfield, MA 01085

MICHIGAN

Clinton River Canoe School
23705 Audrey
Warren, MI 48901

Kalamazoo Down Streamers
6820 Evergreen
Kalamazoo, MI 49002

Lansing Canoe Club
6101 Norburn Way
Lansing, MI 48910

Lower Michigan Paddling Council
8266 Patton
Detroit, MI 48228

Michigan Canoe Race Association
4735 Hillcrest
Trenton, MI 48183

Michigan Trailfinders Club
2630 Rockhill NE
Grand Rapids, MI 49505

Niles Kayak Club
Rte #1 Box 83
Buchanan, MI 49107

Raw Strength & Courage Kayakers
2022 Day Street
Ann Arbor, MI 48104

MINNESOTA

Big Water Associates
1905 River Hills Drive
Burnsville, MN 55337

Boat Busters Anonymous
2961 Hemingway Avenue
St. Paul, MN 55119

Cascaders Canoe and Kayak Club
3128 West Calhoun Boulevard
Minneapolis, MN 55416

Minnesota Canoe Association Inc.
Box 14177
Union Station
Minneapolis, MN 55414

MISSISSIPPI

Bayou Haystackers
112 Grosvenor
Waveland, MS 39576

Msubee Canoe Club
P.O. Box 3317
Mississippi State University
State College, MS 39672

Paddle Pushers Canoe Club
All Saints School
Vicksburg, MS 39180

MISSOURI

Arnold Whitewater Association
480 Pine Court
Arnold, MO 63010

CMS College Outing Club
% Biology Department
Warrensburg, MO 64093

Meramec River Canoe Club
26 Lake Road
Fenton, MO 63026

Ozark Cruisers
#1 Blue Acres Trailer Court
Columbia, MO 65201

Ozarks Wilderness Waterways Club
Box 16032
Kansas City, MO 64112

University of Missouri
Wilderness Adventures Committee
18 Read Hall
Columbia, MO 65201

MONTANA

Montana Kayak Club
Box 2
Brady, MT 59416

Adventures West
1401½ 5th Ave So.
Great Falls, MT 59405

Studies in Recreation
Dept. of HPER
University of Montana
Missoula, MT 59801

NEBRASKA

Fort Kearney Canoeists
2623 Avenue D
Kearney, NB 68847

NEVADA

Basic High Canoe Club
751 Palo Verde Drive
Henderson, NV 89015

NEW HAMPSHIRE

AMC New Hampshire Chapter
175 St. Anselm's Drive
Manchester, NH 03102

Androscoggin Canoe & Kayak Club
Lancaster, NH 03584

Coos County Cruisers
% Weeks Memorial Library
Lancaster, NH 03584

Ledyard Canoe Club
Robinson Hall
Hanover, NH 03755

Mad Pemi Canoe Club
93 Realty
Campton, NH 03223

Mad Pemi Canoe & Kayak Club
Box B
Campton, NH 03223

Merrimack Valley Paddlers
40 Dracut Road
Hudson, NH 03051

Mt. Washington Valley Canoe &
Kayak Club
Box 675
North Conway, NH 03860

Nulhegan Paddle Company
Box 381
North Stratford, NH 03690

NEW JERSEY

Adventures Unlimited
Box 186
Belvedere, NJ 07823

Kayak & Canoe Club of New York
6 Winslow Avenue
East Brunswick, NJ 08816

Knickerbocker Canoe Club
1263 River Rd.
Edgewater, NJ 07020

Mohawk Canoe Club
455 West State Street
Trenton, NJ 08618

Murray Hill Canoe Club
Bell Laboratories
Murray Hill, NJ 07974

Neversink Canoe Sailing Society
Oak Tree Lane
Rumson, NJ 07760

New York-New Jersey River
Conference
52 West Union Ave.
Bound Brook, NJ 08805

Red Dragon Canoe Club
221 Edgewater Avenue
Edgewater Park, NJ 08010

Rutgers University Outdoor Club
RPO 2913
New Brunswick, NJ 08903

Wanda Canoe Club
47 Summit Street
Ridgefield Park, NJ 07660

NEW MEXICO

Albuquerque Whitewater Club
804 Warm Sands Drive SE
Albuquerque, NM 87112

Rio Grande River Runners
2210 Central Avenue, SE
Albuquerque, NM 87106

NEW YORK

Adirondack Mt. Club
769 John Glenn Road
Webster, NY 14580

Adirondack Mt. Club
Genesee Valley Chapter
581 Lake Road
Webster, NY 14580

Adirondack Mountain Club
Schenectady Chapter
Schuyler 16 Netherlands Village
Schenectady, NY 12308

AMC New York Chapter
23 High Street
Katonah, NY 10536

AMC New York Chapter
Midland South, Box 1956
Syosset, NY 11791

American Youth Hostels
6 Cardinal Court
West Nyack, NY 10994

Boulder Bashers Canoe Club
353 Seneca Road
Hornell, NY 14843

Champaign Canoeing Ltd.
Brayton Park
Ossining, NY 10562

Colgate University Outing Club
% Recreation Office
Colgate University
Hamilton, NY 13346

Genesee Down River Paddlers
RD – 2 Proctor Road
Wellsville, NY 14895

Hibernia Canoe & Kayak Association
Masten Road
Pleasant Valley, NY 12538

Inwood Canoe Club
509 West 212 Street
New York, NY 10036

Ka Na Wa Ke Canoe Club
26 Pickwick Road
Dewitt, NY 13214

Kayak & Canoe Club of Cooperstown
Riverbrink
Cooperstown, NY 13326

Kayak & Canoe Club of New York
6 Winslow Avenue
East Brunswick, NJ 08816

Metropolitan Canoe & Kayak Club
150 Amsterdam Avenue
New York, NY 10023

Niagara Gorge Kayak Club
41 17th Street
Buffalo, NY 14213

Northern New York Paddlers
Box 228
Schenectady, NY 12301

New York Whitewater Club
110 Bleecker Street
New York, NY 10012

Otterkill Canoe Club
5 Yankee Main Lane
Goshen, NY 10924

Sebago Canoe Club
9622 Avenue M
Brooklyn, NY 11236

Sierra Canoe Club Committee
5 Lakeview Avenue
North Tarrytown, NY 10591

Sport Rites Club
Brayton Park
Ossining, NY 10562

Tasca Canoe Club
P.O. Box 41
Oakland Gardens, NY 11364

Wellsville Downriver Paddlers
Proctor Road
Wellsville, NY 10701

Wild River Canoe Supplies
Ludington Road
Holmes, NY 12531

W.I.M.P.S.
4671 West Ridge Road
Rochester, NY 14626

Yonkers Canoe Club
360 Edwards Place
Yonkers, NY 10701

NORTH CAROLINA

Asheville YMCA Kayak Club
30 Woodfin Street
Asheville, NC 28801

Carolina Canoe Club
Box 9011
Greensboro, NC 27408

Nantahala Outdoor Center
Star Route Box 68
Bryson City, NC 28713

Raleigh Ski & Outing Club
5117 Melborne Road
Raleigh, NC 27606

River Runner's Emporium
3535 Hillsboro Road
Durham, NC 27705

Watauga Whitewater Club
State Farm Road
Boone, NC 28607

OHIO

American Youth Hostels
Columbus Council
1421 Inglis Ave.
Columbus, OH 43212

Antioch Kayak Club
Physical Education Department
Antioch College
Yellow Springs, OH 45387

Cincinnati Inland Surf Team
7360 Aracoma Forest Drive
Cincinnati, OH 45237

Columbus Council
American Youth Hostel
1421 Inglis Avenue
Columbus, OH 43212

Cuyahoga Canoe Club
Box T
Mantua, OH 44255

Dayton Canoe Club Inc.
1020 Riverside Drive
Dayton, OH 45405

Keel Haulers Canoe Club
1649 Allen Drive
Westlake, OH 44145

Madhatter's Canoe Club
1390 So. Belvoir Blvd.
South Euclid, OH 44121

Mr. Canoe
425 Anthony Wayne Trail
#214
Waterville, OH 43566

Outdoor Adventure Club
2845 Liberty Ellerton Road
Dayton, OH 45418

Pack & Paddle
4082 Erie Street
Willoughby, OH 44094

Toledo Area Canoe and Kayak Club
5837 Elden Street
Sylvania, OH 43560

Valley Voyageurs
5848 Montgomery Road
Cincinnati, OH 45212

Warner & Swasey Canoe Club
406 Millave, SW
New Philadelphia, OH 44663

Wilderness Adventures
256 Forrer Boulevard
Dayton, OH 45419

OKLAHOMA

O.K. Canoers
3112 Chaucer Drive
Village, OK 73120

Tulsa Canoeing and Camping Club
5810 East 30 Place
Tulsa, OK 74114

OREGON

Lower Columbia Canoe Club
Rte 1 Box 134E
Scappoose, OR 97056

Mary Kayak Club
830 Northwest, 23rd #17
Cornallis, OR 97330

Northeast Outward Bound School
3200 Judkins Rd
Eugene, OR 97403

Oregon Kayak & Canoe Club
Box 692
Portland, OR 97205

Oregon Rafting Club
Rte 1 Box 300
Hubbard, OR 97032

Outdoor Recreation Centre
Oregon State University
Corvallis, OR 97331

Southern Oregon Kayak Club
8890 Rogue River Way
Rogue River, OR 97537

Sundance Expeditions
14894 Galice Road
Merlin, OR 97532

Wilderness Waterways
12260 Galice Road
Merlin, OR 97532

Willamette Kayak & Canoe Club
P.O. Box 1062
Corvallis, OR 97331

PENNSYLVANIA

Allegheny Canoe Club
755 West Spring St.
Titusville, PA 16354

Allentown Hiking Club
124 South 16th Street
Allentown, PA 18102

AMC Delaware Valley Chapter
306 Crestview Circle
Media, PA 19063

American Youth Hostel Delaware
    Valley Chapter
4714 York Road
Philadelphia, PA 19141

American Youth Hostel Pittsburgh
6300 5th Avenue
Pittsburgh, PA 15232

Appalachian Trail Outfitters
29 South Main Street
Doylestown, PA 18901

Benscreek Canoe Club
RD 5 Box 256
Johnstown, PA 15905

Bottoms Up Canoe Club
RD #2 Box 266
Pittsfield, PA 16340

Bucknell Outing Club
Box C 1610
Bucknell University
Lewisburg, PA 17837

Buck Ridge Ski Club
986 Anders Road
Lansdale, PA 19446

Conewago Canoe Club
2267 Willow Road
York, PA 17404

Delaware Canoe Club
14 South 14th Street
Enston, PA 18042

Endless Mountain Voyageurs
285 Shorthill Road
Clarks Green, PA 18411

Eastern River Touring Association
Box 451
State College, PA 16802

Explorer Post 65
22 Caralpa Place
Pittsburgh, PA 15228

Fox Chapel Canoe Club
610 Squaw Run Road
Pittsburgh, PA 15238

Harrisburg Area Whitewater Club
Box 2525
Harrisburg, PA 17105

Harrison Area Community College
    Outdoor Club
3300 Cameron Street
Harrisburg, PA 17110

Indiana University Outing Club
Chemistry, IUP
Indiana, PA 15701

Keystone River Runners
1785 Water Street
Indiana, PA 15701

Kishacoquillas Canoe and Rafting
% Wilderness P.O. Box 97
Ohiopyle, PA 15470

Lehigh Valley Canoe Club
P.O. Box 877
Easton, PA 18042

Mohawk Canoe Club
6 Canary Road
Levittown, PA 19057

Mt, Streams & Trails Outfitters
Box 106
Ohiopyle, PA 15470

North Allegheny River Rats
1130 Sandalwood Lane
Pittsburgh, PA 15237

North Hills YMCA Wildwater Club
1130 Sandalwood Lane
Pittsburgh, PA 15237

Oil City Canoe Club
Rte 62 Rd 2
Oil City, PA 16301

Oil Creek Valley Canoe Club
214 North 1st Street
Titusville, PA 16354

Paoli Troop 1 BSA
432 Strafford Avenue
Wayne, PA 19087

Penn State Outing Club
118 South Buckhout Street
State College, PA 16801

Penn Hills Wildwater Canoe Club
12200 Garland Drive
Pittsburgh, PA 15235

Philadelphia Canoe Club
4900 Ridge Avenue
Philadelphia, PA 19128

Pittsburgh Council
American Youth Hostel
6300 5th Avenue
Pittsburgh, PA 15213

Post 42 B.S.A.
Rte 2
Palmerton, PA 19053

Scranton Kayak Club
118 Crown Avenue
Scranton, PA 18505

Scudder Falls Wildwater Club
795 River Road
Yardley, PA 19067

Shenonga Valley Canoe Club
863 Bechtal Avenue
Sharon, PA 16146

Slippery Rock State College
Outing Club
Slippery Rock, PA 16057

Sylvan Canoe Club
132 Arch Street
Verona, PA 15213

Wilderness Voyageurs
Box 97
Ohiopyle, PA 15470

Wildwater Boating Club
LD 179
Bellefonte, PA 16823

Wildwater Rafting Club
326 West Gay Street
York, PA 17404

Wild Rivers Photo Service
Box 1049
Uniontown, PA 15401

Williamsport Y.M.C.A. Canoe Club
343 West 4th Street
Williamsport, PA 17701

RHODE ISLAND

Rhode Island Canoe Association
64 Eleventh Street
Providence, RI 02906

Rhode Island Whitewater Club
10 Pond Street
Wakefield, RI 02879

Summit Shop
185 Wayland Avenue
Providence, RI 02906

SOUTH CAROLINA

Carolina Paddlers
112 Pine Street
Walterboro, SC 29488

Carolina Wildwater Canoeing
  Association
3412 Harvard Avenue
Columbia, SC 29205

Palmetto Kayakers
210 Irene Street
North Augusta, SC 29381

Sierra Canoe Club
P.O. Box 163
Clemson, SC 29631

Savannah River Paddlers
Explorer Ship 121 Sea Scout 404
1211 Woodbine Road
Aiken, SC 29801

TENNESSEE

Baylor School Kayak Club
Chattanooga, TN 37401

Bluff City Canoe Club
Box 4523
Memphis, TN 38104

Carbide Canoe Club
104 Ulena Lane
Oak Ridge, TN 37830

Chota Canoe Club
Box 8270 University Station
Knoxville, TN 37916

East Tennessee Whitewater Club
Box 3074
Oak Ridge, TN 37830

Footsloggers
P.O. Box 3865 CRS
Johnson City, TN 37601

Nolichucky Expeditions Inc.
Box 484
Erwin, TN 37650

Outdoor Expeditions
P.O. Box 396
Tellico Plains, TN 37385

Sewanee Ski & Outing Club
University of the South
Sewanee, TN 37375

Tennessee Hiking and Canoe Club
University of Tennessee
Rte 6
Concord, TN 37730

Tenn-Tucky Lake Canoe & Camping
   Club
Rte 1 Box 23-A
Tennessee Ridge, TN 37178

Tennessee Scenic Rivers Association
Box 3104
Nashville, TN 37219

Tennessee Valley Canoe Club
Box 11125
Chattanooga, TN 37401

TEXAS

Down Hill Yacht Club
12802 La Quinta
San Antonio, TX 78233

Down River Club—Dallas
1412 Oak Lea
Irving, TX 75061

Explorer Post 425
708 Mercedes
Fort Worth, TX 76126

Explorer Post 151
2008 Bedford
Midland, TX 79701

Greater Fort Worth Sierra Club
River Touring Section
525 NW Hillery
Burleson, TX 76028

Heart of Texas Canoe Club
Box 844
Temple, TX 76501

Houston Canoe Club
3116 Broadway
Houston, TX 77017

Kayaks Limited
4110 Markham Street
Houston, TX 77027

Permian Basin Whitewater Association
501 A, 56th Street
Odessa, TX 79762

R & M Outfitters
2534 Teague
Houston, TX 77080

Texas Explorers Club
Box 844
Temple, TX 76501

Texas Whitewater Association
P.O. Box 5264
Austin, TX 78763

Trinity Univ. Canoe Club
Box 180 715 Stadium Drive
San Antonio, TX 78284

UTAH

VTE Alpine Club—River Trips
Union Building University of Utah
Salt Lake City, UT 84112

Wasatch Mountain Canoe Club
904 Military Drive
Salt Lake City, UT 84108

Wasatch Whitewater Association
161 South 11 East
Salt Lake City, UT 84102

VERMONT

Brattleboro Outing Club
Cedar Street
Brattleboro, VT 05301

Johnson College Whitewater Club
Box 649
Johnson State College
Johnson, VT 05656

Marlboro College Outdoor Program
Marlboro, VT 05344

Northern Vermont Canoe Cruisers
Box 254
Shelburne, VT 05482

VIRGINIA

American Canoe Association
P.O. Box 248
Lorton, VA 22079

Blue Ridge Voyageurs
8119 Hillcrest Drive
Manassas, VA 22110

Canoe Cruisers Association
1623 Seneca Avenue
McLean, VA 22101

Coastal Canoeists
RFD 4 Mockingbird Lane
Spotsylvania, VA 22553

Explorer Post 999
3509 North Colonial Drive
Hopewell, VA 23860

James River Runners Inc
Rte 1 Box 106
Scottsville, VA 24590

Roanoke Valley American Red Cross
352 Church Avenue SW
Roanoke, VA 24018

Shenandoah River Canoe Club
Box 1423
Front Royal, VA 22630

University of Virginia Outing Club
Box 101X Newcomb Hall Station
Charlottesville, VA 22901

WASHINGTON

Boeing Employees Whitewater &
   Touring Club
15804 47th Street, South
Seattle, WA 98188

Desert Kayak & Canoe Club
450 Mateo Court
Richland, WA 99352

Natural Designs
2223 North 60th
Seattle, WA 98103

Pacific Water Sports
1273 South 188th
Seattle, WA 98195

Seattle Washington Canoe Club
6019 51 NE
Seattle, WA 98115

Spokane Canoe Club
N. 10804 Nelson
Spokane, WA 99218

Tacoma Mountaineers Kayak & Canoe
   Committee
3512 Crystal Spring
Tacoma, WA 98466

Takoma Kayak & Canoe Club
3512 Crystal Spring
Tacoma, WA 98466

Tri-C Camping Association
17404 8th Avenue
Seattle, WA 98155

University of Washington Canoe Club
I.M.A. Building
University of Washington
Seattle, WA 98105

Washington Kayak Club
P.O. Box 24264
Seattle, WA 98124

Washington Paddle Trails Canoe Club
Box 86
Ashford, WA 98304

Whitewater Northwest Kayak Club
Box 1081
Spokane, WA 98105

Whitewater Sports
6820 Roosevelt Way NE
Seattle, WA 98115

WEST VIRGINIA

Canoe Association of West Virginia
111–18th Street East
Wheeling, WV 26003

West Virginia Wildwater Association
2737 Daniels Ave.
South Charlestown, WV 25303

Whitewater Canoe Club
Mt. Lair Recreation Center
West Virginia University
Morgantown, WV 26506

WISCONSIN

Fond Du Lac Voyageurs Canoe Club
114 Harrison Place
Fond Du Lac, WI 54935

Kayaks Ltd.
5980 Dawson Court
Greendale, WI 53129

Sierra Club
7541 South 31st Street
Franklin, WI 53132

Sierra Club, John Muir Chapter
6561 Hillridge Drive
Greendale, WI 53129

Wild Rivers Club
4901 36th Avenue Apartment 206
Kenosha, WI 53140

Wisconsin Hoofers Outing Club
Wisconsin Union Directorate
800 Langdon Street
Madison, WI 53706

Wisconsin Whitewater River Runners
5530 West Cold Spring Road
Milwaukee, WI 53220

Wolf River Canoe Club
Wolf River Lodge
White Lake, WI 54491

WYOMING

Croaking Toad Boat Works
Game Hill Ranch
Bondurant, WY 82922

Western Wyoming Kayak Club
General Delivery
Wilson, WY 83014

ARGENTINA

Federacion Argentina de Canoas
Florida 229 3 piso- of. 332
Buenos Aires, Argentina

AUSTRALIA

Canoe & Paddle Centre
212 Parramatta Rd
Stanmore Sydney
Australia 2048

Indooroopilly Canoe Club
Box 36 Indooroopilly
Queensland, Australia

AUSTRIA

Osterreicheischischer Kanu-Verband
Bergganse 16 1090 Vienna, Austria

BELGIUM

Federation Belge de Canoe
% A. Vandeput Geerdengemwaart
79 B. 2800 Mechelen, Belgium

BULGARIA

Bulgarian Canoe Federation
Bulevar Tolboukine 18
Sofia, Bulgaria

CANADA

British Columbia Kayak & Canoe Club
1247 A Cambie Rd
Richmond, British Columbia, Canada

Camp Ecole Keno
2315 Chemin St. Louis
Sillery Quebec Canada
G1T – 1R5

Canoe Ontario
559 Jarvis Street
Toronto Ontario
Canada M4Y 2J1

Edmonton Whitewater Paddlers
Box 4117 South Edmonton PO
Edmonton Alberta
Canada T6E 458

Federation Quebecoise de Canot-Kayak
Inc.
881 Est Boul de Maisoneuve
Montreal 132 PQ
Canada H21 L49

North West Voyageurs
10922 88th Avenue
Edmonton, Alberta Canada

Ontario Whitewater Association
21 Vanity Court
Don Mills, Ontario
Canada

Ontario Voyageurs Kayak Club
166 St. Germain Avenue
Toronto, Ontario
Canada MSM 1W1

Sports Resource Information Center
333 River Road
Ottawa Canada
K1L 839

Tumblehome Canoe Club
4 Acacia Grove Court
Frederickton, N.B. Canada
E3B 1YZ

Whitewater Nova Scotia
Box 1180
Middleton, N.S., Canada
BOS 1P0

Wascana Institute
4635 Wascana Parkway
Regina, Saskatchewan, Canada
S4P 3A3

CHILE

Club Canoas Santiago S.A.
Antonio Bellet #309
Santiago, Chile, S.A.

CHINA

Canoeing Association of the People's
Republic of China
9 Tiyukuan Road
Peking, China

CYPRUS

Cyprus Canoe Association
P.O. Box 1384, Nicosia, Cyprus

CUBA

Federation Cubana de Canotaje
% Comite Olimpico Cubano
Hotal Habana libre, Havana, Cuba

CZECHOSLOVAKIA

Czechoslovak Canoe Federation
Naporici 12 – 11530
Prague 1, Czechoslovakia

DENMARK

Dansk Kano of Kajak Forbund
% J. Cronberg, Engvej
184–2300 Copenhaven, Denmark

ENGLAND

British Canoe Union
Flexel House 45–47 High St
Addlestone
Weybridge, Surrey KT15 1JV
United Kingdom

The Advanced Sea Kayak Club
32 Glebe Rd. West Perry
Huntington, Cambs.
PE 18 ODG United Kingdom

FINLAND

Suomen Kanoottilitto ry,
Topeliuksenkatu 41a 00250
Helsinki 25, Finland

FRANCE

Federation Francaise de Canoe-Kajak
87 Quai de la Marne – 94
340 Joinville Le Pont France

GERMAN DEMOCRATIC REPUBLIC

D.D.R.
1055 Berlin
Storkower Strasse 118
D.D.R. (East Germany)

GERMAN FEDERAL REPUBLIC

Deutschen Kanu-Verbandes
Bertallee 8
D-4100 Duisburg 1
Federal German Republic

HONG KONG

Hong Kong Canoe Union
Room 502 Man Wai Commercial
    Building
102 Wellington St.
Central
Hong Kong

HUNGARY

Magyar Kajak-Kanu Szovetseg
Rosenberg Hazuspar u. 1,
Budapest V, Hungary

IRAN

Federation Kakh Varzesh str.
P.O. Box 3396
Teheran, Iran

IRELAND

Irish Canoe Union
% Cospoir The National Sport Council
Floor 11, Hawkins House, Hawkins St.
Dublin 2, Ireland

ISRAEL

Israel Canoe Association
8 Haarbaa St. PO.B. 7170
Tel Aviv, Israel

ITALY

Commissione Italiana-Canoa
70 Viale Tiziano – 00100
Rome, Italy

International Canoe Federation
Via G. Massaia 59
1–50134
Florence Italy

IVORY COAST

Ivory Coast Canoes and Pirogue
Federation B.P. 1872
Abidjan, Ivory Coast

JAPAN

Japan Canoe Association
% Ishi Memorial 1–1–1 Jinnan
Shibuya-ku
Tokyo, Japan

KOREA

Canoe Association of the Democratic
People's Moosing-Dong
Dongdawon District Pyongyang Korea

LUXEMBOURG

Federation Luxembourgeoise de Canoe-
Kayak
Boite postale 424
Luxembourg 2

MEXICO

Federation Mexicana de Canotaje
Sanchez Ascona 1348
Mexico 12 D.F.

NETHERLANDS

Dutch Canoe Union
NL–1561 BD Krommenie
J H Dunantstraat 62
Netherlands

NEW ZEALAND

New Zealand Canoeing Association
P.O. Box 5125
Auckland
New Zealand

Canoe Camping Ltd.
112 Ohiro Bay Parade
Wellington 2
New Zealand

Nelson Canoe Club
Box 793
Nelson
New Zealand

NORWAY

Norges Kajak-Forbund
Hauger Skolovei 1
N. 1346 Gjettum, Norway

PERU

South American Explorers' Club
Casilla 3714
Lima 1 Peru

POLAND

Polski Zwiszek Kajakowy
ul. Sienkiewicza 12 00-010
Warszawa Poland

ROMANIA

Federatia Romana de Caiac-Canoe
Str. Vasile Conta 16
70139 Bucarest, Romania

SPAIN

Federacion Espagnola de Piraguismo
% Miguel Angel num. 18
6 Madrid 10 Spain

SWEDEN

Kuiva Granspaddlare
Box 2074
950-94
Overtornea Sweden

SWITZERLAND

Kanu Club Zurich
Dufourstrasse 3
8008 Zurich
Switzerland

Schweizerischer Kanu-Verband
Brünigstrasse 121
CH-6060 Sarnen
Switzerland

UNION OF SOUTH AFRICA

South African Canoe Association
% W.F. van Reet
13 Leopold Street, Bellville
Union of South Africa

U.S.S.R.

Canoe Federation of the U.S.S.R.
Skatemyi pereoulok 4
Moscow 69 Russia

YUGOSLAVIA

Kajakaski Savez Jugoslavije
Bulevar Revolucije 44/1
11000 Beograd, Yugoslavia

Index